Single, White, Slaveholding Women in the Nineteenth-Century American South

Single, White, Slaveholding Women in the Nineteenth-Century American South

MARIE S. MOLLOY

The University of South Carolina Press

© 2018 University of South Carolina

Published by the University of South Carolina Press
Columbia, South Carolina 29208

www.sc.edu/uscpress

Manufactured in the United States of America

27 26 25 24 23 22 21 20 19 18
10 9 8 7 6 5 4 3 2 1

Library of Congress Cataloging-in-Publication Data
can be found at http://catalog.loc.gov/

ISBN 978-1-61117-870-8 (cloth)
ISBN 978-1-61117-871-5 (ebook)

Portions of chapters 2 and 3 were previously published in "A Noble Class of Old Maids":
Surrogate Motherhood, Sibling Support, and Self-Sufficiency in the Nineteenth-Century
White, Southern Family, *Journal of Family History*, Vol. 41 (4). October 2016. pp. 402–29.

For my husband, Darren, and our daughters,
Olivia, Heidi, and Scarlett.

Also for my parents, Jenny and Graham Phillips.
Thank you for believing in me.

Contents

Illustrations

Acknowledgments

This book is the result of almost ten years' work, and it has developed out of a love for southern history. My work began at Keele University in the American Studies Department. When I embarked on this exciting journey, I was a young mother, with two (now three) small children to raise, and I often burned the midnight oil, in pursuit of balancing family life with my passion for researching and writing about southern women's lives in the Civil War era. In following this dream, I have accumulated many professional and personal debts. I am sincerely grateful to the David Bruce Centre at Keele University for their long-term financial and academic and personal support, which has made this book possible. Special thanks to Professor Axel Schäfer and Dr. Laura Sandy for providing their time, expertise, and guidance, and to Professor Martin Crawford and Professor Karen Hunt for their early input into the book, which helped to shape my preliminary ideas that can be traced throughout the book. Professor Ian Bell has demonstrated his unswerving support and keen interest in my work, always offering great encouragement to me in pursuing an academic career. Fellow scholars and friends have likewise kindly given their time and energy in offering to read and comment on various draft chapters, which has further enhanced the final product. I am extremely grateful to Leslie Powner and to my friend Mary Goode in particular.

Throughout the research and writing process, I have benefited from several generous travel grants that have helped to fund my research trips to North Carolina, Georgia, South Carolina, and Virginia, which were essential in writing the book. These include the Peter Parish Memorial Fund (which is part of the British American Nineteenth Century Historians), the Archie K. Davis Fellowship in North Carolina, the Frances Mellon Fellowship from Virginia Historical Society, and Royal Historical Society funding. Gathering the relevant material on single, white, slaveholding women across the South has been a momentous task, which has led me to several archives in the South. I have mainly worked in six archives: the Southern Historical Collection at the University of North Carolina, David M. Rubenstein Rare Book and Manuscripts Library at Duke University, Virginia Historical Society in Richmond, Georgia Historical Society in Savannah, South Carolina Historical Society in Charleston, and South Caroliniana Library at the University of South Carolina, Columbia. In each repository I discovered some invaluable collections in addition to helpful and knowledgeable staff. Two individual archivists who deserve a special mention are Barbara Illie at the Southern

Historical Collection, who shared her extensive knowledge, but also her southern hospitality with me, and Frances Pollard at the Virginia Historical Society, who always went the extra mile to offer her expertise and advice. It was a great honor to work in such plentiful archives, and to also have the opportunity to explore such beautiful parts of America.

I have benefited enormously from my involvement in conferences, colloquia, seminar series, and workshops in the U.K. and overseas that have provided a richly stimulating and intellectually fruitful environment to learn about and to share my own and other scholars' research. I have had the pleasure of speaking at various conferences in the U.K. and the United States, including the Southern Association of Women's Historians at the University of South Carolina in 2009 and the British Nineteenth Century American Historians (BrANCH) special conference in Houston, Texas, in 2013. Here I met several leading scholars in southern history, who fueled my enthusiasm for research, writing, and teaching. The experience of discussing issues such as race, class, and gender in these collegial forums has profoundly enriched my understanding of the South and of southern women's history.

The greatest debt in writing a book such as this is to my family, for their love, support, and encouragement, which has sustained me on this long journey. To my husband, I owe a very special debt of gratitude for listening to all my stories and dilemmas along the way, for fixing computer problems for me, and for the many days that he entertained our three lively daughters; I am so grateful. My three lovely daughters have shown an ongoing interest in what I am writing about and why I am writing it. We even named our youngest daughter Scarlett as she arrived in the midst of my writing, and so it seemed a fitting namesake. There have been countless occasions that I have heard a gentle tapping at my study door, with a voice enquiring, "How many words have you written today?" It is a wonderful feeling to now tell them that the book is complete. I am enormously thankful to my parents, who have instilled in me a strong desire to succeed. The greatest gift they have given me is self-belief, and the belief that if you have a goal, you should keep going until you achieve it. For as long as I can remember, I have loved to write. As a child, I sat up late at night, writing grandiose stories on my typewriter, and posting the stories off to publishers. I had a dream that I would write stories that would one day be read by other people. I believe my book is the fulfillment of that personal goal, which brings me to my last point, which is to say that first and foremost, this book is inspired by other women's life stories, diligently written and recorded in their letters and personal diaries so many years ago. I remain so grateful that these women kept a record of their lives, so that we as historians might have the privilege of glimpsing a snapshot of the past, and in doing so gain a far better understanding of what women's lives were like in the nineteenth-century American South.

INTRODUCTION

G race Elmore Brown was born in 1839, the fourth-youngest child in a line of eleven, into a privileged, slaveholding family from South Carolina. As a young lady growing up in the heart of the South, in a society in which rigid ideologies of race, class, and gender dominated white women's lives, she wrote with distaste about the gender conventions forced on her as a single, white, slaveholding daughter, which is illuminating. In September 1864, at the age of twenty-five, she confided in her diary: "I feel like a bird beating against its cage, so hemmed in am I by other people's ideas, and forced by conventionalities to remain where I cannot live up to, or according to my own. It ought to be with the human family as with all other creatures, each one seeks for themselves the life best suited to them."[1] Grace was referring specifically to her family ties and to the expectations placed on her to conform to nineteenth-century gender conventions that she felt at times limited her autonomy. Grace longed for independence and claimed that she had once "shocked" her sister with the revelation that "married or not I hoped and trusted I would one day have my own establishment independent of everyone else. Marriage has precious little share in my plans for the future. . . . Marriage would hardly be a happy state."[2]

Grace's comments seem revolutionary for their time and place; she rejected not only marriage but also a future life in which she would have to be dependent on others. She spoke for a new generation of young women, who chafed against the gender conventions placed on them, but also recognized the need to work within their constraints, in order to pursue a life that best suited them. As Grace freely admitted, "self is my idol, however, I may disguise it in benevolence, or in doing it for others, self is my first thought."[3] Grace was therefore fully prepared to show a veneer of acceptance concerning what was expected of her, as an unmarried, white, southern lady. She was prepared to demonstrate "benevolence" and "usefulness" in her everyday life as a single woman if it meant that she could work toward having her "own establishment," which would allow her to exercise a degree of autonomy in her life and the way she chose to live it. Grace Elmore Brown was not alone in her quest for personal agency, as the women in this book will demonstrate.

This book is about constraint and agency in single white women's lives. It is based on the letters and diaries of over three hundred white, native-born, southern women. The single women in this study are predominately from privileged families, who had benefited from owning slaves in the antebellum and Civil War eras. Even for women who came from less wealthy slaveholding families, with fewer slaves, the benefits of slavery were apparent in the way they lived, with black servants doing the menial and household labor, until the end of the war and the emancipation of the slaves, and as such are reflective of the experience of that particular group. They often replicated gender hierarchies, or at least showed an outward willingness to accept them in their lives, which raised their public persona and credited them as virtuous, useful, and valued members of southern society. A small number of women openly rejected them, but many single women did so only in the privacy of their personal diaries or in letters of correspondence. As members of the slaveholding class they were expected to be paragons of southern femininity, because of their elevated racial and class position within the southern hierarchy.[4] They conducted their lives within a framework of acceptable gender conventions that at times constrained them, but that could also set them free—used as a springboard for achieving personal autonomy, particularly during and after the Civil War. These changes often sprang from conservative roots that originated in the antebellum era but were then accelerated by the Civil War, which acted as a catalyst for further social change.

The central hypothesis in this book is that singleness was ultimately a route to female autonomy for slaveholding women in spite of certain restrictions placed on them. Many of the single women discussed throughout the book did not automatically fit into the traditional model of southern womanhood. They were permanently single or had married late, were widowed, divorced, or separated.[5] Geographically they were born and raised in the eleven states that made up the Confederacy: Mississippi, Georgia, South Carolina, Alabama, North Carolina, Virginia, Florida, Texas, Arkansas, Tennessee, and Louisiana. Yet, in spite of their different pathways to female singleness, they shared in the fact that their lives operated within the gender conventions that dominated the South. This framework of analysis helps to view singleness in a much broader light than has previously been acknowledged in the literature and helps us to understand the ways in which single women's lives were circumscribed by the prevalent ideals of femininity that existed in the antebellum period and up to and beyond the Civil War.

This book builds on the growing literature on single women that has broken away from earlier scholarship that viewed single women's role in southern society in a more pessimistic light.[6] Unmarried women from the elite classes were often far from marginal, shadowy creatures within the family unit, and they were increasingly valued for their contribution and services to the family; during the civil war and postwar period they were often integral to it. They were also increasingly active outside of the family unit, often driven by economic need or a desire to broaden their sphere. Lee Chambers-Schiller's *Liberty a Better Husband: Single Women in America; The Generations of 1780–1840* was the first work to draw attention to, and raise awareness of, a small, independent group of nineteenth-century spinsters in the American Northeast.[7] Even though Chambers-Schiller's work focuses on female singleness in the American Northeast, it has tremendous resonance with the southern experience, in that it highlights a "a new affirmation of singlehood, a Cult of Single Blessedness [that] developed in America in parallel to the Cult of Domesticity."[8] Schiller highlighted a similar opening for single blessedness that occurred much later on in the South for women born between 1840 and 1850, who came of age in wartime, and benefited from the blossoming of new opportunities that came alongside war, which is a theme echoed throughout this book.[9] Chambers-Schiller drew attention to the rise of companionate marriage and concluded that "it was better to remain single than to accept anything less than a true marriage," which raised the status of unmarried women.[10] She contended that northern women were primarily motivated by the desire for economic security, and a desire to expand intellectual horizons. Although she claimed that family lay at the center of the Cult of Single Blessedness, she argued that family also held women back, by preventing them from fulfilling all their personal goals, which is a point that will be explored further in the context of the southern family. Zsusza Berend revisited the idea of single blessedness over a decade later, in the context of the nineteenth-century Northeast and underlined an "ethic of worldly usefulness," as opposed to economic gain, that motivated women to work in their quest for single blessedness.[11]

Family, work, and identity are clearly important areas that require further exploration in order to understand the impact that they had on single women's lives. Scholars of women in the North and South have different interpretations of how single women have been affected by the family. Christine Carter's *Southern Single Blessedness: Unmarried Women in the Urban South 1800–1865* focuses on the experiences of unmarried women exclusively in urban areas. She argued that what made southern single blessedness unique from that in the American Northeast was the fact that elite white women were not motivated by economic need or by the need for personal autonomy; they were already well supported by their privileged, well-to-do families and therefore did not need to work but were instead motivated by a desire to find a place for themselves within the family. However, while this was the case for some women, there is evidence to suggest that single women, previously supported by slavery, were increasingly motivated by fiscal gain. This came into sharper focus in the post–Civil War world, when previously wealthy slaveholding or elite families, became the "genteel poor," because of their ruined land and loss of wealth and slaves. Therefore, in this war-torn context, southern women could clearly be driven by economic motives. Elite women also saw the personal fulfillment that could be gained from work and economic remuneration, which led to an increased desire for personal agency.[12]

In this book, "family" is perceived as critical to developing single women's identity in the South and can be viewed as a powerful precursor that transcended old opinions on spinsterhood, by gaining women appreciation and respect from others, which enabled single women to construct new identities, thereby building a bridge to greater opportunities and self-advancement in the public sphere. Single women often strove to be accepted within the mainstream of southern womanhood, as a vehicle to expand the viscous boundaries of true womanhood. Unmarried women from elite southern families were increasingly valued for their contribution and services to the family, and during the war and postwar period they were often integral to it. Single women were also increasingly active outside of the family unit, often driven by economic need or a desire to broaden their sphere.[13] Jennifer Lynn Gross suggested that the spinster in many ways played the same role as married women but beyond the nuclear family, which in turn gave her independence and autonomy in limited measure. Single women acting as nurses and teachers were acting out "mother" to the nation, which gained the respect of the community.[14]

Single women's lives were going through a slow but definite process of change in the antebellum era, in how women's single state was perceived by others, but also in the everyday reality of their lives. This can be demonstrated in the roles and responsibilities single women had in the southern family, which helped the cohesiveness of the family unit. Their roles often conformed to traditional models of femininity. This also led to an enhancement of personal autonomy because it required women at times to step outside of, or beyond, the domestic sphere in preservation of the family. In the Civil War years this process of change intensified as single women's roles expanded more rapidly outside of the family unit and domestic sphere. This was in response to the demands of war that required women to revise their understanding of southern womanhood in order to aid the Confederacy in wartime. In the antebellum era, slaveholding women managed large plantations in the temporary, or permanent, absence of their husbands. Yet the Civil War resulted in an unprecedented number of southern women being left alone to manage plantations, or to become involved in wartime work that previously lay beyond their sphere of influence. As single women's roles and responsibilities expanded in wartime, women demonstrated that they fitted into a new and developing "Cult of Single Blessedness," which stated that unmarried women could prove positive contributors to their homes and families, and to society, through benevolence and usefulness to others. The Cult of Single Blessedness developed alongside the Cult of True Womanhood and came into its own during wartime.[15] It helped to further expand the boundaries of true womanhood, by giving single women the opportunity to prove that they could also be true southern women. It marked a positive step forward in how unmarried women were perceived and treated, as well as providing a platform to self-fulfillment and enhanced personal agency.

Hence the war was a catalyst for further social change not only in the destruction of race-based slavery but also in challenging conventional gender roles. Planter women were forced to reconsider how appropriate their gender roles were in the crisis of wartime. Thus the quest for southern independence also inadvertently challenged the construction of southern womanhood, at the center of which stood the plantation mistress or southern lady.[16] Unlike any other social group, the war challenged the elevated racial, class, and gender position of the southern lady. Drew Gilpin Faust argued that the Civil War forced women to reconsider their gender roles in the light of altered circumstances. As many more women were left on their own, as temporarily single women, they were required to readjust their roles and responsibilities in order to accommodate the exigencies of wartime. As Faust demonstrated, "war has often introduced women to unaccustomed responsibilities and unprecedented, even if temporary, enhancements of power. War has been a pre-eminently 'gendering' activity, casting thought about sex differences into sharp relief as it has both underlined and realigned gender boundaries."[17]

As single, slaveholding women expanded their domestic roles by becoming plantation managers, nurses, or teachers, the traditional gender conventions of southern society were inadvertently challenged. The Civil War highlighted female singleness in an unprecedented way as many more women became "manless women" or women who were on their own.[18] In the light of the war, a clearer definition of who was considered to be single emerged, as the boundaries between married and single became redefined and elasticized. The war therefore illustrated in a very graphic way how the boundaries between married and single were often fluid, and over the course of a woman's life it was common for her to traverse several different roles: typically as a southern belle, a plantation wife and mother, and for many, through widowhood. In the postwar period the process of change in single women's roles that began in the antebellum period continued to gain pace. Female autonomy was enhanced by traditional ideals of protection about women that could be used to their advantage in seeking a divorce or to gain their due in widowhood. Thus from conservative ideology sprang radical social change. The central hypothesis in this book is that singleness, in spite of its restrictions, was a route to greater autonomy for women in the nineteenth-century South in the antebellum, Civil War, postwar, and Reconstruction eras. Singleness, in spite of some social scorn in the early nineteenth century, gradually became accepted as an alternative model for unmarried women, albeit within a conservative social ethos that continued to try to dictate what their behavior should be as single women. Often if women showed themselves to conform to the standard, this resulted in greater female autonomy.

The women in this book were predominately born in the period 1810–60. Information on each individual was collected and stored on a basic database as a collective biography. Information recorded included dates of birth and death, place of residence, age, marital status, duration of marriage, number of marriages, class, type of dwelling, and the number of slaves owned. This included women who were never married, late married, widowed, divorced, or separated. There are a small number of social widows (women who were married but who lived alone for months or years as their husbands were away on business, or later fighting in the war). Initially the information on the women in the sample was gained through printed sources and primary sources available online. Mining online resources, such as DocSouth, initially achieved this. As the research project developed, key repositories were quickly identified that contained family papers, valuable correspondence (letters), and women's diaries. The main archives utilized during the research process included the Southern Historical Collection at the University of North Carolina, the Virginia Historical Society in Richmond, the David M. Rubenstein Rare Book and Manuscripts Library at Duke University, the Georgia Historical Society in Savannah, the South Carolina Historical Society in Charleston, and the South Caroliniana Library at the University of South Carolina. The main sources used in this book are letters, diaries, and journals, though for the final chapter the Race and Slavery Petitions Project was a vital source for court cases, petitions, and inheritance laws.

The diary or journal was a literary genre that enabled women of the slaveholding class an opportunity to express their opinions within the safe confines of a personal diary, and it was an important way to vent hopes, dreams, and personal ambitions, as well as frustrations. Michael O'Brien described the intimacy of women's diaries over time as a "veil between the self and the world."[19] For single, slaveholding women who lived in a society that severely circumscribed their behavior, the diary represented an outlet through which they were able to "confront power and control."[20] It also provided women relief "from an alienating and narrowly defining real world."[21] In this context single women's diaries provide an opportunity for unraveling the complexities of women's lives. They allow the reader to "track the intellectual and emotional independence and life journeys" of women, and to place them within the wider framework of other women's lives. The act of writing itself implies self-assertion, and it boosted women through difficult times, particularly during the Civil War. Sarah Morgan, a young southern woman, at the time unmarried, from Baton Rouge, Louisiana confided, "Thanks to my liberal supply of pens, ink and paper, how many inexpressibly dreary days I have filled up to my own satisfaction. . . . It has become a necessity to me. . . . Just as I am fit for nothing in the world and just before I reach my lowest ebb, I seize my pen, dash off half a dozen lines."[22] Writing in the form of a diary allowed southern women to express their anger, frustration, joy, and delight in a genre that gave them a real voice. Amy Wink explained how women tried to maintain their individual sense of self in their writing because it was the thing they had most control over.[23] "Even within the culturally acceptable and restrictive models of appropriate gender identity, individual identity still involves personal interpretation and moments of individual agency within that same framework," Wink argued.[24] In analyzing the language and expressive styles in women's diaries it is possible to point to historical continuity and changes in the self, in social relations, in work, and in values.

Writing was a luxury for elite women, but it also reflects a certain class and race bias that favored white, planter-class women. They were well educated, literate women, who left an array of personal correspondence, in the form of letters and diaries, in which they often spoke quite candidly about the realities of their daily lives, and the ways in which they felt constrained or liberated by their status as unmarried women. In their letters women were expected to adhere to certain letter-writing conventions that often give a different impression than the personal diaries they left behind. Letters are by their very nature scattered and involve a dialogue between two people. Therefore it is important to understand the significance of how the writers employed, experimented with, or altered the conventional forms alive in their time. Letter writing therefore provides a useful record of how women embraced or resisted the conventions that they were expected to adhere to.

This book has also utilized court records for the final chapter, "Law, Property, and the Single Woman," which was essential for assessing how the legal framework aided or abated autonomy for single, slaveholding women in the antebellum, Civil War, and Reconstruction eras. The court records illuminate the key argument regarding the relevance of gender models in the reality of women's lives. The Race and Slavery Petitions Project was a valuable resource and includes civil litigation cases, divorce petitions, inheritance laws, court actions, and widows' cases to retrieve their property or dower share, thus revealing the relationship between single women and the law. The Race and Slavery Petitions Project was established in 1991 in order to collect and publish "all extant legislative petitions relevant to slavery" as well as county courts records "from the fifteen slaveholding states from the American Revolution to the Civil War."[25] The project holds almost 3,000 legislative petitions and 14,512 county court petitions, many of which have been copied onto microfilm, with 151 reels in the collection. The project covers a wide range of subjects, but the most relevant were the divorce petitions and widows petitioning for their dower share (or requests to be granted permission to move property, to sell land, or to deal with their minor's slaves). These petitions shine a bright light on single women's lives from an alternative perspective as they reveal the similarities and differences between those women who became single through divorce and those living in involuntary singleness, through widowhood.

I found that I could best tell the story of these women's lives by organizing the book thematically rather than chronologically, in order to focus on central aspects of single women's lives that reveal patterns of autonomy and constraint. This method makes it possible to construct a more detailed, textured analysis that reflects the complexities of single women's lives in the antebellum, Civil War, and Reconstruction eras.

What was life like for single women living in the antebellum South, with its sharp focus on class, race, and gender? There were the prevalent gender conventions of the Cult of True Womanhood, tied to the institution of race-based slavery that was of particular importance to the slaveholding class.[26] Given the relevance of the "feminine ideal" to unmarried women's lives, single women tried to forge an identity for themselves in a society that valued marriage and motherhood so highly. Research indicates that attitudes toward, and about, single women were already changing in the prewar period. There is evidence that unmarried women were slowly expanding their roles by showing an adherence to traditional models of femininity, while gradually expanding their roles outward. Also in the air were the influence of the new ideal of companionate marriage but also, the growing awareness of the Cult of Single Blessedness.

A single woman's role within the family can best be understood by examining the nature of the southern family unit and how single women fitted into it, in theory and in practice.[27] Elite, white, southern women enjoyed a relative degree of "power and freedom" compared to black people, and nonslaveholding white people, but they "remained subordinate to men of their own class and race."[28] By exploring their place in the southern family, it is clear that these upper-class women replicated traditional gender roles in some areas of their lives. They demonstrated resistance to the normative roles of marriage and motherhood by remaining single, but in other ways they reinforced gender expectations or patterns by duplicating caregiving roles as the family helpmeet or the maiden aunt, and in their relationships with siblings. These roles reveal how single, slaveholding women's lives operated within a rigid framework of traditional gender conventions that were particularly marked because of their class and race. Their roles in the southern family demonstrated devotion to the same ideals of true womanhood—on the face of it at least—and led inadvertently to an elevated and more privileged position in the family. By upholding the family as central in their lives, single, slaveholding daughters, sisters, and cousins carved out a place for themselves in southern society. They helped to revise old notions that single women were redundant women, and by the time of the Civil War, when they were needed in caregiving roles outside of the family, they were ready to step up to the mantel. The Civil War highlighted the extensive contribution of single women and thus further accelerated the pace of social change in wartime. These temporary changes in wartime became more permanent in the postwar era, as the number of women living alone rose in line with the demographic devastation of war.

It is difficult to establish the exact number of single women in the South from 1830 to 1870 owing to limitations in the antebellum census records, and estimates vary considerably from region to region among historians. Michael O'Brien estimated that before 1860 "about a fifth to a quarter of all adult white Southern women were unmarried for life."[29] However, in an 1848 census of Charleston it is known that "exactly half of all adult white female Charlestonians were married, almost a third were single, and a fifth were widowed."[30] In an earlier estimate based on 750 members of the planter elite born in the period 1765–1815, Catherine Clinton found only 2.1 percent of women never marrying.[31] Finally, the number of unwed, native-born women, across the entire United States as a whole, is estimated at around 7.3 percent in the 1830s.[32] From these figures alone, particularly with reference to the estimates based on Charleston and the South as a whole, it is clear that the number of single white females was a significant number that requires further investigation and explanation.

Single, slaveholding women—often widows—managed plantations or filled other traditional working roles as teachers and nurses. Women would run large plantations in the absence of a male and in doing so confronted certain challenges but also enjoyed opportunities for self-advancement. Single women were already starting to embrace the ideal of single blessedness in the antebellum period. During the Civil War the necessity for single women to fulfill the calling of single blessedness intensified, and women used the exigencies of war as a reason to expand their domestic roles in the family onto a more public stage as nurses on the front line. They also worked as teachers both inside and outside of the domestic setting, and in doing so they expanded the internal and external divisions of work.

The Civil War led to the development of new opportunities for women. It challenged old notions of female dependency and male protection. It also confronted the idea that women were physically weak and timid in nature. As widows and spinsters responded to the demands for help in wartime, they faced difficult and testing situations that they often overcame. They stepped up to the challenge of wartime work, as nurses in Confederate hospitals and in caring for men who were strangers to them. They overcame the initial prejudice of others for taking up "unladylike" occupations, which fell outside of the internal divisions of the southern family, but eventually drew strength and praise from their valiant actions. In the postwar era single women had further carved out a place for themselves in the public world of work, and the temporary changes of war often became more permanent.[33] The war also had a devastating effect on class, as it literally wiped out the livelihoods of some planter-class families. With the loss of their slaves, families were left in financial ruin, a blow from which they never fully recovered.[34]

Single women benefited from considerable freedom in their same-sex friendships in the antebellum era, for the very reason that these friendships were perceived as temporary, and had no possibility of becoming more permanent. They were fixed within the overarching framework of traditional gender roles that perceived women as nonsexual and thus nonthreatening to the conservative status quo. Female friendships therefore reflect the dominant gender ideologies of the nineteenth century, on the surface at least. For within these same-sex friendships lay a culture of resistance to marriage and motherhood, which actually challenged prevalent gender models.[35] The form and function of female friendship was often complex and depended on where women lived, with whom they lived, and stage of life.[36] Romantic friendships were considered a natural part of girlhood, conducted in boarding schools or through letters of correspondence to one another, almost as a precursor to marriage. They were seen as temporary in nature and, as a result, harmless. In the postwar period, attitudes to female friendships began to alter. As female friendship between nonmarried women threatened to become more permanent owing to social, economic, and demographic changes brought by war, perceptions of them changed. The postwar conservative ethos saw women as sexual rather than nonsexual beings and started to interpret same-sex friendship as a threat, and possibly subversive.[37] Changes in women's lives included their growing personal autonomy, and worth noting is the way in which southern conservatism reacted to these changes in the postwar years.

The southern legal system was also motivated by an ethos of patriarchal control that extended its protection only to the most deserving southern women, who were defined by the courts as upper-class women who clearly demonstrated that they were "true women" in their behavior and conduct. In marriage these women had to show that they had been innocent victims of their husbands' abuse and be able to substantiate their claim with evidence. Married women who voluntarily sought a divorce from their husbands were at the mercy of the courts, and therefore they were reliant on them to grant them dissolution of marriage and a return to their status as femme sole. Success or failure hinged on them being able to prove that they had upheld the tenets of true womanhood in marriage.[38] Slaveholding widows were dependent on the courts' discretion in any disputes concerning the dower share they received after their husbands' death. A widow's return to femme sole status was often fraught with difficulties. A widow had to demonstrate her "ladyhood" (in upholding her class, race, and gender roles) but also had to possess determination and grit in order to survive as a woman alone. In the antebellum period legal changes were already in effect, in that the Married Women's Property Acts, particularly in 1848, had inadvertently provided single women with some power. The property acts were the product of conservative concerns regarding men's property in difficult economic times but resulted in significant legal changes in single women's lives.

Chapter 1 THE CONSTRUCTION OF FEMININITY IN THE ANTEBELLUM SOUTH

On 2 December 1829, Mary Telfair, a well-to-do spinster from Savannah, Georgia, wrote a letter to her lifelong friend Mary Few on the topic of single blessedness. In her analysis of the single state she made two important observations. First, "a married woman is always of more consequence than a single one."[1] Second, for a single woman to manage on her own "it requires a vast deal of independence and a variety of resources."[2] Yet for Mary Telfair these issues did not prevent her from choosing to remain single. Since she came from one of the richest and most privileged slaveholding families in Georgia, it seems fair to deduce that her experience of single blessedness was colored by her social, racial, and class position as a southern lady.[3] Mary was careful to be *seen* to uphold the tenets of true womanhood and openly admitted that marriage remained the most desirable status for a woman. At the same time the mere fact that she chose to remain single displayed a covert resistance, by consciously rejecting marriage and motherhood in her own life.[4]

As Mary Telfair's example attests, the construction of femininity in the Old South had already begun a gradual process of change long before the Civil War. This is reflected in the fact that women from the highest echelons of society were consciously choosing a life of single blessedness in the antebellum period. Mary claimed that the Telfair family was devoted to "single blessedness." Therefore, her decision to reject marriage, and with it the opportunity to fulfill the tenets of true womanhood, had begun in the 1820s. Her comments reveal much about southern women's perceptions of femininity as defined by the society in which they lived.[5]

The boundaries of true womanhood were far less rigid than they were often perceived to be.[6] Single women often upheld marriage and motherhood as the hallmark of femininity, but this was predominately as a means to gain social acceptance in southern society, which in turn cultivated the soil for single blessedness to blossom. This in turn provided single women with a route to greater autonomy.[7]

The Antebellum Setting: Cult and Reality

As early as the 1800s, the South had metamorphosed into a distinct region characterized by plantations, cotton, and black slavery.[8] It was a vast geographical area that spread from the upper states of Virginia, North Carolina, and Tennessee down to Mississippi, Alabama, and Georgia (the Lower South). The South was dominated by its agriculture and defined by its slaves who worked on the land. It was also characterized by class, and the stratification of labor meant that all white men, regardless of their wealth, rank, or class, were higher up the social hierarchy. The existence of slavery was therefore crucial as it bound together different social groups and elevated all white people above their enslaved property, in a racial hierarchy distinctive to the South.[9]

Within this complex web of southern social relations stood the figure of the ideal "southern lady." She was both a myth and a reality, but often the two did not match up. The southern lady was a distilled version of the Cult of True Womanhood in the sense that she held a cultural capital unlike any other southern woman.[10] Anne Firor Scott argued this was fundamentally linked to the fact that the South was a slave society, and "because they owned slaves and thus maintained a traditional landowning aristocracy, southerners tenaciously held on to the patriarchal structure," which included their vision of southern womanhood, which pinned ladyhood at its proverbial core.[11] The experience of planter women contrasted sharply with many other groups of southern women (black slaves, the lower class, frontier women) who could never hope to attain its high standards, either because of their racial or class position. Whereas slave women "answered to a master who was not of their natural family, class or race," the southern lady was firmly under the control of male family members (her father, husband, or son), which made her in a sense, compliant in her subordination.

Historians such as Elizabeth Fox-Genovese have suggested that planter women accepted their subordination in the southern hegemony because they were bound to a patriarchal society in a way that black women were not.[12] In other words elite women had a vested interest in protecting the institution of slavery because it elevated their own status above black women and lower-class white women and gave them a degree of power and authority albeit within the limitations of their gender. Likewise single, slaveholding women replicated class, race, and gender hierarchies in the way they conducted their lives. They were keen to demonstrate their deference to the broader patriarchy of the South in the hope of gaining acceptance from their family and from society in general, which inadvertently led to a greater degree of autonomy. Planter-class women subscribed to the same conservative worldview as white men, and they often replicated existing hierarchies by accepting their own subordination within the patriarchal order.[13] Women were taught to accept their subordination as wives and mothers in light of their racial (and for slaveholding women, class) "superiority" over black people.

Slaveholding women in particular had a vested interest in upholding slavery, owing to their unique role in southern society as southern ladies, which upheld them as paragons of moral virtue and ideal womanhood. For women within the slaveholding class or for other elite women who were beneficiaries of slavery in port cities such as Charleston or Savannah, the roles and expectations of them—as southern ladies—were heightened with their elevated social status. The ideal of the southern lady "constituted the highest condition to which women could aspire to," and consequently the pressure for them to attain the feminine standard of perfection was intense.[14] Elizabeth Fox-Genovese noted, "the activities of even the most prestigious lady remained carefully circumscribed by the conventions ordained for women in general, and southern culture placed a premium on her meeting the responsibility in accordance with her station."[15] Therefore, for women who were single, the same pressure to conform to a standard that did not really fit them must have been just as intense, which led many women to show an outward veneer of acceptance of their "required" gender roles. This pressure to conform came in various different guises: from institutions (such as the church and schools), from family and community, and in the form of the printed press (magazines and advice literature). Women could not escape the powerful rhetoric of their community and embedded in institutions, which led to internal conflicts, as women—both married and single—wrestled with their own conceptions of themselves (and for their desire for autonomy), with the competing need to fit in with societal stereotypes of nineteenth-century womanhood.[16] As Reverend T. Carleton Henry of Charleston reiterated, even women without husbands were answerable to the overarching patriarchy of the South, inculcated in his firm warning that "if there be neither husband nor father to complain, community will."[17]

There was a disjuncture between the myth of ideal womanhood and the reality of women's everyday life as a means to understand how female singleness fitted into nineteenth-century ideals of femininity. The Cult of True Womanhood was a social construct that encouraged and inspired middle-to-upper-class white women to fulfill certain models of femininity, based on marriage, motherhood, and domesticity.[18] It had particular resonance for the upper class, who were seen as the exemplars of ideal womanhood, connected to their elevated racial and class position. The Cult of True Womanhood had a strong racial and class bias that was particularly marked in the South because of slavery. Not all women fitted into the mold of nineteenth-century ideal womanhood that was so heavily emphasized and encouraged in the South.[19] Yet women were continually exposed to societal demands to construct, and then control, their femininity. The four "cardinal virtues" of True Womanhood were piety, purity, submissiveness, and of course, domesticity. The church was intent in instilling piety in their female congregation, and "women were encouraged to find solace in religion," but not power.[20] There was generally a fear of powerful women in the church, with ministers who spoke out "against women usurping men's place in religious service" or against those who threatened to move from "pew to pulpit."[21] Piety was more about "effect[ing] conversions among family members" and "bolstering [female] endurance," which "aided them to achieve self-discipline"—a further institutional tool utilized to control women.[22]

Religion was seen as a central "lynchpin" and effective "means of self-control" designed to guide women through the trials and tribulations of life; it also represented a means of social control over women.[23] On the one hand religion provided women an escape from the drudgeries of their daily lives, with the promise of a glorious afterlife, but on the other it limited women from exercising autonomy. For example Laura Comer, the ever-complaining widow from Columbus, Georgia, regularly recorded her religious sentiments in her diary, which spanned the 1860s to the late 1890s. Comer referred repeatedly to the terrible sufferings she endured throughout her earthly life and looked to God for strength, describing herself as "weak, helpless and in distress."[24] Frequently preoccupied by thoughts of death and the promise of salvation in the afterlife, Comer displayed a general malaise and dissatisfaction with her life. In the post–Civil War period, she chronicled her intolerance with "free negroes," whom she dubbed "indolent" and "perplexing," presumably because she could not control them in the way she wanted to, and she found she lacked the authority of her late husband.[25] Following James Comer's death in 1864 (which it must be noted ended a deeply unhappy marriage), Laura Comer turned to God for protection. "O Lord, what wilt thou have me do? Of myself I am nothing, only as God invites, directs and enlightens and strengthens me," she wrote in 1867, adding, "I am done with earthly friendships and loves! I shudder and shrink from assuming any responsibilities. My only hope now hangs in faith I have in God's promises."[26] The case of Laura Comer makes a wider conjectural point about single women, who were caught in a conundrum. On the one hand they drew strength from God, but on the other they were curtailed by their devotion to organized religion, which was ultimately controlled by men, who preyed on female insecurities.[27]

Charleston's Sisters of Charity of Our Lady of Mercy are a good illustration of this point, as they were manipulated and controlled by a figure of male authority within the church. The story as it is retold describes how the Sisters of Charity, under the directive of a Santo Domingan refugee Julia Datty, established an independent school for young ladies, which was thriving as an independently run entity under South Carolina law.[28] After Datty's death "the sisters were dismayed" when the bishop, John England, "ordered [them] to curtail their educational efforts" despite the school's independent status and their volition to continue running the educational establishment as they had done previously.[29] Yet their voices were silenced by Bishop John England as a dominant figure of male authority within the church, who was able to demand female submission and eliminate their free will. It was not until later in the nineteenth century that southern women began to exercise greater control and autonomy in organized religion.

Likewise, in the field of education, women were both entrapped *and* empowered. This dichotomy was tied to the fact that education for women was "carefully refined and adapted to mirror existing traditional values," and "nineteenth-century southern schools were in reality extensions of the home, which meant education was yet another means of family control."[30] Education for women was therefore encouraged within a very specific context. Friedman argued that in spite of this context "education contributed to southern women's self-confidence and a more positive self-image," as young ladies also realized the power of education in promoting future independent living.[31] Minnie Hooper, from Charleston, South Carolina, adorned her father with gratitude for agreeing to continue paying for her education, as it enabled her the opportunity "to earn a subsistence" and "to be independent and to cease to be a burden" later in life.[32]

In the Civil War and postwar periods, young southern girls continued to value a good education. Julia Tutwiler, born in Tuscaloosa, Alabama, in 1841, spoke with deep regret when her father suspended her education when she was seventeen years old. In writing to her sister Ida Tutwiler some years later in 1872, she confessed how much she regretted that her formal education had ceased so prematurely. She readily admitted: "I hated to put father to more expense [in educating me]. . . . I did not know . . . what a large income Father had [at the time], and what an excellent investment of it he would make giving opportunities for cultivation to one of his children who would make use of every minute with enthusiasm."[33] Yet she later admitted, "I have missed and needed that systematic and thorough teaching that is given in boys colleges. . . . I could not exaggerate the need I have had for this training and the trouble I have had for want of it."[34] While this did not prevent her from achieving considerable success as an educational (and prison) reformer, it clearly highlights the correlation between knowledge and power— power in the sense of autonomy and freedom from the shackles of dependence on others. The role of institutions, and the messages that they embodied in southern society, therefore had the ability to shape southern women's identity, regardless of their marital status.

In nineteenth-century women's magazines and prescriptive literature, women were praised for being weak, timid, "dependent," and frail. The *Young Ladies Book* summarized the passive virtues of a good woman, which included "a spirit of obedience, . . . submission," "pliability of temper," and "humility of mind." *Godey's Ladies Book* emphasized "wifely duties and childcare" and said women had to ensure the home was a "cheerful, peaceful place" to keep men satisfied and away from outside temptation.[35] The ideal southern woman was expected to be a wife and mother. Men by comparison were the adventurers, the doers, the hardier sex, who thrived in the public sphere of work, politics, and business, which allowed their weak and dependent wives to enjoy the peace and quiet of the home and family, which better suited their delicate nature.[36] The doctrine of separate spheres thus separated men and women into distinct zones of work and family, dominance and submission. It was an ideology that hallmarked the early-to-mid-nineteenth-century South and targeted the middle to upper-class and slaveholding women, all of whom were heavily cajoled to live according to its standards.[37] It was also an ideology that kept women in their proper social and familial roles, by severely circumscribing their autonomy beyond the household and limiting their roles even in church and education. By telling women that their moral influence and power lay in the home and domestic sphere, men tried to limit women's sphere of independence, and thus bolster their own position.[38] Female activity was heavily circumscribed in all areas of women's lives—a woman was not permitted to travel alone; she had to curtail her physical activity, dress according to custom, and walk, talk, and even express her emotions within a framework of ladylike decorum. A *true* lady was never outspoken, nor coarse, and was seldom driven by intellectual pursuits, and she had to, above all, be guided by what made *her husband* happy.

George Fitzhugh, a sociologist and spokesman on the role of women, wrote in *Sociology for the South* in 1854: "So long as she is nervous, fickle, capricious, delicate, diffident and dependent, man will worship and adore her. Her weakness is her strength, and her true art is to cultivate and improve that weakness. Women naturally shrinks from public gaze, and from the struggle and competition of life. . . . In truth, woman, like children, has but one right, and that is the right to protection. The right to protection involves the obligation to obey. A husband, a lord and master, whom she should love and honor and obey, nature designed for every woman. . . . If she is obedient she stands little danger of maltreatment."[39] In George Fitzhugh's view, a woman was worthy of protection only if she showed her willingness to obey male authority. Much like the African American slave accepting the authority of his or her master, women were also expected to show their deference to men. This placed unmarried women in an awkward position. Since they had not married, they could be accused of failing to conform to gender stereotypes or to the rule of a master, which was particularly marked for slaveholding women.

This was further complicated by women's legal status under common law. In short women should mold their identity—to conform—and then become subsumed into the identity of their husband. Herein lay one of the main dilemmas for southern women. They were encouraged to marry in order to fulfill their expectations of true womanhood, but upon meeting this demand, they relinquished all identity and power of their own. As Wyatt-Brown argued: "Whereas women's social existence largely depended upon her being married, her legal identity ended the moment the ceremony was performed," which meant that she had to sacrifice her legal identity in exchange for her social acceptance in southern society.[40] In this context it is hardly surprising that some women developed an inherent fear of marriage. In spite of the vast literature that encouraged women to fulfill their feminine duty by becoming good wives and mothers, a significant minority of women continued to fear their loss of autonomy. As a consequence of their malaise toward matrimony, some choose not to marry at all, and southern women were beginning to look to alternatives to the dominant ideal.

Martha Foster Crawford, who later became a missionary in China, was anxious at the prospect of her impending marriage. She confided in her diary: "I have the blues—I can't help it. And why? I am continually haunted by the idea of *being married*. I feel like a prisoner. . . . I formerly felt free . . . but now I feel I have my part to act—that I am no longer independent."[41] Martha was not the only woman to use metaphors of imprisonment to describe marriage; other single women spoke of being "hemmed in," submerged, and trapped by the mere thought of marriage.[42] Her sentiments are a common theme expressed in single women's diaries and correspondence. Crawford's intriguing choice of words reveal how she, like many other impending brides, felt trapped by society's expectation that she *should* marry, which led some women to delay, or to avoid it altogether. Martha's knowledge that she would have a "part to play," almost outside of herself, which involved "act[ing]" in an appropriate way in order to fulfill her new role, presumably as a wife, and later, as a mother, is telling of the anxieties women harbored about the realities of married life. These included fears of the wedding night (and their first sexual encounter), and fears of pregnancy, childbirth, and the responsibilities that they would likely encounter as a southern wife. The act of marriage ultimately meant a personal act of sacrifice for southern women. They were expected to give up their former identities (and legal status as femme sole) and become "empty vessels," objects malleable to their husbands' demands, in exchange for being elevated onto an imaginary pedestal and commended as "True Women" by those around them.[43]

Joyce Broussard uses the metaphor of married women literally becoming stripped, "naked before the law," as they exchanged their status as a femme sole for that of a femme covert.[44] In English and American law, coverture referred to a woman's legal status after marriage. Legally, upon marriage, the husband and wife were treated as one entity—the husband's—and the woman forfeited any legal identity she previously had in her own right. Simply put marriage foreclosed a woman's legal existence in relation to her property rights, and a married woman became legally prevented from owning her own property, unless specific provisions had been made before the marriage took place, which were relatively uncommon in the antebellum period. Married women "could not file lawsuits or be sued separately, nor could they execute contracts. The husband could use, sell or dispose of her property without her permission," rendering her invisible in the eyes of the law and therefore powerless. William Blackstone's authoritative legal text *Commentaries in the Laws of England* on 1765 summarized the key features and consequences of coverture: "By marriage, the husband and wife are one person in law: that is the very being or legal existence of the woman is suspended during the marriage, or at least incorporated and consolidated into that of the husband: under whose wing, protection, and cover she performs everything; and is therefore called a femme covert."[45] The importance of understanding the meaning and implications of coverture as a defining factor in the loss of southern women's identity therefore cannot be overstated. It correlates to the ideology of true womanhood and reiterates a married woman's position in law as one of anonymity, which ties in with George Fitzhugh's description of a "nervous," "weak" woman, "shrinking from the public gaze."[46] Religion also encouraged women to take solace in God to stave off "rebellious emotions" and as a positive means of "self-control" that buttressed notions of feminine passionlessness.[47] Yet, oddly enough, the same did not apply to a single woman's legal identity. While single women were repeatedly warned about the necessity of marriage, increasing numbers of young ladies started to question its centrality in their own lives.

Mary Telfair described marriage as a "lottery" that she would rather not partake in.[48] Elizabeth Ruffin thought that spinsterhood might be a "more peaceful station" than marriage and motherhood. She prized the "sweets of independence as greatly preferable to . . . charming servitude under a lord and master." Julia Southall, who never married, chose work over the marital union. She remarked: "Doing too well to think of marrying am I not. . . . Freedom is too sweet to think of changing my present situation," and therefore she made a deliberate and self-conscious choice to remain single.[49] In terms of their legal status, single southern women had an identity and a presence that married women could only dream about, which again helps to explain some women's reluctance to marry. Unlike her married counterpart, a single woman to all intents and purposes had the same rights as most men in law: to file lawsuits, to buy and sell property, and to sue or be sued. Here again the disjuncture between the propaganda on female domesticity, claiming to protect women in marriage, and the reality of women's lives was considerable. Marriage signaled the loss of "property rights and obligations" and held few "immunities [and] exemptions" for married women.[50] By contrast never-married women and widows retained the freedom to operate a farm or a plantation with the ready workforce of slaves.[51] Widowhood also fell under the umbrella of female singleness. Widowhood forced women into new roles; they managed plantations, slaves, and families. They learned to tread carefully to uphold their image as planter ladies while simultaneously demanding an increased share of power in their role as head of household or plantation mistress. These women had the potential to wield tremendous socioeconomic power, particularly if they held a large number of slaves and productive plantations.[52]

This was not the experience of all widows, and Catherine Clinton argued that most widows "did not fare well" as they were "besieged by financial debts," family breakdown, and legal and social wrangling.[53] Scholars of widowhood have stressed how widows faced the challenge of constructing new identities as single women following the loss of their husbands. Chagsin Lee, working on widowhood in northern Kentucky, 1862–1900, describes the difficulties women endured as widowhood stripped them of their status, roles, and identity as married women.[54] The "powerless institution" that Lee described for soldiers' widows (on the Union side) hinged on the premise that widowhood was a negative identity. To say "I'm a widow" in the North elicited only pity from others, and according to Lee, "widows were expected to live up to an image [of virtuous widowhood]" that fell in line with nineteenth-century conventions of the "grieving widow."[55] As highlighted by Lee's analysis of widows in the North, the status of widowhood also placed constraints on women, as women without husbands were expected to live up to an image of virtuous widowhood inextricably bound to the Cult of True Womanhood. Deviation from this ideal was not countenanced by society, and therefore widows were forced to operate within these tight constraints or to manipulate them as best they could in order to exercise a sense of agency in their lives.[56] Lee's widows in the North were "soldiers' widows" with little or no money and a matching social standing.

In contrast Kirsten Wood's *Masterful Women: Slaveholding Widows from the American Revolution through the Civil War* represents a very different class of widow —white, slaveholding widows across Virginia, the Carolinas, and Georgia in the late eighteenth and nineteenth centuries.[57] The widows that Lee described in the North and the wealthy plantation-class widows of Wood's investigation fall at opposite ends of the social spectrum. As Wood noted widowhood left "most women socially marginal and even destitute" in the period following the American Revolution and through to the Civil War, in large part owing to the economic difficulties encountered by lower-class widows.[58] Slaveholding widows, cast in a safety net of relative wealth, often experienced widowhood quite differently, which linked to the terms of their husbands' wills. These women formed a small minority who were buffered by their wealth, property, and social position—and with it their autonomy. As wealthy widows these women were respected and revered within the social hierarchy as they utilized their elevated position to reexert both ladyhood and power, which gilded them with an air of superiority unparalleled by women from the lower social classes. Their class standing afforded them protection from public criticism and sheltered them seeking work outside of their plantation. They manipulated their status as southern wives and ladies following their husbands' death in an effort to provide them with the protective cushioning necessary when dealing with their slaves, property, and family as women on their own.[59] Slaveholding widows therefore took pride in their identity and recognized their privileged position in the southern class, race, and gender hierarchy, often trading on their good name. This can be seen in many of the petitions used in the final chapter of this book.

Male and female slaveholders believed that widows held important responsibilities for maintaining the status quo and therefore failed to extend much sympathy to women who allowed excessive grief to interfere with their new duties as plantation mistresses. Many cases in this book reflect a more positive picture of self-reliance and ingenuity. Elite, slaveholding widows did all they could to protect their stake within the southern hierarchy. Elizabeth Fox-Genovese argued, "Elite, white women themselves preferred a hierarchical society in which they were subordinated, if that was the price for slavery and its exploitation of the poorer classes."[60] The position of elite, slaveholding widows lay outside of the boundaries of a typical planter wife, and therefore by emphasizing an ongoing dedication or allegiance to their deceased husband, widows attained a privileged position associated to their previous marital status as a slaveholding wife in a way that never-married women did not. Widows therefore continued to be defined by their relationships to men, even when their husbands passed away. In the development of new identities as single women, widows donned masculine behavior in conducting business transactions such as slave trading and in executing slave punishments, and as executors of their husbands' wills. Widows therefore combined an apparent contradiction between helpless femininity and widowed responsibility to good effect as they navigated between masculine and feminine gender roles. Tellingly these new roles of autonomous and independent widowhood were not only tolerated but also accepted within southern society, because widows were perceived as acting on behalf of their deceased husbands—rather than for their own self-interest.[61]

Virginian widow Martha Cocke stood firm in her resolve to prove that she was a capable plantation manager after her husband died. Her sister-in-law Caroline Cocke mused: "I suppose they think, as she is one of the fairer, I will not say weaker, sex, she will lack capacity, industry, & for carrying on such business, but really I think she will be quite a Manager, and if she be not, she must at least be rid of the perplexity of a multiplicity of Agents, who seldom prove faithful—by concentrating her business, a great inducement to her."[62] Martha and Caroline were united in their resolve that Martha had potential to become "quite a manager," but they were shrewd enough to recognize that even if the plan did not go well, she would be "rid" of her former agents. As Wood recognized, thousands of slaveholding widows reigned successfully over their plantations, slaves, children, and households in the event of their husband's untimely death. These women rose or fell in their endeavors largely as a result of their success or failure in crafting new identities for themselves. Widowhood demanded a blend of feminine and masculine gender traits, in order to overcome adversity. Ada Bacot, a slaveholding widow from South Carolina, understood this and wrote in her diary on 11 February 1861: "I find some of my young Negroes have been disobeying my orders, they were found away from home without a pass. I hope I may be able to make them understand without much trouble that I am mistress and *will* be obeyed."[63]

In reality widows rarely emulated masculine behavior per se but instead interpreted male authority in their own unique manner. Women were reluctant to use violence to achieve their means where masters would not hesitate.[64] This point is illustrated again by Ada Bacot, who worked as a housekeeper (and later as a nurse) in Maupin House during the Civil War. She recorded an "unfortunate incident" with a slave boy named Willie that resulted in her, rather uncharacteristically, losing her temper and slapping him "in the mouth." In response "he ran off yelling as if I had hit him with a cudgel, he never rested until he made his nose bleed, than ran to his mother saying I had done it."[65] The ugly incident ended with an intense argument with the child's mother, who she described as "perfectly frantic," "like a lioness in a moment."[66] Her reaction to the slave boy, from a race, class, and gendered perspective, requires attention. In spite of Bacot's anger with the "impertinent" boy, she nevertheless displayed a guilty conscience at having slapped him, for when Dr. Macintosh returned and decided to whip the "Negroes" in punishment for their insolence, Ada tried to intervene and pleaded with him not to, as they were generally "good" slaves. Her words evidently fell on deaf ears, as she recounted that the slaves had a "dreadful time of it," finally being taken to "gaol" until Dr. Maupin returned. Ada described how she had been being "worried sick about it all."[67]

The incident revealed the limitations of her own and other white women's power to control external situations. In other contexts Ada Bacot demonstrated that she had considerable power and autonomy (such as managing her own plantation), but here in the social confines of the boarding house, she was not "mistress" and therefore remained compliant to the higher authority of Dr. Macintosh and Dr. Maupin, who represented the patriarchal figures in the boarding house. This particular incident highlights some important points: that Ada Bacot usually enjoyed a satisfactory relationship with her slaves and was generally averse to using corporal punishment to reprimand them; on the rare occasion that she did, she felt guilty about her loss of control and perceived it as unladylike behavior. A distinction can clearly be deduced regarding how slaveholding men and women dealt with recalcitrant slaves; men resorted to violence in order to protect their honor, while women shied away from it in order to protect their own ladylike decorum.

Widows then remained fixed by certain gender conventions concerning feminine behavior even though they were now single. An exception to this rule was the case of social widowhood (women who were married, but who spent months or years living alone in the temporary absence of their husband), which demanded that married women act as temporary heads of households in the absence of the male patriarch. These women remained bound by their coverture as married women but were granted special privileges to act on their husband's behalf in order to enable him to "enjoy" his "privileges fully" as a man.[68] In the antebellum (and Civil War) South, husbands were frequently absent from home owing to political, economic, business, or social responsibilities. When their husbands were away, often for extended periods of time, married women acted as temporary heads of households; managed plantations, households, slaves, and children; and to all intents and purposes functioned as "temporarily single" women.[69]

Virginian slaveholder Paulina Pollard lived apart from her husband for five years, a burden she simply described as "an additional responsibility."[70] Rebecca Pilsbury endured months of living alone in her new home in Brazoria, Texas, when her husband, Timothy Pilsbury, served as a member of the U.S. Congress in Washington in 1848. During this time Rebecca kept a detailed diary in which she expressed the difficulties that she faced as a woman on her own. Living in Brazoria, Texas, Rebecca lived as a social widow, and her life revolved around the management of her slaves, household, and domestic chores, and around the inadequacies she felt as a woman left to manage a plantation alone.[71] "Today has been a sad day for me. My dear husband left me for Washington, he will be absent five months at least, but I shall try to do what I think will please him and thereby pass the hours more pleasantly," Rebecca commented in her diary on 14 November 1848.[72] This must have been a hard task, faced as she was with the constant duties as housekeeper and manager of a small plantation. Her daily tasks included caring for slaves; attending to the pigs, pigeons, and poultry; and "toil[ing] diligently" in all her "duties" in the hope of making her (absent) husband happy.[73]

While social widows often kept up a detailed correspondence with their absentee husbands, the reality was that their letters often took days, if not weeks, to reach them, particularly if they lived in a remote locality, as many of them did. Therefore, by the time they actually received word from their husband, on anything from what crops to plant, to the management of slaves, or other day-to-day management of the plantation, it was often too late, and the decisions had already been made. As a result these women, who acted as temporary plantation managers, or as head of household, had learned to develop a wide range of skills that had been born of the necessity to manage their husbands' duties. Mary Steele was forced to adopt surrogate mastery (acting as a lady with temporary power) while her husband, John Steele, performed his role at the Treasury. "The Steele marriage illustrated the chief reason why slaveholding wives acted as deputy masters: for white men to enjoy their privileges fully, wives simply had to act [out] a manly part when men left their enclosures."[74]

Social widowhood was also an important training ground that prepared women in the eventuality they would ever be faced with a permanent state of widowhood. Ruth Stoval Hairston married Peter Wilson, a planter of Berry Hill, Brierfield, and Goose Pond in Pittsylvania County, Virginia. The marriage, apparently a happy one, resulted in five children. However at the age of thirty Ruth was widowed for the first time, and in 1816 she married again. Her second marriage to Virginian planter Robert Hairston, of Leatherwood plantation in Henry County, was by contrast a tumultuous one. In 1837 Robert moved to Mississippi, with the intention, he claimed, of managing his properties there. Meanwhile he left his wife in Virginia to singlehandedly manage their plantation, for what amounted to literally *years* at a time. There is much speculation surrounding Robert Hairston's decision to relocate to Mississippi, culminating in the controversy after his death in 1852, when he left a slave child his entire estate and Ruth nothing.[75] Ruth Hairston's case accentuates how social widowhood was at times a pretext for masking more ingrained marital problems, thus avoiding formal separation and divorce. Certainly this seems to resonate with Ruth Stoval Hairston, who spent over a decade living alone as a social widow, before her husband died in 1852. For elite white women preserving the façade of a good marriage was important to their image and "respectability" as good southern women. At times the façade became impossible to maintain, as a small but growing number of married women reclaimed their femme sole status through the avenue of divorce. Female divorce petitioners frequently complained that their husbands had failed to live up to their promise of protection, while men criticized their wives for failing to behave according to the tenets of true womanhood. This linked to traditional notions of southern womanhood, and to the marriage contract, whereby a woman gave up her identity in exchange for the protection of her husband, which played an important part in replicating conventional gender hierarchies.

However, in the case of divorce it was critical that upper-class women could prove that they had been virtuous women throughout the marital union and were able to demonstrate to the court that they had tried, against all odds, to be the perfect southern wife. In addition they had to prove that their husband had failed to live up to his promise of protection and provision in marriage thus highlighting his masculinity (or lack of it). By couching their divorce petitions in the language of benevolence, and by painting themselves as morally pure models of womanhood, who were at the same time physically weak and dependent in nature, women demonstrated that the best way to gain a divorce was by displaying an outward submission to the overarching patriarchy of the courts.[76] Divorce petitions filed by female complainants in Florida, Georgia, Tennessee, Arkansas, and Louisiana slowly began to be granted, as early as the antebellum period, though the rate of divorce accelerated in the postwar period in line with the broadening of the divorce laws to include reasons such as drunkenness, cruelty, neglect to provide, infidelity, and miscegenation with former slaves. For example Martha Smith Green, a planter-class woman from Tennessee, accused her husband of mistreating her so badly that she was ill "for eighteen weeks."[77] She also said that he was having an illicit relationship with a female slave, which further demeaned her name. In seeking a divorce, women like Green were presented with a real dichotomy; women had to demonstrate their femininity (which included weakness, dependence, and so on), while at the same time being assertive enough to challenge their husband's authority by filing a divorce petition in the first place.

Widows faced a similar dilemma in presenting their petitions to the courts, in claiming the right to their dower share, or seeking permission to move or sell property. They too had to show a respectful deference to southern femininity, by showing their continued femininity or embodiment of virtuous widowhood. Elizabeth Kirkpatrick, a widow from Arkansas, displayed fortitude and agency in disputing a minor's claim on her property following her husband's death. She insisted that the courts recognize that her dower share was separate from the property left to the children, which the courts endorsed.[78] Likewise on 15 April 1830, Louisiana widow Sarah Anne Moore petitioned to Orleans Parish in order to recover her "dower property" from her husband, William B. Beldon, which included $9,096.73 in property, including six slaves. Her petition was successful, her appeal granted, and her dower share returned.[79] As these examples bear witness to, for most widows financial concerns were paramount. Remarriage brought with it significant risk, and if a widow had children from a previous marriage, she had to consider whether her potential new husband would make an adequate stepfather. Even childless and laboring widows thought twice about reentering covertures beset with concerns regarding compromising their own wealth.[80] The financial consequences of losing a husband—at any age—were thus undeniable. However, certain variables, such as the age of a widow, the number (and age) of her children, her social class, and where she lived, directly affected the receipt of a widow's dower share, the share for life of her husband's estate. Younger widows were often left with small children to raise, as well as plantations to safeguard and manage, until their children reached maturity and could take on the responsibility of plantation management themselves—this took time and money.

Sarah Alston of Halifax County, North Carolina, was given the power to "use and manage" her underage children's estates as "to her seems best."[81] Wood argued, "A widowed mother left with a houseful of little children also stood a good chance of being given more than a dower. These widowed mothers often bore the weighty responsibility of managing the entire estate for the benefit of their young children."[82] Thirty-five-year-old Sarah Witherspoon from Hartsville, Darlington County, in South Carolina was widowed in 1861, with two young children to raise, and the family plantation and other property near Darlington and Spring-ville, South Carolina, to manage.[83] For widows without children, such as Keziah Brevard, a fifty-seven-year-old widow living in Richland District, near Columbia, South Carolina, the experience of widowhood was quite different. In 1861, following on from her husband's death, Brevard lived alone at her Sand Hills plantation (later renamed Alwehav) with two hundred slaves for company.[84] Brevard was an "indomitable widow" and "remarkable woman" who managed her plantation with "consummate skill" in a patriarchal world in which she handled her role admirably.[85] Each woman's experience of widowhood was intimately woven into the fabric of her personal life—the proximity to friends and family, whether she lived alone or had dependents, and then according to where they lived, and their ages.

As the nineteenth century progressed there was a steady transformation, or what Chambers-Schiller described as a "cultural re-assessment of singleness."[86] Single women helped to alter their image as redundant women and proved that they could contribute to the patriarchy of the southern family. They did this by upholding their femininity but also by showing that they were both willing and useful in their service to others in the family and wider community. These women pledged allegiance to an alternative model of womanhood, referred to as the "Cult of Single Blessedness" that began to remove the stigma of remaining single. Rather than being seen as a curse, the single state began to be seen as a blessing. In advice manuals, such as *Godey's Lady's Handbook* or *The Young Lady*, writers began to advise "that no marriage" was better than "an unhappy one contracted out of self-ish motives," which coincided with the rise of companionate marriage and a slow but definite revision of acceptable gender roles.[87]

Single Blessedness

The state of single blessedness gradually gained acceptance as a viable alternative to marriage, which dovetailed with the new ideal of companionate marriage that emerged in line with it. As the name suggests it reflected a more optimistic attitude to the single state, viewing nonmarriage as more of an opening for doing good and hence a blessing, rather than a curse. Female singleness began to gradually move away from less favorable stereotypes, which had prevailed in the early to mid-nineteenth century, though evidence of some social scorn persisted in some cases.[88] A particularly harsh depiction of the single woman surfaced in the *Southern Literary Messenger* in 1862: "A leech is about as lovely as an old maid of forty-six," it professed. An unidentified single woman also wrote in a somber tone: "I soak myself in the warm water of interest and sympathy in the lives and happiness of others—in charity—in various other tepid baths—but it's of no use. I am not really alive—like the poor leech, I have at best a miserable semblance of existence. Who but I has such a dreary and lonely existence?"[89] The publication of articles such as "The Reverie of the Old Maid" highlights that while views toward single women were slowly altering, derogatory stereotypes continued to exist. Terms such as "spinster" and "old maid" conjured up negative connotations specific to women who never married. As Lisa Tickner argued, ridicule is "a powerful weapon in the maintenance of hegemony. . . . It operates as a kind of short circuit to argument in the interests of preserving the status quo," which was certainly true in the South.[90] By using words and constructing images that belittled single women, such as redundant or odd, power remained with the white, male hegemony. In this context it is hardly surprising that women like Mary Telfair or

Grace Brown were keen to show a veneer of cultural acceptance on a woman's place. Paradoxically by doing this single women maintained a greater degree of personal autonomy and had more flexibility in how they chose to live their everyday lives.

In the South girls were expected to marry young. Based on Clinton's statistics, the mean age of first marriage for a southern woman was much lower than in northern states, meaning that by the age of twenty-five an unmarried woman was officially considered a spinster.[91] "Twenty-five today and an 'old maid'! Well it's not disgraceful to be with that much abused truce of mortals to belong to the sisterhood through life," penned Anna Holt in her diary on 25 January 1861.[92] Holt was well aware that she had passed the typical age of marriage for a young lady in her position, and she had already reconciled herself to a life of single blessedness. Ann Reid was still unmarried by thirty but later considered her single state as a relief and good fortune, as she was "free from household duties and [instead] dedicated herself to religion."[93] Grace Elmore Brown similarly recognized she was not suited for marriage, assuring herself, "I am not trusting enough to let myself be guided by a human creature. I could scarcely be happy with any man."[94] Angelina and Sarah Grimké, the daughters of a wealthy South Carolinian slaveholder, also had little inclination to marry. The Grimké sisters had formed part of an antislavery duo and had exiled themselves from the South. They stood out as radicals, women who "rejected their birthright, moved north and became abolitionist crusaders."[95] The sisters' philosophical and political ideas blacklisted them as "pariahs within slaveholding culture."[96] Consequently the Grimkés were considered loquacious and unfeminine by society. In their failure to conform—or at least to show that they conformed to conventional gender models—they became a threat to society and therefore faced ridicule and abuse. Many observers saw the publication of *An Appeal to the Christian Women of the South*, written by Angelina Grimké in 1836, as a juvenile outburst that did not befit a woman's place. Women were supposed to be passive and submissive and shun the glare of public scrutiny. Yet for the sisters the pursuit of marriage was surpassed by a love of politics, of righteousness and morality for all—black and white. Perhaps surprisingly at the late age of thirty-three Angelina did eventually marry. Her sister Sarah Grimké remained single for life but lived in the home of her sister and brother-in-law in an unconventional living arrangement that suited the triumvirate.[97]

For many of these women their future happiness firmly rested on being able to remain single—rather than pursuing marriage and motherhood. In contrast to the unfavorable simile of the leech, increasing numbers of well-to-do southern women paid homage to the blossoming of an alternative culture of singlehood, supported by literature written by and about single women. Domestic novelist Augusta Jane Evans provided an alternative vision of southern femininity in her novels, which were not only popular but important in changing the perception of female singleness.[98] The so-called Cult of Single Blessedness was rooted in the belief that women could fulfill a useful role outside of marriage. It was part of the cultural reassessment of singleness that had gradually begun after the revolutionary war that had made "some Americans dramatically change their attitudes towards marriage and singlehood."[99] Chambers-Schiller described how attitudes toward singleness began to change first in the North and later filtered down into the South, crystallizing in the Civil War period.[100] The Civil War rapidly escalated the process of the cultural reassessment of female singleness as women's lives altered dramatically in wartime; for slaveholding women this was particularly marked because of the destruction of slavery, which took the ideal of southern womanhood down along with it. Another important social change in nineteenth-century society was the rise of a new marital ideal, "companionate marriage," which moved away from the "standard formula for successful marriage," which focused on "property, earning capacity and social standing," to be replaced gradually by a formula that "placed love and emotions at the center."[101] This became more entrenched in the postwar period, as the separate spheres ideology that separated male and female roles started to disintegrate and marital expectations altered. In the antebellum South women began to assert themselves in their families and voiced their demands that they must marry for love rather than to secure their family the best calculable assets possible, which gained pace as the century progressed.[102]

Sarah Morgan from Baton Rouge, Louisiana, balked at the idea of marriage and motherhood, clearly stating that she wanted "no man for her lord and master," and she stuck to her resolve until she was in her early thirties, when she married widower Frank Dawson, with whom she discovered the "companionate ideal" of love and companionship in the postwar period.[103] Mary Wylie also married late (at the age of twenty-five) to a man she clearly adored; she was the envy of her two unmarried sisters, who recognized the special bond between the doting couple. In a letter to her unmarried sister Susan, Hannah Wylie wrote, "You may guess that I compared our old maidism with the blissful married state [of Mary and Dr. Mobley] but no hints to Dr. and M. for I must confess that there is an exception in all rules," and they were it. [104] Other women echoed Susan Wylie's view that companionate marriage was still relatively scarce. Even women who were married recognized its shortfalls. Civil War diarist Mary Boykin Chesnut from Charleston, South Carolina, who was wealthy, married, and childless, took a cynical view of marriage: "It is an odd thing. In all of my life how many persons have I seen in love? Not a half-dozen and yet I am a tolerably close observer, a faithful watcher of men and manners. Society for me has been only an enlarged field for character study. Flirtation is the business of society. That is play at love-making; it begins in vanity, it ends in vanity. It is spurred on by idleness and a want of other excitement. . . . it is a pleasant but very foolish game."[105]

Posthumous portrait of Mary Telfair (1791–1875), by Carl Ludwig Brandt, 1896. Courtesy of the Telfair Museum of Art, Savannah, Georgia.

Other well-to-do women compared marriage to the state of single blessedness, and the former still came up short. Mary Telfair was convinced that she would never find a suitable mate: "I never have, could, or will see a soul in a man worth loving," she admitted in May 1818.[106] Mary likewise was a keen social observer, who often wrote about other people's marriages. On one occasion she used the metaphor of two birds trapped in a cage to emphasize how not all marriages were companionate ones. This correlated to her earlier reticence toward marriage, because she could not find a suitable mate. In a letter written in the early 1800s she wrote that "two people coming together in holy wedlock always reminds me of two birds in a cage unless they sing in Concert, what discord ensues—far better to chirp tune their notes on some lonely spray, unseen unheard in 'single blessedness,' for a solus well performed, is preferable to an indifferent duet."[107] The contrast of the "solus well performed" to the "indifferent duet" is a reference to companionate marriage. She vocalized the wider opinion of increasing numbers of women that started to take root in the early nineteenth century, which was that it was better to remain single than to marry for convenience or endure a lifetime with the wrong mate. This new philosophy made room for alternative models of femininity to take root—and develop—in the Old South.

Of course not all women wanted to marry. South Carolinian Grace Elmore Brown confessed at the tender age of twenty-two her hopes for the future, which did *not* involve matrimony. "Marriage has precious little share in my plans for the future," she confided in her journal on 13 September 1862. That "marriage for me would hardly be a happy state" was a conclusion she had reached by virtue of the fact that none of the men who she might want to marry would want to marry her.[108] Even prior to that Mary Telfair wrote disparagingly in reaction to a rumor circulating that she was to marry. Telfair said in disgust:

> Neither Jew nor Gentile has any chance in drawing me as a *prize* in the great lottery of matrimony. I am too great a lover of *liberty* to resign it particularly to an Israelite besides I belong to a family devoted to "single blessedness" therefore my dear Mary believe any thing you hear of me sooner than I am going to be married, not that I am an enemy of the *holy institution* I approve highly of the state when two persons enter into it from disinterested affection and when there exists a congeniality of character, but I have always thought the number of happy matches considerably less than unhappy and always conclude that there are faults on both sides, among the whole circle of my acquaintances, I know of but one couple who came up to my idea of a *rational* pair.[109]

In this extract three key points require further attention. First, the way in which Telfair equated "matrimony" with the loss of "liberty." Second, her observation that only one couple, out of all her married friends (which was probably a considerable number as Telfair was twenty-three years old when she wrote this letter in November 1814), were well suited. Third, Telfair demonstrated that spinsterhood was a *rational* choice, and one that she had consciously made, and not one that had been made for her. She freely admitted that she did not "envy a woman her husband" and noted that "I have never viewed the state of single blessedness with horror."[110]

Another tactic used by some women was to try to delay marriage, rather than put it off altogether.[111] Anya Jabour's work on young women in the South describes "a culture of resistance" in youth. For example young girls deliberately delayed marriage by extending the length of time they spent at boarding school thus prolonging the period of time they remained single. If they had agreed to marriage already, they might make the courtship as long as possible.[112] Some of the women in this study clearly exhibited a "culture of resistance" by marrying late. However, research suggests that a significant minority of single women did more than resist cultural pressures to marry; they rejected it altogether. Some women did this by developing a "culture of compliance" in that they showed a veneer of acceptance, but only as a platform for enhanced personal agency. "Let people talk as much as they choose about engagements being happy, my late experience does not increase my faith in the idea. Engagements lead too certainly to matrimony," confessed Lucy Breckinridge after calling off her engagement to Lieutenant Thomas Jefferson Bassett, convinced that he was the wrong match.[113] Anya Jabour argued that the prolonging of life stages was indicative of girls' "reluctance to accept the socialization into their assigned roles" as wives and mothers, and not simply fear of making the wrong choice. It was a symbol of women's silent resistance to the prescribed norms of nineteenth-century southern society, and an attempt to hold on to their identity as single women.[114]

What is striking about these young, white, slaveholding women was the passion and determination with which they delayed or rejected marriage, and the positive metaphors they often attributed to the unmarried state. Three main factors seem to have influenced the development of new attitudes toward female singleness: the rise of companionate marriage, single women's real or mimicked desire to replicate traditional gender roles in being useful to others, and of course the impact of the Civil War in challenging gender constructions. As attitudes started to change toward marriage, parents also began to advise their daughters to choose their husbands carefully or at least by a different set of criteria. As early as 1782, John Gregory wrote a popular advice book, *A Father's Legacy to His Daughters*, in which he "urged his daughters and readers to remain unmarried rather than marry the wrong man for the wrong reasons," which was a revelation at the time.[115] Clearly the importance of having positive relationships with male authority figures in the family, who openly encouraged women to marry for affection and love, further heightened women's resolve to embrace singleness as a respectable alternative to marriage if necessary.

This point is well illustrated in the case study of the Wylie family. Susan Wylie came from a well-known slaveholding family from upstate South Carolina. Her parents, Peter and Anne Wylie, had eight children. Of the five daughters, two remained unmarried and a third (Mary) married late but chose to remain childless (an active display of autonomy in itself). This was most likely a conscious decision, achieved through abstinence, in order to exercise control over both her body and her life, as she wanted to live it. Hannah and Susan remained unmarried, and Mary married late, at around twenty-five years of age, to a doctor, William Mobley. Of all the daughters, Susan clashed most obviously with the men in her family—in her views on politics, marriage, and men (normally in that order), which are conveyed in her copious letters of correspondence with members of the family, both male and female. Yet her views were not only tolerated, but encouraged, thus effectively challenging traditional ideas that women should be submissive and meek.[116] Her opinions were expressed with drama and conviction and revealed an image of a woman dissatisfied with the role in which she was placed, yet also a woman who had the freedom to express herself in the context of her family. As Jeff Hoffman observed, "There was a longing for more autonomy but also a realization that this longing could not be fulfilled" beyond certain boundaries.[117] Susan Wylie's relationships with the men in her life, which were almost exclusively limited to the men in her family, were open and companionate in nature, and yet she still remained constrained by societal expectations of her that lie outside of the family.

The overall impression gleaned from Susan Wylie's correspondence is one of "independence and outspokenness in a period that did not honor such behaviors in women."[118] Her identity was afforded space to breathe and grow, even though she often complained about it, and there is rarely any indication that the Wylie family tried to curb their sister's enthusiasm. Nor did this fact seem to alarm the Wylie sisters, or their father, who would have been *expected* to try to discourage such outspokenness in his daughters. On the contrary Peter Wylie often "grumbled about politiks and sometimes branche[d] out into religion" when being nursed by his unmarried daughter, and he clearly enjoyed their conversations on topics usually reserved for men. It would seem single women were afforded a degree of leeway in how outspoken they were within their own families, perhaps because they simultaneously mirrored conventional gender roles in their caregiving roles and service to the family. For example Susan nursed her father during his long period of ill health. In her obituary she was noted for her "assiduous and untiring attendance on the sick of her extended family circle."[119] The obituary continues, "her neighbors also, in sickness and distress, never failed to receive her active sympathies, exhibited by those kind services which she could so intelligently and efficiently render. . . . Although her sphere was limited, few can claim a life so entirely devoted to acts of benevolence," thus stressing her feminine virtues above all else. Susan Wylie's obituary paints a picture of a woman who embraced southern femininity and of an individual who was satisfied in her caregiving role and service to neighbors and extended family. Yet rather interestingly it gives no indication of the vexations, frustrations, and general outspokenness that also characterized her life.

Historian Jennifer Lynn Gross argued, "Positive images of single womanhood and an acceptance of marriage as the best place for women coalesced because [single women] still behaved within the bounds of true womanhood that confined married women."[120] Gross was writing with reference to the work of domestic novelists such as Augusta Jane Evans, who wrote about single women as the protagonists in her novels. Evans turned to writing and proved to be one of the most successful domestic novelists in the South of her time. In her novels she often praised the single woman but continued to make it clear that marriage and motherhood remained as the most favored ideal for southern women.[121] As a novelist Evans gained a good reputation and honorable identity for herself in her public role as a writer. In the act of writing domestic novels centered on courtship,

Portrait of Augusta Jane Evans Wilson, 1835–1909. Courtesy of the Alabama Department of Archives and History, Montgomery, Alabama.

marriage, and female singleness, and by portraying the last in a new, positive, and more useful light, Evans helped to change societal perceptions of female singleness and forged a "respectable" identity for herself as a female writer.[122]

It seems rather ironic that Evans's public endorsement of marriage and motherhood provided a platform for her to broaden her own social space as a writer. By writing, Evans and domestic novelists like her shielded themselves from public criticism and elevated themselves to a position of moral authority that allowed them to fit in and be accepted within the existing status quo, rather than be seen to be balking against it. In constructing alternative identities for themselves as single women, southern women therefore often subscribed to, and replicated, the key attributes of true womanhood. In doing so they gained respectability and social acceptance and were no longer seen as a threat to male authority.

Not all single women found their role an easy one. Sarah Varick Cozens, a young unmarried woman from North Carolina, managed a school in the mid-1830s. She wrote of her "incapability of training up little mortals" and her need to look to God for help and reassurance: "I know I can do nothing. To thee, O my God do I look for help."[123] This may have been true, but by expressing her inability to manage independently, she displayed her outward submission of feminine dependency. By seeking God's help and reassurance, she also clearly demonstrated her piety, which would have been readily accepted in a society that valued meekness and submission in women. Piety, purity, submissiveness, and

Augusta Jane Evans Wilson, 1835–1909. Courtesy of the Alabama Department of Archives and History, Montgomery, Alabama.

domesticity were important watchwords for single women. Single women therefore had to show that they were submissive to a higher (male) authority in order to fulfill the ideal of single blessedness. This was of course more difficult because as unmarried women they had seemingly rejected male authority by remaining single, but they also had an elevated legal status as a femme sole that afforded them certain legal rights that married women were stripped of. Submissiveness could be shown in a variety of ways, most commonly by devolving power to their family and by rallying to its needs, which linked to the attribute of domesticity.

An unmarried woman's identity was therefore very much tied to her family of birth. An unmarried daughter could, for example, demonstrate her submission to the family's needs by sacrificing her own, particularly in the event of sickness or a death in the family. North Carolinian Margaret Bain Cameron delayed marriage in exchange for caring for her younger siblings and sick father when her mother died in 1842. Likewise Henrietta Augusta Drayton forfeited marriage to stay at home and care for her sick parents; and Harriott, Frances, and Anne Percy delayed matrimony to help their father manage plantation affairs. These single women often discovered that death in the family was a harbinger of change that signaled a shift in their own identities as unmarried women, often turning their temporary single status into something more long lasting and permanent. The loss of a girl's mother marked a traumatic period in girls' lives, particularly in their personal and social development because of the additional commitments consequently demanded of them. The eldest unmarried daughter within the family circle was often expected to shoulder the extra household and familial duties of their deceased mother, especially if younger siblings who required care and attention were present. A mother's death thus foreshadowed new expectations and identities for unmarried daughters, who were automatically expected to manage their natal family (which included their father) in the event of their mother's death. Death in a southern family affected many, but its impact on single women was particularly marked. It may have opened a doorway to prove their usefulness and devotion to a life of single blessedness, which inevitably helped to revise conventional gender models, but it also represented a source of hard work and personal constraint.

There are many cases of the maiden aunt who took on the additional responsibilities of raising nieces and nephews following the death of a family member. Mary Susan Ker, a single woman who grew up in a planter-class family in Natchez, Mississippi, took on the lifelong responsibility of bringing up her two nieces, Mamie and Nellie Ker, after the death of her sister-in-law at the end of the Civil War.[124] Mary Telfair also assisted her sister-in-law in bringing up her niece, Margaret Long, after her brother Thomas's death in 1818. Death within the extended family significantly altered single women's responsibilities, such as becoming surrogate mothers to their relation's children.[125] For some the added responsibility was a delight, which helped shape their lives accordingly. For others it was a heavy burden, which they took on out of a sense of duty and as a demonstration of their usefulness to family, friends, and community. In doing so they were able to show that they had fulfilled their calling to single blessedness.[126] By the time of the Civil War, the Cult of Single Blessedness was rapidly maturing as an alternative model of femininity that unmarried women could aspire to. The coming of the Civil War thus further accelerated a growing societal acceptance of unmarried women. Even in the planter class there was an awakening to the reality that the necessities of war might lead to a temporary revision of gender conventions, as so many southern men went off to fight, and women were called on to fill their roles. The war itself also spurred on a wave of new activities for southern women; they became plantation managers, nurses, teachers, government workers, factory workers, and milliners, in addition to a variety of other occupations, dependent on their social position, class, and marital status.

The Civil War

As Alabaman Augusta Jane Evans made clear in her wartime novel *Macaria: Altars of Sacrifice*, the war represented a unique opportunity for single women to prove they were useful by doing good deeds that would breed self-fulfillment. Evans was an unmarried woman who had worked for a short time as a nurse in the Civil War, caring for Confederate soldiers (though it should be noted that she was initially dissuaded from doing so by her brothers, who considered such a vocation unsuitable for a young lady of her class), and it was from these formative experiences that she penned her wartime novel *Macaria*.[127] What is interesting about Evans's novel is the central character, an unmarried woman named Irene, who dedicates her life to the pursuit of "Womanly Usefulness" after the loss of her lover. Irene in many ways represents the single women of the Confederacy, the never-married and widowed women, whose mantra in life was to be "useful." As in the story of *Macaria*, "it is the blessing—and *Macaria* also means blessing in Greek—of the single woman to be more useful because she belongs exclusively to no one, her heart expands to all her suffering fellow creatures."[128] Certain parallels can be drawn between the novel and the reality of single women's lives in the Civil War. The war offered them a unique opportunity, even more meaningful and pronounced than those of their married counterparts, to do something important, thereby fulfilling their potential as women, and establishing their true identity. Single women, like the fictional Irene, could literally sacrifice themselves to the cause and in doing so gain acceptability and respectability. For these unmarried women, their willingness to dedicate themselves to cause and country, in whatever capacity it demanded of them, was not something to be feared, but something to be "celebrated." It cemented their identity as "useful" and "virtuous" single women but also offered them the opportunity for self-fulfillment.[129]

As Anne Firor Scott noted, "The challenge of war called women almost at once into new kinds and into new degrees of activity," both within the home and also outside of it.[130] As men dashed off in defense of their fledgling nation's right to independence (and their right to own slaves), women started to extend their own sphere of influence in response to wartime demands. Virginia Hammett was a young lady of Oakland in Stafford County, Virginia. When the war began she was just eighteen years old and lived a quiet life with her parents and sister on their large family farm.[131] Virginia, a fervent secessionist and a despiser "of all things Yankee," threw herself into her new wartime responsibilities with enthusiasm. "Necessity is the mother of ingenuity," exclaimed Virginia in August 1863, in reference to her nursing of the wounded soldiers, which she described in graphic detail. "I saw a great many wounded, some with eyes shot out, noses shot away, ears off, fingers off, arms, hands, flesh wounds through legs, arms, and shoulders."[132] Living in such close proximity to the battlefield, just "six miles north of Fredericksburg," meant that the Hammett family and their neighbors had regular contact with injured soldiers as well as Yankees, who frequently trespassed on their property. In February 1863 Virginia penned in her diary, "I have been cursed, abused, robbed, insulted, my life threatened, and I have been <u>seized by a Yankee solider, rudely shaken and struck over the head with a stick</u> . . . have heard my grey haired father cursed by the lowest soldiery, have heard them threaten to hang him in his own yard . . . have seen my home and that of my neighbors made desolate, been robbed almost to starvation."[133] Yet Virginia did not whimper or cower with apprehension or fear but emboldened herself, emblazoned in a new image, as a young, unmarried woman, who is capable, steely, and strong in the face of adversity.

In numerous entries in her journal, Virginia confided her fear of Yankee intruders, of lack of food, and of bad treatment. She even admitted, "I have slept night after night with an axe at my bedside and an unsheathed dagger under my pillow, with the terrible determination to defend myself if possible."[134] The fact that Virginia felt the need to protect herself speaks volumes about the war and the way it changed southern women's lives. In the absence of the men, and even in the presence of those few men who had remained, women felt unprotected and at risk. The war then did not simply alter the roles and responsibilities of southern women; it also forced them to temporarily change their nature as true women. Virginia talked about hiding an "unsheathed dagger" under her pillow each night, a decision that challenged every notion of femininity. She also imagined herself as a soldier and daydreamed of fighting as a man in the war, though she admitted, "I confess these are not very womanly feelings but one thing I know let nay one who had any spirit or love for country, be placed in my situation and they will sometimes feel as these lines express."[135] Other southern women also shared her sentiments. Grace Elmore Brown longed to "battle with life as men do, and expend in action those energies that work but to excite fretfulness because denied the true outlet."[136] Elizabeth Collier wrote a simple note in her diary in 1862, "Would God I were a man."[137]

Drew Gilpin Faust argued that these sentiments conceal an even deeper dissatisfaction with women's assigned gender roles as well as a nagging belief that men had let them down, because of their failure to adequately protect them during the war.[138] According to Faust southern women, particularly those from the slaveholding class, had been the ones who had encouraged secession in protection of their way of life, and for the preservation of their social position, but they were also the first ones to feel dissatisfaction when men faltered in their failure to protect them.[139] For these women the code of honor that had made women look up to their men as strong, patriarchal, and protective figures was broken.

War also affected attitudes toward marriage. For some women who were single, the response was one of panic, to marry any man, and fast, in order to secure them a measure of protection and to avoid what they still considered the blight of spinsterhood. Virginia Hammett spoke of a "marrying disease" that "had taken possession of our neighborhood and there is no telling who it will attack" next.[140] She spoke in horror about a young girl "just grown" who was marrying "an old man of fifty" so desperate was she to be wed.[141] However, many southern women had the opposite response to marriage, which was simply to avoid it altogether. Lucy Breckinridge was sixteen when the war broke out and lived at Grove Hill plantation in the Shenandoah Valley. Though "countless" men pursued her, she remained for a long time quite steadfast in her desire to remain single. She had carefully deduced that marriage (for many) was not a happy state. It was dominated by hard work, caring for children, and husband pleasing, and she would not do it unless she met a suitable match.[142] Virginia Hammett had no desire to marry while the guns were still firing in the not-so-distant background. As she pointed out rather sensibly, she did not want to marry in wartime: "I do not approve of it, I have no fancy for being married to-day and probably widowed tomorrow," which was for some slaveholding women an all too familiar story.[143] Virginia wrote in her diary that many of her contemporaries would be "compelled to spend our days in single blessedness" owing to the countless "slaughters" of the battle field that would leave many young girls "matchless."[144] No doubt the "slaughters" were a reference to the unprecedented loss of life in battles such as Gettysburg in June–July 1863, when the Confederate army lost a staggering twenty-eight thousand men (a third of the army under Robert E. Lee's command) in a harrowing blood bath that lasted three days.[145]

The reality of war meant that many southern women lost men: husbands, fathers, sons, and brothers. As one southerner exclaimed, "War makes its widows by the thousand," and this was certainly true in the case in the Confederacy.[146] Both inside and outside of wartime, widows had to prescribe to certain codes or gender conventions in order to fit in or gain respectability. For elite and upper-class women who were widowed, it was important that they continued to uphold the image of "virtuous womanhood" in spite of the fact that they were newly single. In the Civil War and postwar eras the definition of "virtuous womanhood" that had dominated the antebellum era was ever present.[147] According to Chagsin Lee this was an important image that widows were expected to uphold following the loss of their husband, because virtuous womanhood was seen as an extension of female propriety and a visual symbol that women continued to act in the best interests of their husbands, as opposed to their own self-interest.[148] A broader point can be drawn from this statement, which is that widows, who were also legally defined as single women, were often able to explain more autonomous behavior (in managing plantations, buying and selling property, and managing slaves) by claiming that they were acting in the interest of their late husbands.

Slaveholding widow Ada Bacot from Darlington, South Carolina, was thrice widowed, once prior to the war, again during it, and a third time well into old age.[149] After the death of her first husband (and also her two small children), Bacot galvanized herself into action, fueled by her steely determination and successful management of her Arndale plantation and the maintenance of its tobacco and cotton production. Ada Bacot was atypical in that the level of responsibility she shouldered and the power concentrated in her hands was far greater than that of many planter-class women. Her wealth and position as a slaveholding widow provided her with additional freedoms that her married sisters did not share. "Under early American law, widowhood turned a wife bound by coverture into a free and legally independent woman. Widows were their own people both legally and economically. . . . They needed no guardians, sponsors or patrons and often became heads of productive households, with authority over space, capital and labour."[150] Ada Bacot's is only one story, but it reflects two wider points. First, that if a widow was unusually wealthy, she often tended to fare better than poorer widows, which highlights the relationship between class, marital status, and independence. Second, it reflects the difficulty in any attempt to try to categorize women by virtue of their marital status, as invariably women shifted between nonmarriage, marriage, widowhood, separation, and divorce. This is reminiscent of Mary Telfair's opening statement that "it requires a vast deal of independence and a variety of resources" for a never-married woman to enjoy a good life.[151] Ada Bacot's marital status shifted considerably during the course of her life cycle, but she remained wealthy and to a degree powerful, because of her class and status. The Civil War was a time of unprecedented change, with a marked increase in women living alone, as their husbands were fighting during the war. Women were also left alone for vast periods of time, with few marriageable partners to choose from. Clearly the lack of "available" men to marry began to alter attitudes toward the single state.

Summary

For single women the postwar period was important in helping to determine how permanent the changes in their lives were. In terms of the figure of the southern lady, whose elevated social position was secured by the presence of slavery, the postwar period held special significance. All women's lives changed in the context of war and its aftermath; they had to in order to mobilize women's efforts in aid of the families and for the Confederacy.[152] Yet for more than any other group in southern society, the war had been waged in the interest of the planter class, in order to protect the institution of slavery on which their privilege and class position was based.[153] Therefore, by the end of the war, when southerners faced defeat, and Lincoln freed the slaves, the lives of planter families, and women in particular, changed in profound ways.[154]

Southern women increasingly understood that in waging war, men had failed in their promise to protect them. They had been left as defenseless women, to manage in a whole raft of new roles. In this context old notions of male authority and female submission and dependence started to slip away. Slaveholding women, whose position as southern ladies had hinged on patriarchal authority and the presence of slavery, found the vagaries of war helped to break down traditional gender roles. In connection with this, planter women who were single had stepped out from the shadows and clearly demonstrated their willingness to fulfill the Cult of Single Blessedness. They took on additional roles and responsibilities in wartime that highlighted their valid place in southern society. The old stereotypes of the redundant "old maid" who was a drain on her family and community gradually died out. Instead female singleness was perceived as a positive good or a blessing to southern society that had come into sharp focus in the war years.

In this sense the war had sped up and highlighted certain changes in single women's lives that were already afoot in the Old South. In the war years and during the years of Reconstruction, an increased number of women were single. Many women had become widows during the war; other young women coming of age simply decided not to marry if they did not find the right partner. This linked to the burgeoning of the new ideal of companionate marriage that encouraged women only to marry for love and affection. A combination of these factors meant that the construction of femininity in the postwar period had shifted in order to reflect the social, demographic, and economic changes that had occurred in the South. As notions of single blessedness slowly transfused old stereotypes of social scorn, the war further revised and expanded traditional gender conventions.

As Jennifer Lynn Gross rightly pointed out, single women were offered a new "portrait of exemplary feminine wartime behavior" in the model of single blessedness that developed and matured in the postwar years.[155] By the time of the war's end in April 1865, single women's lives had altered considerably. Not only had they taken on new roles and responsibilities inside and outside of the household, but they were also called on to revise their identities as women in order to adapt to the challenges of war. Old notions of female dependency were revised in the light of the Confederacy's demand for women's assistance on the home front, and as women stepped up to the new challenges of wartime responsibility, they also reshaped other's perception of them as respectable and useful single women. The war brought into sharp focus the fact that many southern women were now single, mostly through nonmarriage and widowhood. In the postwar years a new generation of single women continued to emerge. They had successfully built on the foundations of their past, in the antebellum era, during the war, and now into Reconstruction.

Chapter 2   SINGLE WOMEN AND THE
          SOUTHERN FAMILY

"Duty" is a word that regularly surfaces in the letters and diaries of single women: duty to parents, to siblings, and to extended family. The DeRosset family from Wilmington in North Carolina provide a fascinating insight into single women's roles and responsibilities within the southern family and shed light on single women's valued contribution to the family unit, supporting siblings, children, and ageing parents. The DeRosset family first became established in North Carolina in the 1730s. They owned a rice plantation in Brunswick, North Carolina, and they had slaves in North and South Carolina, in addition to their professions as physicians and merchants.[1] The family patriarch, Armand John DeRosset Sr., married twice, first to Mary Fullerton, and second to Catherine Fullerton (her daughter), whom he had five daughters with. Eliza Ann and Magdalen Mary never married, and a third, Catherine (Kate) Kennedy, was later widowed.[2] The women kept up a lively and detailed correspondence throughout their lives, which included letters among themselves, and between cousins and close friends. In their letters the women, both married and single, spoke repeatedly of their duty to home, family, community, and God. In hard times the women repeatedly referred to their faith as a source of strength that bolstered them in overcoming adversity and enabled them to carry out their familial duties.

It is especially striking that all the women—regardless of their marital status —reiterated their duty and commitment to the family throughout their correspondence.[3] For example Eliza Ann DeRosset, one of the unmarried daughters of Armand and Catherine Fullerton, reproached herself for failing in her duty of care to her sister. She openly reprimanded herself for leaving the family home prematurely, while her sister remained there unwell. In writing to her married sister, Catherine Kennedy, she admitted "a great deal of self-reproach" for not fulfilling her "duty." She confessed, "Your duty was to go [as she was married] mine to stay, at least for a few days or week longer. . . . I did not as much as I ought—take duty into consideration and it makes me feel unhappy."[4] Married women were also tied by a strong sense of duty to home and family. The DeRossets' married cousin expressed her own frustrations in a letter to Magdalen DeRosset, highlighting the constraints that familial duty placed on her. "I cannot leave home again for such a long period. Duty is in strict opposition to inclination, and however hard the struggle, I hope I will have strength to overcome and obey the stern voice of the former."[5]

Duty and usefulness were clearly important watchwords for white, southern women of a certain class, which were further accentuated by the racial and class limitations attached to familial "duty." Black, enslaved women were repeatedly denied the right or "duty" to care for their own family; their children were the property of their master, who bought and sold them at his whim. Consequently for black women, the legal right to their children (and family) was denied, and with it they were also stripped of their womanhood. Middle-to-upper-class white, southern women, by contrast, expressed their womanhood in the service to the family and in doing so wanted to prove that they were useful members of society, thereby cultivating respect and self-worth. Many scholars have argued that family was an important prism through which women cultivated a greater understanding of themselves and of their role and function within southern society.[6] Considerable interest has focused on the role of the plantation mistress, but less concentration has been devoted to the role of single women in the planter-class family. As members of the slaveholding elite, this small subset of southern women operated within the parameters of their social position, which was an important marker that separated them from other women—from the North and the South. For planter-class women who were single, the family could be a tremendous source of support, as well as an opportunity to prove how useful they were. Others found their responsibilities in the family simply an unwanted burden.

Women's attachment to "usefulness" often replicated gender roles, which enhanced the outward perception of their "femininity" in the context of a culture that prized the family. This helped reshape traditional notions of femininity in the prewar South and inadvertently resulted in an advancement in female autonomy. It also represented a springboard in helping to achieve a limited degree of personal autonomy. This point is illustrated by Kate DeRosset Kennedy, who was widowed in 1840 when she was forty years old. Kate proved she could overcome the constraints of her personal circumstances, which included raising her ten-year-old daughter singlehandedly. In 1861, having raised her daughter, and now sixty years old, Kate Kennedy reinvented herself again. The war had just begun, and Kate rechanneled her energy into her new role as a volunteer at the military hospital in Petersburg. She noted in a letter to her sister, "We have yet no other lady attendant than myself," and she recognized how "short of assistance they find themselves."[7] Applying the skills she had already cultivated within the private sphere of home and family, Kate clearly relished the opportunity to test her resourcefulness within the community. She cheerfully admitted, "I find it really more pleasure than toil in the duties to be performed. The consciousness of being in the way of duty, and the gratification that flows from being useful to others contribute not a little to my real enjoyment."[8] However, she checked her enthusiasm, adding, "How it gratified me that no bad word from any of them [the male patients] had reached my ears and no unruly temper been exhibited."[9] This short statement highlights the importance of preserving a woman's personal dignity and innocence in a male-dominated environment, in the role of a female attendant. Kate Kennedy clearly understood the value of upholding the tenets of true ladyhood, and she kept her "delicacy" intact while embroiled in her hospital work.[10] Elite, white, southern women thus demonstrated their duty, usefulness, and femininity by melding together the private realm of home and family with work in the public arena. For single women this was more feasible, as they were not tied to a husband or dependents in the same way as married women were, which made it easier for them to branch into new roles without disadvantaging the family.

Family was at the core of a woman's identity and defined her relationship to the wider community. Feminine ideals, such as the "Cult of True Womanhood" and "Cult of Single Blessedness," influenced single women's daily lives and acted as a constraint to keep unmarried women under control, and to a degree it provided a platform for autonomy and self-construction.[11] The "Cult of True Womanhood" was a social construct that inspired and encouraged middle-to-upper-class white women to fulfill certain models of femininity, based on marriage, motherhood, and domesticity. It had a strong racial and class bias that was particularly marked in the South because of slavery. Not all women fitted into the mould of the nineteenth-century stereotype of ideal womanhood that was so heavily emphasized and encouraged in the nineteenth-century South. Its focus on piety, purity, submissiveness, and domesticity immediately excluded black, enslaved women, frontier women, and poorer white women. The racial limitations of southern femininity, and the new gender ideology of which it was part, hinged on the exclusion of black women, who were barred from the legality of marriage, motherhood and family life.[12]

Single women's roles and responsibilities within the southern family both replicated and expanded the boundaries of true womanhood. This led to a recognition of singleness as a viable alternative to marriage, which culminated in an enhanced level of self-sufficiency for women who were single.

The Southern Family

The southern family was "marked by the visibility of race" in a manner distinctive to the South.[13] The existence of race-based slavery permeated every aspect of southern life; the family was no exception. Eugene Genovese and Elizabeth Fox-Genovese discussed how slaveholders used the "ubiquitous phrase" of "our family, white and black," to refer to their white kin and to their slave property. Its roots went back to colonial times "recurring constantly in the slaveholders' private diaries, letters and correspondence."[14] Fox-Genovese shed light on the way that the planter class "emphasized the persistence of the metaphor of family as appropriate representation for various social relations" that supported race, class, and gender hierarchies that white, slaveholding women were enmeshed in.[15] Race, class, and gender became inextricably intertwined in southern society, and consequently slaveholding women (married and single) had a unique role to play in upholding the southern, white hegemony—and with it the institution of slavery. Thus the cultural construction of the Cult of True Womanhood fused with very specific southern ideals of class and race. Orville Vernon Burton emphasized that "white Southerners were an especially family-centered people"; they spoke of their "slave family" and in doing so perpetuated the myth of benevolence and contentment in slave life designed to counteract criticism from abolitionists.[16] The family defined women as part of a larger collective, and elite white women had a designated role to play in southern society as they were considered paragons of ideal womanhood to which the lower classes aspired.

The nineteenth-century southern family extended beyond the parameters of the "immediate" family, reflecting the patriarchal structure of southern society during the antebellum period, with the husband (or patriarch) at the helm, and the wife, children, and slaves dependent on him for protection and support.[17] As Joan Cashin observed, "the planter family had a nuclear core of parents and children [but] its borders were permeable and its structure was elastic, including many other relatives, aunts, uncles, nieces, nephews, and cousins—who were intimate members of the family."[18] Jane Turner Censer described the southern family as a flexible, "unfixed entity" and an amalgam of various family members, who passed in and out of its viscous boundary by virtue of birth, death, remarriage, widowhood, or divorce.[19] The structure of the southern family was also affected by the "vivid presence of close relatives" omnipresent through the pattern of visiting (on a daily, weekly, monthly, or annual basis), which further augmented family ties. The popular practice of "child exchange" often involved maiden aunts caring for their nieces or nephews for extended periods of time, if not indefinitely, in the aid and preservation of the family compact.[20]

The southern family extended far beyond the traditional parameters that might be ascribed to the modern nuclear family, incorporating single women within its broad spectrum. By adopting the language of the family in their wider discourse, southerners knew their place in the antebellum world and where they fitted into the wider schema, which included single women's place within it.[21] Other scholars have similarly described the southern family as "an inclusive" institution that extended "beyond the customary boundaries to embrace more than blood kin, common color, or those of equal status," which set it apart from the northern family.[22] Scholars have long spoken of the containment of southern women in the home connected to the ideal of the southern lady, whereas in the North, the development of the women's reform movement emerged out of the

"Cult of Domesticity," drawing a comparison between them. The role of women in the North increasingly became linked to economic change, with the focus on industrialization and urbanization. In the eastern and midwestern states, new opportunities opened up for women to work (such as for the Lowell Mill girls in the 1820s and 1830s), in addition to the growth of female organizations, particularly for the middle class.[23] These changes were much slower to take place in the South, and the construction of the southern lady was tied to the maintenance and protection of a slaveholding society. It formed part of a conservative worldview that made the experiences of southern women unique.[24] Fluctuations in age of marriage existed, with southern women tending to marry slightly younger than their northern counterparts (often by the age of twenty), often to men who were considerably older than themselves. If a woman had not married by the age of twenty-five she was considered to have married late. According to Hacker this figure was steadily on the rise, particularly during and after the Civil War, with women marrying slightly later still.[25]

Catherine Maria Sedgwick, herself an unmarried woman from the North, reflected rather critically on the status of unmarried women within the family circle, when she penned *Married or Single*. She argued vociferously that single women needed to be "useful," and her words resonated across the North and South. In 1834 she wrote, "Married life is the destiny Heaven has allotted to us, and therefore, best fitted to awaken our powers, to exercise our virtues, and call forth all of our sympathies."[26] Mary Kelly in her analysis of Sedgwick's work concluded that by elevating marriage to such a high status, Sedgwick was "automatically ascribing an inferior status to the unmarried woman, despite her protests."[27] Sedgwick also stressed the need for women to be useful, another key requirement of the Cult of Single Blessedness, and the idea that in order to be fulfilled as a woman, it was important to prove her usefulness as a means of gaining external affirmation or self-worth in a male-dominated society. In 1854 Sedgwick claimed, "As slaves must be trained for freedom, so women must be educated for usefulness, independence, and contentment in single life . . . as a mode of life in which one may serve God and humanity, and thus educate the soul, the great purpose of this short life. So considered, single life would not long be regarded as either helpless, joyless, or ridiculous," and that dreaded stigma, "old maid," would soon "cease to be a stigma, and in the lapse of ages possibly become obsolete."[28] Northern writers like Sedgwick, who argued that single women needed to be "useful," had considerable influence both in the North and the South. Sedgwick drew a parallel between race and gender, likening the position of slaves needing training for freedom to women requiring education and direction, in order to attain usefulness both inside and outside of the family unit. As the century progressed, there was a growing belief that single women could prove their usefulness by committing themselves to doing good deeds for others, and by focusing their attention on the service of their extended family or community.

In this context single women attempted to replicate the behavior of true womanhood in their service and contributions to their families. On the face of it, it would seem that there was no acceptable place for unmarried women who fell outside of this remit. Catherine Clinton argued that southern "culture provided no primary role for unmarried women [and they were forced to] devote themselves to their parents, nieces and nephews, and in general provided supplemental care whenever required within the kinship network," owing to a lack of available options open to them.[29] In practice the roles of unmarried women were muddied by some women consciously choosing to integrate themselves within their extended family, which provided a platform for gaining credibility and self-respect. Single women honed a sense of identity from their various roles within the family, which could be constraining at times, but it could also be used to unmarried women's advantage to expand their sphere and gain a measure of personal autonomy, albeit within certain limitations.[30]

In the postwar setting, elite white women continued to order their lives around the family but at the same time pushed at the boundaries of their prescribed roles, in large part out of necessity tied to the catastrophic changes in the social, economic, and demographic landscape. By demonstrating an outward submission to feminine ideals, single, slaveholding women eased "the transition to a society in which white women would increasingly be called upon to stand by themselves or to stand with the aid of other women."[31] In a sense the ideal of womanhood had naturally shifted—or expanded "to include a more active, outspoken and courageous aspect" of womanhood.[32] In the formation of the Ladies Memorial Associations in the postwar period, southern women demonstrated a strong allegiance to honoring the Confederate war dead and fallen heroes of the South, in assuming the responsibility for Confederate memorialization and the creation of the "Lost Cause" mythology. Inadvertently it opened up another opportunity for single, southern women to demonstrate their ability and usefulness in the postwar context, while proving again that they were true southern women.

The Family Helpmeet

On 1 February 1853 Margaret Cameron received a letter from her cousin Adelaide praising her for the support she had provided for her family, and especially to her father, during his ill health, and in the final hours before his death. "To think how many blessings you have and the means of doing good. In helping those around you—do look above this world and then you will be comforted. What a blessing that you were able to attend to your Father to the last, in that you were at home, surrounded by all your family and friends, who were able to give assistance when required."[33] Margaret Cameron, the eldest daughter of the slaveholder Duncan Cameron and his wife Rebecca Cameron of Orange and Durham Counties in Raleigh, was a single woman in her thirties who had filled the role of the family caregiver or helpmeet, tending to her younger siblings and to her father since her mother's death ten years before.[34] As the eldest unmarried daughter, it was expected that Margaret would take over the mantel of responsibility as the family matriarch in the absence of her mother, thus replicating gender roles, and emulating the mother's care that she would have given had she still been alive. Even when Margaret announced that she wanted to marry her long-time beau, George Mordecai, it was a request that was temporarily blocked by her father, who was unwilling to give her up while he still needed her. By refusing to consent to the pair's marriage, he demonstrated the limitations of his daughter's free will. As Jane Turner Censer contended, "elderly Duncan Cameron did not wish his mid-thirtyish daughter Margaret, who managed his household and cared for her invalid sister, to marry George W. Mordecai, a banker of Jewish descent. Still, Cameron, who cited 'domestic' reasons for his refusal, took no steps to guard against Margaret's marriage in his will drawn up shortly after."[35] Evidently it was not that he was against her marrying per se, but simply that he was against her marrying during his lifetime, as he not only relied on her for practical support, but he also needed her to manage his affairs. In the light of this information, cousin Adelaide's praise takes on a whole new meaning, as Margaret's desire to marry was usurped by her father's own agenda. Immediately after his death, Margaret, aged forty-two, married George, and the pair remained happily married until George's death in 1872.

Mississippian-born single woman Mary Susan Ker similarly contributed to her birth family. The Kers were a slaveholding family from Mississippi who lost much of their wealth during the Civil War. This had a profound effect on them all, compounded by the fact that the family patriarch had died some years earlier, followed by their mother's death in 1862. During the war the family made a series of unfortunate wartime investments, and the family had been left financially devastated, which must have been a culture shock to a generation who had grown up alongside luxury and wealth. For Mary in particular, her childhood expectations of growing up to become a plantation lady—marrying and having a family of her own, with slaves and servants to do the bulk of the household work for her, would have been in stark contrast to her later life as a single, working woman. Therefore, by the time the war reached its conclusion, and the slaves were freed, Mary's expectations of becoming a plantation mistress (and all that it entailed) fell into tatters, alongside the model of ideal ladyhood. By the war's end and the destruction of slavery, the Ker family became representative of what was known as the genteel poor—a hitherto wealthy slaveholding family who were torn asunder by the vagaries of war. Destitution culminated in insecurity in employment, lifestyle, and family relationships. The Ker men, accustomed to traditional patriarchal roles

Portrait of Mary Susan Ker, 1838–1923, as a young lady. Courtesy of the Southern Historical Collection, Wilson Library, University of North Carolina, Chapel Hill.

and well-established gender stereotypes, became frustrated by their economic impotence and the reality of seeing their wives, daughters, and sisters struggle for subsistence in a way that they never thought possible. Across the South countless women had lost male relatives or lovers in the war, and others had started to lose faith that their men could protect them at all, which led to the reshaping of family boundaries and groups and individual roles.[36]

It is in this context that Mary Ker, the youngest unmarried sibling of the Ker family, was plunged into new and uncharted territory. With the family matriarch gone, the mantel of responsibility was passed on to Mary. She helped manage the family business, financially supported her brother by selling her silver to provide enough money for him to buy land, and perhaps most important, she took on the responsibility of raising her brother's two daughters after their mother died. Furthermore Mary found formal employment in order to support herself and her two young nieces. In doing so she proved to be a "a fine specimen of the noble class of old maids who in addition to their professional duties, cared for two generations of orphaned nieces and great nieces."[37] Mary Ker was in many respects an inspirational woman, who showed tremendous resilience and adaptability throughout her life, where other members of her immediate and extended family regularly faltered. Not only did she rely on her own judgment, but other family members relied on it too. Consequently she crafted new and important roles and responsibilities for herself, and she represented the glue that held the family together. Though never married, she demonstrated her unwavering commitment to the family unit and her strong desire to keep the family together, as reflected by her determination to become the guardian for her brother's children.

*Portrait of Mary Susan Ker,
1838–1923. Courtesy of the Southern Historical Collection, Wilson
Library, University of North
Carolina, Chapel Hill.*

Narcissa Josephine Varner, or Miss Joe as she was commonly called, was another single woman equally propelled by a strong commitment to her family and to her ongoing contribution that she made to it. The youngest child in a large family of thirteen children, born to Edward Varner and Cynthia Fitzpatrick on 17 June 1837, Josephine grew up as a typical planter-class daughter in Jasper County, Georgia, where the family remained until their relocation to the Indian Spring, Georgia, in 1850.[38] Josephine's early childhood was spent living on the family cotton plantation, and along with her brothers and sisters, she received a good standard of education in Georgia and Tennessee at Eatonton Female Academy and LaGrange College that led her to a teaching career in her early adult life. In 1849 her father purchased the Indian Spring Hotel in Butts County, Georgia, and this is where Josephine went on to spend the majority of her adult life.

Josephine loved home and family but reported mixed feelings when she spent time apart from them, especially when she was teaching in her early adult years. On the one hand she savored the freedom that came from living alone, but on the other she missed her family and craved for the closeness of the family compact. This is reflected throughout her personal journal. On 21 April 1863, now in the height of the Civil War, when Josephine was about twenty-six years old, she guiltily confessed, "It may be wicked, it may be weak, but I greatly enjoy being

The Varner House, Indian Spring, Georgia. Courtesy of the Georgia Historical Society, Savannah.

mistress of my own movements. If I am to steer my boat alone all through life, God grant that I may do it cheerfully, as I feel that I can now do."[39] Her choice of words is interesting as they reflect commonly held ideas on gender. She used the words "wicked" and "weak" in describing the enjoyment she experienced "being mistress of my own movements." In admitting her enjoyment, she also recognized that she was challenging traditional gender roles, which dictated that women should be dependent and deferential to male authority. It was not considered ladylike to be "mistress" of your own movements, hence her admission that she was "wicked." Two short years later, at this stage writing at the end of the war, her sentiments shifted considerably, and all talk of being mistress of her own affairs and manager of her own destiny melted away, as she described her uneasiness living away from home and family, no doubt intensified by the fact that her anxieties were heightened because of wartime. "I am almost sick at heart that I ever left home, even the smallest things I do cast me a struggle, sometimes I heartily wish I had never left home," she confided.[40]

Clearly Josephine was a woman of mixed emotions—of considerable highs followed by periods of depression, as substantiated in her private journal. Her personality colored her perceptions of the world and the way she saw it at different stages throughout her life course, making her view her single status as liberating

Josephine Varner, 1837–1928, as a young woman. Courtesy of the Georgia Historical Society, Savannah.

one day, and constraining the next. These fluctuations in mood are less evident in her personal correspondence, where she tended to mask her true feelings and conform more rigidly to the conventions of Victorian letter writing (in itself a sign of constraint). Yet, when she was sitting alone, penning her thoughts in her private journal, she was more at ease to mention the inner conflict that she felt regarding the role expected of her, and the conflicting emotions she harbored in performing them. This dichotomy between autonomy and constraint was often hidden behind closed doors, and rarely discussed, in line with acceptable gender conventions, but on occasion it surfaced in single women's private journals. At times Josephine, and single women like her, must have inhabited a difficult world, isolated by their perceptions of how things were, contrasted to how they would prefer them to be. It was during these dark moments that women drew strength from the familiarity of the home and family.

Joe Varner is a good example of a single woman who chose to make a life for herself within her birth family, in spite of sometimes feeling pulled outside of it; she did not have the role imposed on her against her will. Much like Mary Ker, Joe Varner seemed to view her role within the family as a vocation in life, and she found tremendous comfort and well-being from the connections with her immediate family. She revealed on 23 February 1863, "I love them all so much. This short life time, judging their hearts by my own, we love each other strong enough to last forever and ever."[41] At several key points in her diary, Josephine referred to the close relationship with her family, especially to her mother and older sister, Amanda Varner, who likewise never married.[42] When her mother went through a period of ill health, Joe fretted, "Ma is not very well tonight. The whole world might be sick but it would not give me half the uneasiness as it does for Ma to be the least ailing," mirroring the strong maternal bond shared between them.[43] Throughout her life Josephine invested much time and energy into her relationship with her parents and sister, providing her mother with round-the-clock care when she became seriously ill, right up until her death in December 1881. On the night her mother passed away, Josephine described the scene: "She sat before the fire, ate a good supper, enjoying it so much. I was ready to get in bed, when she said, 'what a pain is in my right shoulder.' I said, 'turn over' and she did. I took her in my arms and she never breathed again."[44] In memorializing the scene of her mother's death, Josephine depicted her mother as "lovely and as sweet as a white flower," and herself as "a baby child."[45] Josephine's description is typical of a deathbed narrative, in which she painted her mother as serene and pure as a "white flower" and described herself as a "child" dependent on her mother's care, even though in reality their roles had now reversed. Joe tended to her mother's needs and provided her with the love, care, and support that typified the role of the dutiful daughter or family caregiver.

Single women took their roles and responsibilities within the family very seriously, which reinforced the pivotal role of the family helpmeet or dutiful daughter within family circles. Carter referred to the "dutiful daughter" in her critique of single women and the family in Charleston and Savannah.[46] She evoked images of usefulness, servitude, and selfless contribution to the family that again show the way that single women's roles often replicated traditional gender roles. These roles tied to the "servant ideal"—the idea that single women could find fulfillment and purpose by serving the patriarchy. Single women were able to affirm their self-worth by devoting their lives to their parents, to their siblings, and to the wider community.[47] Carter revealed how single women flourished in their roles as dutiful daughters, single siblings, and maiden aunts in the urban centers, which is a useful blueprint for examining single women's lives across the South more broadly.

The Maiden Aunt and Surrogate Motherhood

An important avenue to self-advancement for single women was the role of the maiden aunt. From 1820 to 1850 significant changes to the family affected single women's status within the family circle and to their role in helping to raise children.[48] The "Cult of Domesticity" was a gender ideal that had gradually infiltrated nationwide. Carroll Smith-Rosenberg described it as "a rigid gender-role

Josephine Varner with Ann Campbell at Indian Spring, Georgia. Courtesy of the Georgia Historical Society, Savannah.

differentiation within the family," "between and within society as a whole," that resulted in "the emotional segregation of men and women."[49] In the North this may have been a conservative reaction to the market revolution, and the rapid urbanization and industrialization of American society. By stipulating that "true women" belonged in the private sphere of home and family, men used women as an anchor of stability amid turbulent and changing times. In the South, however, the ideology of separate spheres was tied to notions of paternalism, chivalry, and honor, which some have argued were becoming redundant by 1850.[50]

Tied to the separate-spheres ideology, child rearing became an increasingly female-centered occupation (with unsurprisingly the mother at the center). As part of this nationwide configuration, single women were frequently seen as vital ancillaries to mothers, because they had fewer household responsibilities of their own and could be relied on to help at short notice. Americans increasingly bought into the notion that the "mother heart beats in all women" and that "women were born to love" regardless of marital status, which was a critical step forward for single, childless women from propertied backgrounds. This was aided by the Second Great Awakening, an evangelical revival that swept the republic in the first half of the nineteenth century. This revivalist frenzy pushed women (married or single) to the center and made them responsible for "rekindling the spirit and enthusiasm among the people."[51] This onus on women to personify religious purity provided single women with the opportunity to prove they were useful, by committing themselves to religious activity and the conversion of others, especially men. This had two main consequences: increased responsibility for single women within the household, and an enhancement in their perceived status (but not necessarily their power) in the family and outside of it.

Commonly held ideas that single women were "superfluous" to the family unit, and to society in general, gradually died out as unmarried women increasingly became viewed as highly prized assets that could aid in the smooth running of the southern family unit. This critical shift in opinion was tied to the belief that *all* women possessed a maternal instinct, regardless of their marital status. Consequently women did not have to be married to be considered "true women"; they were able to satisfy their calling to southern womanhood by fulfilling their maternal role as maiden aunt, surrogate mother, or alternative caregiver. Single women could therefore align themselves with the traditional nineteenth-century ideals of womanhood, by presenting themselves as committed in their servitude to others. The so-called servant ideal bridged the gap between conventional ideals of femininity and the "Cult of Single Blessedness," as it was more mutually inclusive and less bound by marital status.[52]

Advice author Margaret Coxe advised unmarried women to "take to your heart with fond affection, the offspring of your beloved brothers and sisters, and in their sweet caresses and tender love experience a happiness only second to a Mothers."[53] Coxe, similar to Sedgwick before her, continued to emphasize the happiness that single women experienced in loving their nieces and nephews but noted how it remained "second to a Mothers," thereby reinforcing the existing hierarchies based on marriage and motherhood. Yet the love and affection that maiden aunts felt for their nieces and nephews is vividly depicted in the letters and diaries of single women who often dedicated their lives to caring for their siblings' children. One such woman, Margaret Williford, a thirty-five-year-old single woman from North Carolina, cared for her nephew Olly after his mother's sudden death. Margaret became alarmed on hearing that Olly's father (Margaret's brother) had decided to remarry, in large part fearing that her relationship to her nephew might suddenly lie in jeopardy owing to the arrival of a new mother figure, her sister-in-law. In a letter to her own mother, Margaret anxiously confessed, "As long as my dear little Olly is mine, I feel satisfied, but it would grieve me to death to be separated from him."[54] Margaret's confession makes plain an important truth, which was that as much as single women's role in the family was valued and of service to others, it remained vulnerable and restricted and ultimately hinged on the goodwill of others, in particular siblings.

Even though some single women privately voiced their dissatisfaction regarding their role as maiden aunts, rarely did they openly challenge the existing status quo, choosing instead to quietly reinforce preexisting gender norms, thus demonstrating the limitations to single women's personal agency. Margaret Williford was not alone when she confessed, "I do not believe any mother could love a child more than I do him," and while she may have been right, it was an opinion that did little to challenge or alter the existing social hierarchy.[55] Fortunately her new sister-in-law, Carrie Holmes, turned out to be a kind and sympathetic woman who shared in Margaret's sentiments that Olly should remain close to his aunt, which reassured Margaret of her permanent and lasting position in the boy's life and helped to establish a lasting bond between the two women. Carrie Holmes admitted to Margaret's mother, "You must not ask to have Maggie at home with you very soon, I cannot let her go, she really seems like an own sister to me, than any one I have ever met. I love her dearly."[56] Margaret permanently moved in with her brother and sister-in-law, caring for Olly like a mother and assisting Carrie, who miscarried twins in 1850. She remained with her sister-in-law after she was widowed in 1858, and she proved to be a tremendous source of support to her for many years.

The maiden aunt possessed few—if any—legal rights over the children in her care, leaving her reliant and dependent on the goodwill of family members, often sisters and brothers, in keeping to their verbal agreements with her. Mary Susan Ker, a maiden aunt from Natchez, Mississippi, in 1864 took on the care and financial responsibility of raising her two nieces, Mamie and Nellie Ker, after her sister-in-law, Jane Percy, died unexpectedly. Mary felt great apprehension regarding her long-term position in raising the girls, even after she adopted them in 1867. In an attempt to alleviate some of her anxiety, Mary decided to formalize her legal authority regarding the girls and produced a written document that she pressed her brother to sign. A lawyer drafted an admittedly nonbinding but specific resolution that stated that her brother would relinquish all rights to his children to Mary, who was after all raising them as a surrogate mother, thus effectively transferring parental like authority into her hands. The resolution stated, "I, Lewis Baker Ker, do hereby promise my sister Mary S. Ker, that she shall have the charge, keeping and complete control of my children, Mamie and Nellie, so long as she wishes to do so, and she is not to be interfered with in the exercise of such charge, by any person or persons" clearly referring to himself, and any other relevant party.[57] Several points require addressing here. While the drafting of a legal document specifying her "complete control" or the transfer of complete control to Mary from her brother may have given some reassurance to Mary that she had sole power over the girls and their future with her, the resolution nonetheless remained a nonbinding agreement "between relatives." The rights that Mary (and maiden aunts in a similar position to her) had been promised remained intimately bound to the familial ties with their brother, and to the relationship Mary shared with *him* rather than being based on any firm legal foundation. Perhaps Mary

sensed this fact, for in December 1871, she again took further measures to formalize the relationship she had with her nieces, by drawing up a will that divided her
property between them in the event of her death. Mary averred, "I have made this
disposition of my property according to my judgement and feelings combined," as
if to rein in control over her young charges.[58]

Mary had a tendency to be swayed by personal preference or favoritism toward
the children. A clear illustration of this can be seen in the manner that she conducted her relationship with her now grown-up nieces, Mamie and Nellie. Most
obviously Mary favored Mamie over Nellie for reasons that are not always clear,
and she responded to each niece accordingly. In May 1894, after a fatal illness that
resulted in Mamie's sudden death, Mary confided in her diary, "I have lost every
spark of affection for Nellie, since her visit to her dying sister at Moore's Station. I
cannot help her and do my best not to think of her one way or another. Poor Nellie, how I pity her!"[59] Her strong disapproval of Nellie seems particularly marked,
in stark juxtaposition to her adoration of Mamie, which was clearly intensified by
the events around the time of Mamie's death, when Mary felt that Nellie in some
way behaved inappropriately toward her sister. Undoubtedly this was a major
source of friction between the three women even prior to Mamie's illness and
death, as Mary pitted the sisters against each other, which only served to fuel Nellie's sense of inadequacy. Mary deified Mamie in death, with entries in her diary
memorializing her love for "darling Mamie," who she admitted was "constantly
on my mind," while at the same time completely disregarding Nellie, who desperately needed her reassurance and help during a tumultuous stage in her own
life.[60] Mary's actions tell the reader a great deal about her mixed emotions toward
surrogate motherhood and her journey of extreme highs and lows. However, just
as Mary had freed herself from the financial, practical, and emotional constraints
of raising her two nieces to adulthood, the death of Mamie Ker rekindled Mary's
child-care commitments, and she faced the new responsibility of raising Mamie's
two orphaned daughters, Catherine and Tillie (Matilda). This fact clearly riled
Nellie, who was struggling to raise her own children owing to a depressive illness
and an alcohol addiction. Yet Nellie was met with short thrift from Mary at every
turn. Evidence clearly suggests that Mary felt overburdened by her responsibilities
at times, raising four children, spanning as many decades, in addition to teaching
long hours to facilitate their care was arduous, but she refused to give in or let
anyone else take over, determined to manage on her own. On hearing the news
of Mamie's death, and in spite of her grief, armed with the full knowledge of what
raising two children entailed, her response was immediate and purely maternal
in nature. On 19 April 1894 she anxiously wrote in her diary, "My heart and mind
were so absorbed in what to do for the five children left motherless—the same
as homeless—almost the same as fatherless—entirely moneyless—that I could
think of nothing else."[61]

Portrait of Catherine and Tillie (Matilda) Dunbar with friends. Courtesy of the Southern Historical Collection, Wilson Library, University of North Carolina, Chapel Hill.

Her maternal instinct propelled her to step in as surrogate mother to two of the children; she could not afford to raise all five. After temporarily splitting the children up to live with relatives in Natchez, Mary quickly organized herself and ensured she had a job and the accommodation to enable her to raise Catherine and Tillie, the two girls.[62] Mary in her grief demonstrated the tenacity of a single woman dedicated to her goal of bringing up her great nieces, and it is clear that her devotion to the girls surpassed the role of family caretaker or maiden aunt, as she became the girls' surrogate mother. Mary worked steadfastly in her vocation as a teacher in order to provide for their practical, social, and educational needs in the postwar years, and as she approached old age, they also cared for her.[63] In spite of her intermittent protests that raising Mamie's children was a "cruel experience" that she was forced to endure, she clearly adored the girls and wanted to raise them. She admitted that they were her motivation to keep working, often in difficult teaching posts, in order to provide for them.

Yet Mary's diary makes it clear that she found the task of raising her grand-nieces a mixed blessing; she was intent on raising them on her own, but the reality was that she often found it an exhausting occupation, particularly as she grew older. Added to this was the important fact that she was not their birth mother, nor were the children her sole occupation in life. She continually struggled to maintain full-time employment, as a governess, and later as a teacher, in order to afford their care. Her residential living arrangements were often temporary, and she constantly had to prove that she was doing a satisfactory job at work, to keep not only her job, but also a roof over her head, as often living quarters were provided by (and in) the school in which she worked. Mary found this arrangement taxing on her emotions, which often resulted in her becoming run down and ill. She was always anxious to secure longer-term employment, which meant she was continually negotiating her employer's rules, regulations, and requirements, in order to fit in, gain a good reputation, and secure long-term work, but this placed constraints on her personal autonomy.

Mary was determined to be self-sufficient, and when help was offered, she usually rejected it, which revealed a dogged determinism to manage independently. Her brother William, who was a teacher in Port Gibson, asked Mary on several occasions to come to live with him and his wife Josie. He urged her, "If you insist on being independent, I think this would suit you much better than the life you have been living," as if to imply that she would benefit from his care and protection. Yet Mary rejected his offer, insisting that she would not to be separated from the children.[64] Mary was a woman who clearly preferred her limited independence with all the stresses that it might entail to a life of dependence, or worse, breaking the promise she had made to care for her nieces or grandnieces. She moved in with her brother William and his wife Josie on only one occasion, and this was to help care for him when he was ill, in the capacity of familial support as a helpmeet. Even during this temporary living arrangement, Mary felt stifled: she argued incessantly with Josie, and she felt infuriated by the lack of privacy she experienced there, which impacted on her preparation for work. This was an indication of her drive for personal agency, at home and in school. She exhibited strong traits of independence, which pushed against the boundaries of true womanhood, and in doing so she forced them to expand a little further, in her own life at least. Mary Ker's life undoubtedly turned out to be quite different from how she might have imagined it would be, growing up as a young girl in a wealthy, southern family. Though she was born and raised like so many other slaveholding daughters, the Civil War had materially altered the social dynamics of the Ker's lifestyle and stripped the family of their land, property, and slaves.

Her story is indicative of the lives of many other unmarried women from planter families in the mid-1860s, who similarly found that they were in tightened economic circumstances owing to the exigencies of war. The social fabric of society was gradually shifting, and Mary and her generation of single, slaveholding women were particularly important in taking on the mantel of child care in the service of their extended families. Single women often outwardly prescribed to the ideals of southern womanhood, and they hankered after the acceptance of their community in the same way as if they had married. Just because they did

Mary Susan Ker in her advanced years. Courtesy of the Southern Historical Collection, Wilson Library, University of North Carolina, Chapel Hill.

not have husbands or dependents of their own, it did not mean that they were any less committed to the ideals of the southern family that represented the bedrock of the South. Historian Joyce Broussard referred to their commitment as the "servant ideal," in that it allowed women (from all social classes) to fit into the wider hegemony of the South by demonstrating their servitude and commitment to the "larger patriarchal order of life."[65] In other words women were able to bypass social, racial, and class barriers that typically barred single, lower-class, or black women from obtaining the mantel of true womanhood. By pledging their devotion to the more universal ideals of submission, honor, and paternalism, they gained respectability where ordinarily they would have found themselves shut out.[66]

The maiden aunt provided much in exchange for the reward of familial intimacy and a good reputation. She counterbalanced a mother's shortcomings and provided a unique service to the family compact and "offered instruction while maintaining perspective and balance."[67] Mary Telfair, a rich, slaveholding spinster from Charleston, South Carolina, underscores this point well. Following the death of her brother Thomas, and coupled with her lack of faith in and rather low opinion of her sister-in-law, who was now a widowed mother caring for two children, Mary stepped in and took charge of her nieces, Mary Eliza Telfair and Margaret

Long Telfair. Despite Mary's status as an unmarried woman, she deemed it her *responsibility* to actively intervene in the care of her two nieces, as she believed they were being raised inadequately by her sister-in-law. In this rather awkward situation, what seems most astonishing is that Mary garnered both the power and influence to control the situation, even though, strictly speaking, she fell outside of the parameters of the immediate family. Perhaps it was Mary's wealth and family connections, or her strong, even pushy persona that enabled her to interfere in their lives. What remains clear is that her pattern of interference was not an isolated case. In 1839 Mary intervened once again and took charge of her grandniece, when the girl's parents, Pierce Cobb and Mary Eliza Telfair Cobb, died. Mary virtually adopted her grandniece, raising and educating her as if she were her own daughter. However, Mary was soon to discover the limitations of her power, and not even her wealth or social position could protect her from it. Regardless of Mary's authoritarian nature, she remained beleaguered by the difficulties of raising other people's children within a wealthy, slaveholding, southern family. In frequent streams of correspondence to Mary Few, her closest friend, she admitted, "It is not necessary to be a Parent to feel the responsibility and anxiety of one," thus emphasizing the commonality of experience with biological mothers.[68]

In a subsequent letter, Mary spoke of the constraints placed on her as the maiden aunt, which are illuminating given the manner in which she rode rough shod over the feelings of her sister-in-law after her husband died.[69] Even when it came to decisions, such as whether or not the girls should be sent north to continue their education or stay in the South, Mary was simply not consulted on the matter, which made her feel isolated and insignificant. As she confided in Few: "We feel the delicacy of our situation and cannot urge what we wish," highlighting the vulnerability and limitations of a single woman's role in the family.[70] Mary's case demonstrates that even the wealthiest and most well connected slaveholding women found their autonomy was circumscribed within existing gender hierarchies when it came to their designated role in the southern family. Similarly, biological mothers found their autonomy was clipped by the dominant male hierarchy, which dictated the parameters of their maternal roles. Slaveholding mothers faced the dual responsibility in that they were mothers to their own children, but also considered themselves "mothers" to their slave dependents. This strange dichotomy was further complicated by the fact that a planter-class woman's husband (and patriarch) was oftentimes the father of their "slave dependents," which highlights the issue of sexual abuse and rape of black African slaves.[71] The injustice of the fact that black, enslaved women were subject to sexual abuse with white men, and then denied the right to their own children, who could be bought and sold against their will by the white slaveholder, underscores how gender ideals in the South had clear racial limitations. Slaveholding women's elevated racial and class position hinged on the total disregard for black women's maternal nature.

Thus the gendered ideal that "the mother heart beats in all women" was ring fenced by distinct racial and class boundaries.

For some unmarried women, the role of the maiden aunt was thrust on them when they neither expected nor desired it. Ann Lewis Hardeman, a forty-six-year-old spinster from central Mississippi, after years of living with her brother, sister-in-law, and ageing mother, was suddenly commandeered to take charge of her sister's six children. In early 1849 Ann's sister, Sarah Stuart, fell desperately ill and died after giving birth for the last time. She left behind six children and an irresponsible husband who she knew would be incapable of raising their children alone. Safe in the knowledge that her sister was a reliable woman, Sarah in her wisdom decided to nominate Ann to take on the responsibility of bringing up her six children: James, Oscar, Adelaide, Annie Elizabeth, Edward, and Sarah-Jane. It was a request that shaped the rest of Ann Hardeman's life, but one she could not easily refuse, and she rather grudgingly took on the responsibility that accompanied her new role of surrogate mother to her sister's children. "Suddenly the spinster aunt of 46 had become a sort of mother. She had no money of her own, was never to have money of her own [and she] lived upon the charity of her brother and sister-in-law," which did little to boost her self-confidence, independence, or personal autonomy.[72] Ann made it clear in her diary that she occupied a rather shadowy existence within the family unit, and she often described her position as being compromised by her shared living arrangements with her brother and sister-in-law, in addition to her restricted financial independence. This spilled over in the way she disciplined the children, as she found her sister-in-law routinely interfered, which belittled her position. Mary tried to share parental responsibility with Ann, which caused further conflict and confusion and ultimately diluted Ann's authority, making her appear indecisive and at times weak. Although she spoke with great kindness and warmth regarding her relationship with her brother William, she found that her position as surrogate mother was continually undermined by the presence of her sister-in-law, Mary Hardeman. Michael O'Brien described Mary Hardeman as a "stern, authoritative woman," "watchful of her status," and "chilly in her formality."[73] Evidently she was a cold, domineering personality who occupied the center of the family and was a woman who made Ann's life difficult. Ann played second fiddle, rendering her meek and ineffectual by comparison.

Despite these constraints Ann forged strong and lasting bonds with her surrogate children. Her diary revolves around the minuscule details of the children's daily routines, their likes and dislikes, health and education. Later as the war unfolded, she effused her crippling anxiety for her nieces' and nephews' safety in the safe keeping of her diary, indicative of the deep ties of affection she had for the children she had raised. Though Ann evidently worked hard, she lacked the authority and confidence of a true disciplinarian, perhaps linked to her feelings of inadequacy within the family. Yet the home and domestic sphere were all she really knew, hence the focus of her diary on domestic reports, chronicling when the children are ill with whooping cough, chickenpox, colds, and scarlet fever. In a typical entry on 8 July 1850 Ann wrote, "Our dear little Jane has been quite ill of Diarrhea for a fortnight. Looks badly—but on balance doing tolerably well— Adelaide improving—Betty can spell."[74] Her time was dominated by caring for them, monitoring their progress with schooling, and ensuring they attended church, which buttressed Ann's religious beliefs.[75]

When the children grew up, matured, and left home, Ann missed her former dependents and continued to worry about each of them—all adults with their own responsibilities—particularly the boys who left to fight in the Civil War. In December 1860 she wrote, "This Christmas is lonely for me having only two of my dear ones with us," a reflection of how much she missed and drew pleasure from her surrogate family.[76] Her feelings of loneliness intensified as the journal progressed. As Michael O'Brien observed, Aunt Ann sunk into a deep depression: "She sat in her room, ageing and alone, nursing her health and trying by force of prayer and will to preserve the children she loved," but to no avail. This picture of Aunt Ann reveals a complicated image of a single woman—on the one hand ageing and alone, and on the other comforted by her lasting attachment to her grown children and to her role as surrogate mother. This was not a woman who regretted the role thrust on her, but an individual who had battled through difficult circumstances, to enjoy her identity as a surrogate mother, despite of the personal constraints and heavy responsibilities the position had placed on her. Ann's lack of personal autonomy and her rather diluted sense of self within the family compact must not detract from the fact that her role as a surrogate mother enabled her to enjoy a full and contented life, which drew on the positive relationships she shared with her nieces and nephews. Ann may not have initially chosen her role as a surrogate mother, but she certainly seems to have benefited because of it. She may have lacked the fiery independence of Mary Ker, or the economic advantages of Mary Telfair, but she nonetheless shared certain commonalities with them: a commitment to the children and a desire to be *useful*. Ann Hardeman was certainly not an autonomous woman; in fact she found the process of decision making an almost unbearable challenge. However, she represents a good example of a "reliable" woman who could be trusted to hold the family together, particularly in times of crisis. Ann, and women like her, often discovered an inner strength, which enabled them to overcome daily constraints that they faced within their own family, and to ultimately prove that they were worthy caregivers, on a par with their married counterparts, which gave them a sense of belonging and self-worth.

Single women were not defined simply by their marital status, but by many additional factors: their wealth, family connections, geographical location, and personality. Few shared the same confidence, drive, and gumption of Mary Telfair and Mary Ker. Some women lacked the wherewithal to manage alone or to secure a job to support themselves and their young charges. Others had little motivation to pursue employment, as they had grown up in wealthy aristocratic families that sheltered them from the necessity of working for a living. Yet these distinctions notwithstanding, single women were often equally dedicated to domesticity and the family unit as their married counterparts were, even if this was solely to gain acceptance and respect within the family unit. After all, if single women were willing to take on the responsibility of raising other people's children, surely they deserved some recognition for their efforts, even if those responsibilities were thrust on them. Single women therefore demonstrated their commitment to the family by taking on various roles within the family circle. The details of each individual story, while distinct, collectively illuminate general trends or patterns that reveal a great deal about single women's relationship to the southern family. Even though women like Ker and Telfair may have devoted themselves tirelessly to the care of their brothers' children in their role as maiden aunt, it was a role that replicated the tenets of true womanhood and continued to hinge on the wishes of higher male authority that did little to challenge existing feminine ideals or gender hierarchies, in an effort to gain acceptance in a male-dominated world. Even in exceptional cases, when slaveholding women came from extremely prosperous families who retained wealth during and after the war, such as the Telfairs, the maiden aunt discovered that her role was limited by the paternalistic structures of a male-dominated world that did not *visibly* crumble until the American Civil War and beyond. Stemming from this observation, it would seem that single women gained little in growing independence in the family unit, at least in their role as the maiden aunt. This is not to say that unmarried women did not gain any personal autonomy in the family, but rather to suggest that they were simply expanding agency within the existing class, race, and gender hierarchies that were already in place.

Sibling Support

Sibling relationships could provide an excellent source of practical and emotional support for single women. At their best strong networks of reciprocal support that was mutually beneficial to both parties were forged between siblings. Conversely single women also found they were vulnerable to constraint and exploitation, especially in regard to their relationship with their brothers, if they turned sour. Fraternal bonds were a vital relationship that could either make or break a single woman's fortune, determining where she lived, the support she was given, and how family members perceived her. Yet many single women found solace in their special relationship with their brothers. George W. Mordecai, a successful and wealthy lawyer and businessman from Raleigh, North Carolina, proved to be a loyal and supportive brother to his unmarried sisters, in addition to other members of his extended family.[77] He shared a close relationship with his never-married sister Emma Mordecai, who shared a communal living arrangement with George, his wife, Margaret, and their sister-in-law, Rosina Ursula Young. Rosina was a widow who suffered from poor health. Emma often supported Rosina during times of sickness and offered support to the wider family unit. As a single woman, Emma Mordecai was a rock of support to several members for the family as a family helpmeet or caregiver, but she was especially helpful to her brother, who could count on her reliable and steadfast manner to take care of herself (practically and financially in her role as a teacher) and for the wider family. This included caring for her sister, Caroline Mordecai Plunkett, who was widowed in 1824.[78] Caroline Plunkett had left the family home in Richmond, but returned during an extended period of ill health (she suffered from a nervous disorder), during which time her sister Emma cared for her. Unfortunately the situation did not easily resolve; Caroline was so unwell and her mental state so unstable that she eventually required hospitalization in an insane asylum. Throughout the ordeal Emma Mordecai remained stoic, and while the situation at home must have put enormous pressure on her, she remained dogged in her determination to assist in the family compact.

The reciprocal relationship between Emma and her brother George was an ongoing source of support to them both, and theirs is an example of the sibling bond at its most positive. In a letter to her brother George on 29 September 1862, Emma noted wistfully, "How often and how gratefully I think of you, and what ought to be told sometimes, how much I love and admire you."[79] Yet it was clear that the adoration and support were mutual. Emma was a stoical character. She cared for her sick mother, Rebecca Myers, who died in 1863. During this bleak period she remained undeterred in her pursuit to do "good" despite the daily constraints placed on her. After her mother's death she threw herself into war work at a nearby military hospital, applying the skills she had developed at home caring for her sister and mother, by putting them to use for the good of the wider community. This crossover between the private and public sphere, particularly in the context of wartime, helped to alter perceptions of single women's place in southern society. Personal stories such as Emma Mordecai's resonate with a collective number of unmarried women who also made the transition from the domestic to the public realm, in their wartime work to care for soldiers, or to partake in other useful work, in aid of the Confederacy. Single women like Emma Mordecai remained deeply committed to their birth families, but they were also impassioned by their broader commitment to the South. Not all single women were as strong and resourceful as Emma Mordecai, nor were all brothers or male relatives as supportive as George.

A good contrast to Emma Mordecai is Ellen Lazarus Allen Shutt, George's niece—a woman who was widowed when her first husband, John Allen, died in

1858. Ellen characterizes the stereotype of the desperate widow, a woman who was left financially destitute after her husband's death, with several children to support. John Allen had never been good with money, and the couple were seldom prosperous even when he was alive. However, after he died the situation got even worse, as nothing had been settled regarding his limited estate. Ellen, right from the outset, proved to be needy, and on occasion manipulative in sourcing money from George. Rather than expressing a desire to be independent, Ellen regularly turned to her uncle for advice and financial support. Even when she was offered money from her sister, she refused it and explained to George, "I feel assured you would prefer my continuing to make known my wants to you, to resorting to my sister or any other source. Is it not so?"[80] Her continual reference to George in all domestic and financial matters was more common than we might otherwise assume, and she constantly reiterated her need for a male patriarch to replace her husband. She was unwilling to take on advice from anyone else or to trust her own judgments and instead relied on the good nature of Uncle George to solve all her familial, financial, and legal problems.

In the period after the war, Ellen Shutt's affairs dominated George Mordecai's personal correspondence, and it must have been frustrating but also time consuming for George, though he seldom discussed his feelings on the matter. Ellen wrote him long letters detailing her hardships during the war. For example she recounts the sorry tale of how her family had experienced such dire financial straits that she foolishly apprenticed her daughter Minnie and son Urner (now Ernest) to the Shakers for fear that she would not be able to support them as a woman on her own.[81] It was a decision that she regretted but seemed unable to reverse. She claimed that the Shakers used "deception and treachery" to persuade her to give the children up, and in her letters to George she badgered him for advice on how to get the children back.[82] Ellen would often make poor decisions without any consultation with her uncle and then in a panic try and get him to reverse the action she had put in motion. The Shaker story is a good example of this; her eldest daughter, Minnie, had no desire to leave the sect, but Ellen eventually managed to rescue Ernest. In Ellen's case the indoctrination of appropriate gender roles and behavior had a lasting effect and prevented her from developing a direction or voice of her own, which negated her personal autonomy, as she constantly reached out for protection and provision from an alternative figure of male authority. Ellen Shutt's predicament highlights several points: the vulnerability that some single women encountered, particularly widows who were used to having a male protector. Second, it shows how important a single woman's personality was in coping alone, and the value that she placed on having an extended family to turn to. Ellen Shutt was fortunate that she could rely on the support of her Uncle George, who was more than accommodating during her times of need. At the same time, the ease of having a male figure to turn to negated any need for her to foster new skills of self-sufficiency. In many ways George replaced his father as the family patriarch when his father died, and he frequently demonstrated his ongoing commitment to upholding his role in the family on numerous occasions. Independent historian Emily Bingham observes how family came first to the Mordecai clan, regardless of each member's marital status. Members "grounded their identity in and found their place in the world through service to the family," and single siblings were no exception.[83]

In the Cameron household the philosophy was much the same. Siblings Margaret and Paul Cameron from Orange County, North Carolina, demonstrated their continuing commitment to their family throughout their lives. The familial bond, which they shared, was a constant source of support that was reflected in their personal correspondence over several decades. When their father, Duncan Cameron, was dying in March 1853, Paul wrote to his sister, "I wish it was in my power to go to you in this time of need, I know I would be a comfort to you," which he evidently was.[84] Even after Margaret married George Mordecai in 1854 the sibling pair continued to rely on one another for emotional and practical support. Margaret was able to trust and confide in Paul regarding her deep attachment to their birth family, safe in the knowledge that he echoed her desire to be constantly present for their siblings. In regard to their sister Mildred (who suffered from neuralgia and partial paralysis), Margaret felt a special commitment. She confessed to Paul, "I sometimes think that it is my duty to take her to Philadelphia for medical aid," following a particularly severe bout of ill health and spasms for Mildred.[85] It was in the dialogue with her brother that Margaret felt at ease to express her innermost thoughts and concerns, a sentiment that never diminished throughout their lifetimes. The strong fraternal and sororal bonds that existed between many siblings reinforces the ethos of the "collective family," which at its best proved to be a loving, communal, and nurturing environment in which single women rooted much of their identity.

Throughout their adult lives, Margaret and George devoted considerable time and energy to their extended family networks, reinforcing the stereotype of the supportive sibling and family caregiver. Margaret maintained a close and loving bond with her siblings, particularly with her unmarried sister Mildred Coles, which is well documented in the Cameron family papers. Even though George and his wife never had children of their own (except for one stillbirth) they demonstrated much care and compassion to their birth families. Margaret continued in her role as family caregiver to Mildred, who suffered from poor health and paralysis. George also showed care and compassion in his familial relationships, particularly with his unmarried sisters Ellen and Emma Mordecai. When his brother Moses died in the 1830s, George shouldered the responsibility of providing for his widow, Ann Lane Mordecai, who lived with him, and he served as a guardian to her children. When his sister Rachel Mordecai Lazarus was widowed,

George again assumed familial responsibility, becoming the legal guardian to her children.

Not all women could rely so heavily on the solid support of their brothers. Mary Scudder was a never-married woman who had tended to her sick parents for two and a half years. After their deaths she was shocked to discover that the bonds of mutual dependence, which she thought she shared with her siblings, were on shaky ground. While Mary never regretted the decision to invest the days of her youth in her caregiving role, she openly admitted her disappointment regarding her brothers. She had willingly fulfilled her role as the family helpmeet during times of crisis, but found that she was left isolated and unsupported after the crisis had passed. Mary constantly reminded her brothers of the painstaking care she had taken of their dying parents. Despite this she discovered both herself and widowed sister were left destitute, without the financial means to live an independent life.[86] In spite of the fact that it had been her father's last wish that his two daughters be provided for, the reality was that his requests were ignored, and the girls had to fight for what was rightfully theirs. Owing to complications in their father's will, which had originally been written prior to ill health, nothing had been specified in writing as to what he intended to leave them. Consequently Mary's fate had been left in the unsympathetic and greedy hands of her brothers, who refused to share out the family estate. Their actions ultimately clipped her wings of independence (or at least her free choice in the life she may have chosen, or where she might live) and devolved power into her brother's hands. For Mary Scudder and for other single women in her position, the loss that resulted from her father's death was therefore taxing on a number of different levels: emotional, financial, and practical. Not only had Mary lost her father, whom she had devoted so much time and affection to, but she had also been robbed of any degree of personal autonomy. Her brother had stolen her key to personal independence and tightly controlled the limits of her private and public life. With limited options open to her, and heavily circumscribed by her own family, Mary eventually decided to accept the proposal of marriage from her suitor Mr. Magie. She exchanged her life as a spinster for the security of a home and future that had been denied to her by her brothers.[87]

The Holladay sisters were more fortunate in the loving relationship they shared with their brother. The Holladay family were from Prospect Hill plantation, Spotsylvania County, in Virginia. Waller Holladay and his wife, Huldah Fontaine Lewis Holladay, had six daughters, five of whom were unmarried (as well as some sons) at the time of Waller's death in 1860. The daughters were well provided for in their father's will; they each received what would have been considered a traditional provision of being granted permission to live together in the family house, which had been passed on to their brother in their father's will. His will stated: "To my single daughters I give the right to reside in my dwelling house with their brother James M. Holladay if they wish it, so long as he may be the owner of it. In the event of the marriage of any one of them, the right, to such one, shall cease."[88] There are two key points raised here. First, the girls were given the right to live together in a female dominated household, but, second, their autonomy remained checked by their brother, who ultimately owned the house, and therefore they were subject to his desires as to if he wanted to keep it, or sell it on. As single siblings living together, they may well have shared in a camaraderie and special relationship, but even that was subject to the ultimate authority of their brother, which bound them to the patriarchal order even though they had not married. The Holladay sisters luckily shared a good relationship with their brother, and as sisters they were close and depended on each other. Long before their father's death, in the spring of 1848, Eliza Holladay penned a letter to her cousin Elizabeth Travers Lewis, in which she confessed her anxiety regarding the possibility that her unmarried sisters *might* someday marry and break up the intimate sororal circle shared among them. "We have always lived so happily together that I should almost be afraid of any of us to get married for fear that we would not be so happy afterwards, when separated from each other," Eliza admitted nervously.[89] These young women were intimately tied to one another, and their letters show they did not want to break this tie, even after their parents died.

For Eliza, and other single women living in a similar situation to her, her sisters represented an essential part of her life, and they were the embodiment of what the southern family meant to her. Fortunately her sisters also shared in her sentiments, and none of them ever married, and they all lived together on the family plantation throughout the course of their adult lives even though other options were available to them. Having lived together for over thirty-two years, the sisters were loath to alter their living arrangements after their parent's death. The ties that bound single women like Eliza Holladay to their birth family were ones that transcended childhood and kept siblings together on a far more permanent basis. As Eliza freely confessed to her cousin Bet, "I always feel so miserable when I have been from home for any length of time without any of my sisters," adding that her parents would not like to be parted from their children either adding, "of course we cannot do so, so long as they object to it," reflecting a pattern of mutual interdependence.[90] The fact that Eliza and her sisters continued to live in the parental home, even after their parents passed away, is itself proof that the decision to remain at home was a conscious decision rather than parental constraint.

The Holladay sisters' case demonstrates that the fraternal bonds between single women and their brothers were an important aspect of their everyday lives, which heavily influenced, and at times controlled, key decisions in their lives. While not always positive, the significance of the sibling bond remained of fundamental consequence in single, white, southern women's lives. Unmarried women often poured considerable time and energy into their relationships with their siblings, and they were naturally left devastated if their siblings were ill, or worse, died. Mississippian Ann Lewis Hardeman lived with her unmarried sister, Caroline Hardeman, in a family group and was left devastated when she died, admitting she was "close" to her and "depended so much upon her for everything."[91] Caught in a world where she lacked confidence and self-assurance, the loss of her "contemporary and friend made her life dreary." She recognized: "My precious sister though wert all of earth to me—the world seems sad without thee—my poor heart is stricken indeed."[92]

Such deep affection was common among unmarried sisters, and the loss of a beloved sister was keenly felt. Mary and Margaret Telfair tended to their sick brothers on more than one occasion, first to Alexander in 1817, which Mary described as an arduous duty, as she spoke of being stuck on a rural plantation, surrounded by Negroes, with only her sister, Margaret, for company.[93] Fortunately Alexander did recover, leaving Mary to later reminisce: "I sometimes think that I was endued with uncommon firmness to have gone through what I did, but I was so constantly engaged that I had no time to reflect. I only felt as though my existence hung upon his."[94] Her choice of words is illuminating as she described herself as having an "uncommon firmness," which in many respects was an unladylike characteristic, yet one that she seems almost proud of. In fact, in the Telfair household, worse was to follow, when Mary's eldest brother, Thomas, who was thirty-one years old, died on 18 February 1818, which shattered Mary's inner sanctum and turned her world upside down. In her grief Telfair entrusted her innermost thoughts to her lifelong confidante and close friend Mary Few. She admitted, "You knew how beloved was the object I lament, how much I esteemed his virtues, and how I delighted in his conversation; he was Brother, friend and instructor, indeed he was everything to me *and the separation was hard indeed*."[95] The separation, of course, was a metaphor for death. Mary's heartbreak over her brother's death plunged her into extended depression. Nevertheless in time Mary recovered sufficiently to refocus her energies on the care, upbringing, and education of his two daughters (her nieces), Mary Eliza and Margaret Long Telfair. She also developed a closer relationship with her eldest brother, Alexander, whom she and her two unmarried sisters, Margaret and Sarah, shared a home with. Their living arrangements reflect the idea of a collective family that flourished on the ideals of mutual companionship and interdependence. It also demonstrated the fluidity of the family unit discussed earlier.

Single women did not have to live alone to validate their desire for autonomy. In the Mordecai family two distinct family groups formed separate living arrangements following the death of its patriarch, Jacob Mordecai, in 1838. Jacob's son from his first marriage to Judith Myers headed one faction, based in Richmond, Virginia. Members of the household in 1849 included Samuel's single sisters, Ellen and Emma; Julia, a widow; half-sister Laura; and Eliza Kennon (also a widow);

Rosina Young later joined them after her husband died. Rosina suffered from chronic health problems, which rendered her unfit to manage her farm, Rosewood, or her household independently, and she was quickly embraced within the family fold. The second family group lived in Raleigh, North Carolina, headed by George W. Mordecai. This group included Nancy Lane Mordecai (George's sister-in-law); sisters Harriet and Temperance Lane (Moses and Margaret Lane Mordecai's children); and in the 1840s Mary Lazarus. Additionally in the 1850s Margaret Cameron married George Mordecai, and she joined them along with her invalid sister Mildred Coles.[96] These two groups illustrate how the nineteenth-century southern family accommodated various living arrangements that incorporated single women into the fabric of the family.

The Mordecai family comprised men and women of various marital statuses who often pitched in and lived together, as a result of shifting family circumstances: marital breakdown, bereavement, widowhood, or remarriage. These individuals were able to live contented lives, coming together as a family group, yet each willing to exert personal autonomy in the way they conducted their lives. For example Ellen was a teacher in the family school and later worked as a private governess; she also wrote several books, including *The History of a Heart,* which described her conversion to Christianity. Emma was the family caregiver but after the war pursued a successful teaching career, which her family supported wholeheartedly. "I am so glad Emma has occupation which she naturally so much desired," wrote Ellen Mordecai to her brother George on 16 October 1868. "I am very anxious to have a letter from her informing me of everything that I would know if we were together—I am sorry we are so far apart, but if she is prosperous and contented I can find my consolation in that reflection."[97] In the case of the Mordecai family, each member derived great pleasure from the success and well-being of its fellow members, reflecting a strong reciprocal bond of love and concern. For instance, when George was unwell, his sister Emma wrote to him from her teaching post and expressed her concern for him. She stated, "You do not know that everything that hurts you, hurts me—how often I think of your many anxious cares, and how I pray for your welfare and happiness."[98] This is only one of countless letters written between siblings that demonstrate the affectionate bond between family members. This also extended to the strong relationship between the Mordecai women and their new sister-in-law, Margaret Cameron, who quickly became integrated in the family circle.

Records reveal that single women often lived in sibling pairs, or small clusters, or as part of a collective family group. Sibling pairs were relatively common. Angelina and Sarah Grimké were sisters who spent a lifetime living together. The Grimkés were a well-known pair, who were exceptional in their early distaste for and abhorrence of slavery, irrespective of their southern roots. In 1819 the sisters fled to Philadelphia, and later to New York, where they became the first women to lecture for the Anti-slavery Society.[99] Their shared opinions on women's suffrage and abolition bound them together as one and resulted in a lifelong commitment to activism. Even after Angelina's belated marriage to the antislavery campaigner Theodore Weld in 1838, the sisters lived under one roof and supported each other in private and public affairs. Likewise the Edmundson sisters of Montgomery County in Virginia were a sibling pair who lived together. Mary Rebecca and Sally Munford were unmarried sisters who had been provided for in their father's will. In a contracted agreement, the girls were each paid one hundred dollars per year to support their living arrangements, which had been a condition of their late father's will administered and paid for by their brothers, David Edmundson and William Radford Edmundson.[100]

Further case studies, such as the Wylie sisters, demonstrate the advantages of living in a sibling pair. South Carolinian single sisters Hannah and Susan Wylie provided each other with a lifetime of companionship and support; they also retained a close bond with their late-married sister Mary Mobley. In fact when Mary became ill, it was Susan who rushed to her sister's aid irrespective of the fact that she was unwell herself. She dashed to her bedside "and there gave her unwearied attention" to her dying sister. In a strange twist of irony, Susan then became "dangerously ill," and the sisters died within a day of each other. Susan Wylie was described in her obituary as a person one had to "admire," and it also stated that "her faults were but few and were overshadowed by her virtues" (note, however, that it does refer to her as having faults, perhaps a slight at her single status). "She was the bedside attendant of the sick, the comforter of the bereaved, the friend of the oppressed, and the personification of benevolence, charity and virtue."[101] This highlights the way "womanly virtues" were upheld as important attributes in a society that valued piety, purity, submissiveness, and caregiving. Even though she was single, the carefully crafted words in her obituary homed in on these "womanly virtues." There is no mention of the qualities that really set her apart; her fiery disposition, tendency for outspokenness, and independent spirit, which were loved and accepted by all her family—but these would not have been considered appropriate attributes in a nineteenth-century obituary.

After the devastating loss of her dearly loved sisters, Hannah Wylie continued to show her resilience, hardiness, and resourceful character. She maintained a close relationship with Mary's widower, William Mobley, who continued to hold Hannah in high regard and tried repeatedly to persuade her to move out west to Mississippi to be closer to him, though there does not seem to have been a romantic connection between them. In his frequent correspondence to her, he spoke of how much he missed her friendship and good advice and how he worried about the effect her sisters' deaths had on her. "Hannah, I often think of you sitting alone brooding over your great bereavement," he wrote. "I think if I were with you I could comfort and sustain you some in your troubles, as I know you could with me—if ever we get near each other again nothing, so far as I am concerned, shall part us."[102]

Clearly sibling relationships, when they were strong and durable, provided an enviable level of support for unmarried women. No single experience can tell the tale of *all* unmarried women's lives, or of the different relationships with their families. However, certain key points can be drawn from the examples discussed here. First, family was clearly very important in single women's lives, and when their relationships with parents, siblings, and other family members was good, it made home the most perfect place in the world for these women to be. If these women were happy and contented at home, then this was usually a reflection of the strong sibling support they shared there. Home was a special place for many single women. Mary Telfair whimsically noted in a letter to Mary Few, "At home . . . I am a very *important* personae and then I am never happy separated from my own family any length of time," though she regularly enjoyed extended holidays and visits with family and friends in the North.[103] The point was that Mary valued home and family deeply; here she felt at ease, and of great importance. Thus, by telling Mary Few that she did not want to venture far from home, she was attaching a high value on this important element of her life. Yet she qualified her statement, adding: "I doubt whether this state of mutual dependence is not more productive of more misery than happiness," as if to illustrate the vulnerability she also felt.[104]

Josephine Blair Harvie from Amelia County in Virginia was another single woman who felt equally devoted to her family. During her time teaching as a young woman in 1852 Josephine wrote regularly to her mother regarding her pining to return home: "Is home the same pleasant place that it used to be? Or is it changed at all?" she questioned. "I feel that if I could only get there I should be the happiest person in the world." It was in the quiet moments of sitting alone, far from home, that "home" took on the rosiest hue. "I feel very low spirited indeed in my solitary room, my thoughts are far from here, they are at home that sweet far away place," she mused.[105] Home for Josephine was a special place; it was familiar, safe, and comfortable, a place where she could be true to herself and accepted as such, in much the same way that Mary Telfair had described. Connected to this was her strong attachment to her siblings, who she took enormous pleasure in. For example she could not disguise her regret when she learned that her brother would not be home for Christmas. In a letter to him she disclosed, "I can't tell you how disappointed I am that you're not coming home. Xmas will not be Xmas for me without you or any one of my brothers or sisters."[106]

The correspondence between the Harvie family members revealed a close relationship between siblings and the mutual dependence between them. Members of the family each gained something from their relationship with their siblings. When Josephine's eldest brother, Edwin James Harvie, was serving in the

U.S. Army in Washington Territory, he frequently wrote to his sisters and confided in them the details of camp life. "I like to share my feelings, happy or unhappy, with my sisters," Edwin wrote, possibly because it helped maintain a feeling of closeness, even though they were miles apart. This argument appears justified by his parting sentiment that "I love you more than I ever did."[107]

Summary

At the heart of the roles of being a family helpmeet, maiden aunt, surrogate mother, and devoted sibling lay single women's mission to prove that they were useful. As femininity was inextricably intertwined with "usefulness" or servitude to the family, or to the patriarchal ideal of femininity, single women did their best to replicate the role of their married sisters in the commitment they showed to the southern family. If women demonstrated that they were active members of the family circle or of the wider community, it often negated any claim that they were superfluous or redundant women.[108] In the eyes of Georgian society, Miss Joe Varner had proved her worth through unprecedented acts of usefulness and good works within the wider community that had gained her respect and notoriety. Single women, including Varner, Ker, and the Holladay sisters, proved that they were indispensable resources—either within the family or as key contributors in the wider community. This prevented them from being seen as a "drain" on the family and helped to reconstruct the spinster stereotype into one of usefulness and indispensability early on in the antebellum era. Usefulness could be achieved in a variety of roles—as the dutiful daughter, supportive sibling, family helpmeet, maiden aunt, or a mix of all these roles.

Widows could also achieve "usefulness" by proving that they were acting in the interest of their late husbands, an issue that came into sharper focus during and after the Civil War, when so many more women took on the temporary or sometimes permanent roles of deputy husband. In the postbellum period an increased number of single women became heads of household, mostly out of a desperate need for someone to fill the positions that their husbands had previously occupied. Stepping into the role because of their husbands' absence (either because they were fighting, or worse, dead) was initially an act of pragmatism; women were simply acting in the best interest of the family, rather than openly challenging gender roles. Though the exigencies of war thrust many women into new roles, the fact that this was even possible (and in many ways encouraged) indicates the growing flexibility of the family structure in the prewar era. The fact that these women were seen as acting in the interest of an absent or deceased spouse, or because of pressing financial or practical needs, rather than in a grab for personal autonomy, allowed women to take on roles traditionally reserved for their men folk. This links to Joyce Broussard's argument that unattached women could operate as equals to their married counterparts, as long as they demonstrated their dutiful behavior to the servant ideal.[109] Even in the postbellum world, when slavery had fallen and the patriarchal structure started to crumble alongside it, unmarried women were able to appear nonthreatening if they operated under the guise of servitude to the patriarchal ideal (even if that ideal was gone). Nonetheless what it clear is that women were generally accepted in southern society if they managed to demonstrate both their vulnerability (and need for protection as true southern women), together with their willingness to serve the body politic. Nineteenth-century southern society liked to protect "true southern women," and therefore the family often stepped in to care and protect its own.

The question of whether or not the Civil War changed the roles and responsibilities of single women in the southern family is again complicated. Certain patterns of dependence were clear in the antebellum period, right through to Reconstruction, and hinged on the bonds single women did or did not share with parents, siblings, and other family members. However, at the same time other important changes relating to women's legal standing and property rights were already underway in the prewar period. The legal debates and legislation that was passed gave some southern women more authority within the family in inheritance and residential living patterns, which offered them a limited but unprecedented degree of autonomy. Attempting to protect some single women through legal means and the changing perception of their legal status becomes an issue that is more clearly recognizable in the postwar period, and certainly during Reconstruction. However, this does not diminish the fact that attitudes toward single women were, for a variety of reasons, slowly altering to favor their circumstances in the antebellum era, a development that an increasing number of southern women would take advantage of during and after the Civil War.

Chapter 3   WORK

Virginia Hammett, a young eighteen-year-old girl who lived in Stafford County, Virginia, spoke in her diary about how her life had changed in the war. "Necessity is the mother of ingenuity," she mused, as she found herself undertaking a wide range of household chores such as organizing the house, sewing, sweeping, and making shoes and slippers, in addition to nursing the wounded soldiers,and later teaching in the postwar years.[1] The Civil War had acted as a catalyst that accelerated the changes in women's working roles and began to offer them wider access to paid work that white families increasingly relied on. As Mary Elizabeth Massey argued, "the Civil War compelled women to become more active, self-reliant, and resourceful, and this ultimately contributed to their economic, social, and intellectual advancement."[2] This reality is echoed by South Carolinian Grace Elmore Brown, an unmarried white woman in her mid-to-late twenties, who admitted rather uneasily in October 1865, "I look in astonishment at myself, so different am I from what I was by nature, I seem to have lost all elasticity, all buoyancy of temper, and to be settling into a hard, strong willed, go ahead woman. . . . I have also learned to act for and rely on myself alone."[3] Even though Grace came from a well-to-do white, southern family, she still found she was deeply affected by the vagaries of war, which meant she had to adapt her role and "nature" as a woman in order to survive. "We have truly said goodbye to being ladies of leisure, my time seems fully occupied and often I do not have time to sleep. Now our vocation is work, and our people seem to recognize it, for young and old, men and women are pushed by necessity unknown before, the need of bread. The gentry of the land are beggared, and they are turning their hands most bravely to work."[4] Grace Elmore Brown's comments captured the necessity born of war that Virginia Hammett spoke of. The war acted as a catalyst for social change, accelerating and changing women's traditional working roles at an unprecedented pace. These changes had already begun in the antebellum period, as women—married and single—took on additional roles. Married women whose husbands were absent for long periods of time acted as the temporary head of household, and single women, particularly widows, managed their plantations and large numbers of slaves when their husbands died. However, the urgency of wartime led to an increased demand for women's labor on a much bigger scale, as many more women were left alone to manage plantations and financial affairs. This inadvertently led to the honing of new skills, an opportunity for self-fulfillment, and a chance to prove that single women were useful.

The war therefore expedited social change and offered unmarried women new opportunities to demonstrate that they were useful in southern society. Many of the temporary changes in women's lives had a liberating effect on them and led to more permanent alterations in women's lives in the postwar era, which dovetailed with the burgeoning of the Cult of Single Blessedness. Women were keen to show that they operated within the acceptable framework of their gender, but they also argued that the exigencies of war must allow them some flexibility in the temporary expansion of their roles. As Phoebe Yates Pember, a South Carolinian widow, wrote in 1864, "A woman *must* soar beyond the conventional modesty considered correct under different circumstances" because of the *necessity* of wartime.[5] Pember was referring to the role of female nurses in the context of the Civil War. However, she highlighted an important point that lies at the heart of this discussion, which was that the war acted as a catalyst that accelerated changes in women's working lives that had already been set in motion in the prewar period.

The roles and responsibilities of slaveholding women in plantation management inextricably intertwined with race and class. Planter class women represented a small minority of white, southern women. They were privileged because of their class and wealth, which set them apart from lower-class white females. The fact that they were also single meant that they did not automatically fit into existing models of "true" womanhood. Yet by emulating traditional female roles in the prewar period they often gained acceptance in society, which inadvertently led to an increase in self-autonomy.[6]

Nursing came into sharp focus during the Civil War as the Confederacy struggled to provide adequate hospitals and nursing care for injured soldiers. As field hospitals and wayside hospitals sprung up, in an attempt to keep pace with the high number of casualties from the battlefields, so too did the nation's demand for nurses intensify in parallel with it. Single women, particularly spinsters or widows without children, were especially in demand as they had the potential for greater mobility in wartime compared to their married counterparts, who frequently had children to raise. The ability to relocate, often at short notice, was an important factor for women who nursed during the war, as they had to work in areas where the need was greatest, in close proximity to where combat was taking place. Women also helped to supply goods for soldiers, through ladies aid societies or benevolence work, or more important, they acted as caregivers and nurses to Confederate soldiers.

The trend for teaching had already slowly begun in the antebellum period, but during this time it was primarily based in the privacy of the home and family, where single women helped to educate their nieces and nephews, or helped read

Bible passages to slaves. A small but growing number of single women worked as governesses or teachers in the antebellum period, but it was not until the Civil War that teaching became, as one young lady put it, "a vocation rather than avocation."[7] Prior to this point women tended to work as unpaid laborers within their extended families, caring and helping to educate younger siblings or nieces and nephews, in the service of the extended family. In doing so they conformed to gender stereotypes and demonstrated that they were useful to the family, which coalesced with the development of an alternative model of femininity—single blessedness.[8] Wealthy southern families also generally frowned on their daughters going out to do paid work and actively discouraged them from doing so, as they perceived it as an outward sign that the family could not afford to support their own daughters.

After the war teaching became increasingly accepted as a more respectable way in which single, southern women could earn a living without compromising their feminine delicacy, which is evidence of the way that traditional working roles led to new opportunities and autonomy for women. Single women stressed that theirs was a valid contribution in the nurturing of the next generation, helping to mold young minds into becoming good citizens of tomorrow.[9] In the postwar world, an increasing number of single women turned to teaching as a means of making a living. The vagaries of war had altered wealthy families' social and economic positions, and in the postwar world the additional contributions from unmarried daughters and single sisters became valued. Women, both married and single, were conscious that they must tread carefully in taking on new roles, and if they did, they must justify doing so, even in the context of wartime. It was important that women showed a willingness to conform to the conservative roles expected of them, even if in reality they were overstepping its boundaries and gaining a degree of independence. Judith Mitchell echoed an earlier argument by Mary Beth Norton that women "concealed their flouting of convention by subsuming their actions within the confines of womanhood and its proper functions."[10] Mitchell focused on the life story of Ann Pamela Cunningham, a wealthy, southern-born white woman, who overcame her physical disability and single status by initiating a "public crusade to rescue the home of George Washington."[11] By cloaking her actions in a benevolent guise, and by describing her actions as fitting with a woman's role, she showed spirit and agency. As Nancy Hewitt noted, "Women influenced and advocated change, but they did so within the context of their particular social and material circumstances."[12] This links back to Pember's argument that the social changes generated by war made it acceptable for women to step outside of their sphere of home and family, without being perceived as a threat, or as a challenge to male authority.

Pember's words resonated with elite white women, who like her were either unmarried or widowed. These women fell outside of the parameters of "true" womanhood by virtue of their single status. Thus in pursuing war work, many single women wanted to prove that they were useful—as it engaged with the burgeoning of a new Cult of Single Blessedness, which measured an unmarried woman's worth by her contribution to society. Chambers-Schiller suggested that "a Cult of Single Blessedness emerged alongside the much-discussed Cult of Domesticity, and was evident for women coming of age in the Civil War era and finding new opportunities as a result of it."[13] Chambers-Schiller has noted that "the same pattern emerged in the South and West as seen . . . in the Northeast. It began in the South among women born in the 1840s and 1850s and became prominent there, as elsewhere, among women born after the Civil War."[14] At the start of the war, many southern women, married and single, felt redundant after having enthusiastically waved their men off to fight. They initially felt uncertain of what role they had in southern society.[15] As the war gathered momentum, there was a mounting pressure for women to help contribute to the war effort, which eased their concerns and gave them a new purpose.[16]

Plantation Management

Even before the war, evidence suggests that single women managed large plantations when required to do so. Rebecca Pilsbury's husband, Timothy Pilsbury, served in the House and the Senate of the Republic of Texas and was absent for long stretches of time when he was a member of the U.S. Congress from 1846 to 1849.[17] In his absence Rebecca Pilsbury had to take on unaccustomed responsibilities that were extremely taxing at first. In her diary she recorded the new household and farm duties she must attend to in her husband's absence. She noted the new chores were "entirely novel to me," and she described how much she missed the "kindness and support of her husband."[18]

The expansion of her domestic role was arduous to her, and she often commented that she was "not designed for a worker." Nonetheless she was determined to make her husband proud of her, proving that she could manage in his absence.[19] In December 1848 she wrote: "There is a pleasure in doing things you know will meet the approval of those you love, beyond the mere sense of having done your duty, and received the approval of your own conscience."[20] Rebecca Pilsbury's words reveal the importance of gaining external affirmation for her efforts on the plantation in her husband's absence.[21] Paradoxically, in pleasing her husband, she also developed new skills, which made her more independent. Virginian social widow Ellen Moore also echoed the difficulties of managing alone without her husband. On one occasion she bemoaned the fact that the slaves "all think I am a kind of usurper and [that I] have no authority over them" while her husband was absent. Her shrewd observation underlines how slaves recognized the differences between male and female slaveholders and in some instances helped to replicate existing gender conventions, simply by being aware of this.[22]

Daily life tested female slaveholders in several capacities. They honed a variety of new skills—including farming knowledge, business management, and dealing with their slaves (including reprimands and punishments). Thrice widowed, Ada Bacot from Darlington District in South Carolina recalled in her diary on 11 February 1861 how she dealt with disobedient slaves. As discussed previously Bacot made it clear that unlike Ellen Moore, she *would* be obeyed. She also intended to exert control over the slaves regardless of her gender and in doing so replicated class and racial hierarchies, which channeled power into her hands. Ada Bacot proved that the barriers of her gender could be overcome even when dealing with slaves, if women were from privileged and extremely wealthy backgrounds. Bacot exercised a heightened degree of personal agency, by replicating hierarchies of a male-dominated world, rather than transcending them. Female autonomy in these cases was linked to dominance over others, mostly over slaves and poorer white people, which had already become well established before the Civil War. The power that wealthy widows like Bacot displayed was different from that of a male slaveholder, who tended to brandish authority over his slaves by the use of physical force. Female slaveholders generally avoided physical reprimands of slaves, and on the rare occasions that women used physical force to reprimand them, they felt tremendously guilty, almost as if they had tainted their own femininity by reverting to such masculine power traits. Bacot's reaction to slave truancy demonstrated this.

Slave management was fraught with pitfalls. Laura Beecher Comer, a widow from Columbus, Georgia, is an illustration of this fact. On reading through Comer's diary, one of the first impressions the reader gains is that Comer was not a happy woman. She complained incessantly about the slaves, noting, "Oh, it is terrible to be weighed down, with a large family of the ignorant creatures! When shall I be delivered from them?" On another occasion she added, these "obstinate creatures" have "consumed 13 of the best years of my life! And I would gladly now be free of them forever! I love my house but it is continually clouded by these willful and disobedient servants. How much longer can I endure?" Yet, in spite of her apparent abhorrence of them, she found it hard to punish them, describing it as "a terrible duty."[23] It was difficult for single women to uphold their status as "ladies," while at the same time getting their hands dirty in the practical day-to-day running of the plantation, which included the punishment of slaves. As a result women learned to tread carefully in an effort to protect their image as both planter ladies *and* single women by showing that they did not overstep gender boundaries, even though in reality they often did. In the antebellum period, widows were keen to show that they adhered to traditional working roles and that if they extended beyond them it was done so only in the interest of their deceased husband. Kirsten Wood argued that as "ladies," slaveholding women believed they were superior to most of their sex, because of their position in the planter hierarchy. The feeling of moral superiority also extended across gender lines as elite women often considered themselves nobler stock than planter men "in manners, gentility, and piety, qualities that popular opinion deemed white women's special province."[24] Supposedly character-based, "these assessments invariably reflected class and race privilege," but they also represented an avenue to enhanced independence.[25]

Many widows understood how the death of a husband marked a critical moment in their personal lives, which forced them into new roles out of the necessity of their altered circumstances. Material resources were an important factor that helped determine a female planter's level of autonomy. Financial difficulties could become a source of considerable restraint in single women's lives. Laura Beecher Comer was dissatisfied with her life as a planter wife living on a cotton plantation in Alabama. Laura, originally from New Haven, Connecticut, married James Comer, a cotton planter from Alabama, in 1848. Her marriage and later her widowhood were characterized by dark entries in her diary that reflected her dissatisfaction with the life she had chosen and her lack of options to escape it. Throughout the pages of her voluminous diary she referred gloomily to her unhappy marriage and how she hated living on an isolated cotton plantation in Alabama, surrounded by slaves. "It is a terrible life! Who can appreciate or understand anything about such a life but a woman who marries a bachelor; who has lived with his Negroes as equals, at bed and board! What a life many poor wives have to live in uncomplaining silence," she fumed in April 1863.[26] In reality Laura Comer displayed agency by vocalizing her discontent and unwillingness to conform. Her story, like many others, was one of dissatisfaction, but also one of conformity. Women like Laura revealed moments of significant personal agency in describing their dissatisfaction with the lives they led, yet they also conformed, keeping their opinions within the private arena.

For Laura Comer it was widowhood that led to an enhancement of her personal autonomy. Initially, after her husband James died, her diary entries remained bleak. Although she did not mourn the loss of her husband, whom she clearly did not like, she still found it hard to cope with all the practical and financial realities following his death. "I shudder and shirk from assuming any new responsibilities," she confessed in her diary in 1867.[27] Initially widowhood was not as she had imagined it would be. The reality of mounting financial pressures and other anxieties connected to running a plantation imposed additional restrictions on her that she had not envisaged. Liberty and personal freedom were initially not apparent. For Laura Comer it took time to build up the mental fortitude to free her from the constraints of marriage, and then the practical responsibilities that accompanied her widowhood, which were mostly tied up with managing the plantation and financial concerns. Finally, not long after she had turned fifty, she declared: "I have been a slave to my business affairs too long. I have taken care of others and neglected myself—it is high time I should attend to myself."[28] In her use of the word "slave" she likened her status as a woman to the restraints of a slave, which echoes Clinton's observation that all plantation mistresses were bound to the land in the same way as their slaves were.[29] Yet in widowhood Laura Comer removed the shackles of responsibility and recognized that it was "high time I should attend to myself," which demonstrated a burgeoning sense of personal autonomy. In Laura's third and final volume of her personal diary, her entries are injected with a renewed enthusiasm, absent in her earlier entries. As she wrote on 16 June 1872, "A new life seems to dawn upon me," which culminated in her plans to return to her home state of Connecticut and then travel onward to Europe.[30]

Evidently material resources were a critical factor in determining single women's scope for personal freedom. In 1800 South Carolinian widow Catherine Edwards remarked on the interrelationship between wealth and personal agency. "I have lived so long a widow that I no longer find the state a solitary one—besides my children will be greatly benefited by my remaining single and I am desirous to transfer all my good luck to them—Widows in this country are little Queens if they have property—and I have enough to gratify all of the vanity in my heart—have both my country and own house—with a number of servants and an elegant equipage and in addition an unencumbered estate having paid all the debts and this year a great crop of rice."[31] It is clear that even at the turn of the century, wealthy widows such as Edwards understood the benefits associated with property ownership for single women. In the South wealth was invested in goods and property. Therefore, as Edwards wisely deduced, property equaled power, and power equated to personal liberty. According to her assessment, the key to independence lay in bricks and bank notes, which accounts for her conclusion: "Let poor widows my dear Sir get husbands but those who are independent have respect enough without them."[32] A woman's "respect" and "independence" hinged on the procurement of wealth, not marital status, in Edwards's view. Even in the event of widowhood, a woman was able to retain respectability if she could uphold her social or class status (again the idea of protecting one's "ladyhood"). She could raise authority as a result of her wealth and social position, and retain respect by upholding the standards of ladylike decorum. Therefore, as these individual cases indicate, planter-class women who were single were able to overcome the subordination of their gender by virtue of their wealth, which suggests agency in the midst of restraint.

Paulina Cabell Read Le Grand, a wealthy widow and mistress of Edge Hill plantation in Halifax County, Virginia, was proof of how a widow could overcome adversity. After her husband's death, Le Grand employed an overseer to manage her large plantation, which freed her from the daily responsibilities of plantation management. She persuaded a friend, William Huntington, to reside at Edge Hill when she was away traveling, which gave her more freedom. In her letters to him, she was authoritative, even demanding, imploring him to, "stay with me, you can read here as much as will be profitable to you and I feel cheerfully willing to compensate you liberally for your services to me and my poor servants."[33] The tone of her letters borders on dictatorial, as she clearly expects William to submit to her will, with the soft bribe of liberally compensating him, an unusual trait for a woman in the antebellum era. Le Grand takes on the role of pseudopatriarch and in doing so subverts the commonly held notion of female dependency. Her wealth enabled her to broaden her domestic sphere to such a degree that she flouted all notions of feminine inadequacy and gained her own power. Leonora Whiteside also broke the model of "true womanhood" by displaying tremendous self-direction following her husband's death. Leonora had married James Anderson Whitehead, an influential and successful businessman, originally from Danville, Kentucky. They settled together at Ross's Landing (Chattanooga) and had nine children. James died in November 1861, and Leonora inherited his vast estate. Under her competent management, the estate accumulated substantially, reputedly making her "the richest woman in Tennessee."[34] These examples illustrate how slaveholding women were in a particularly advantageous position to overcome adversity and to demonstrate independence that resulted from their wealth and class, in stark contrast to lower-class white women.

Ada Bacot, Keziah Brevard, and Rachel O'Connor were well-known female planters who wielded enormous coercive power over their slaves and over poorer white people. Bacot's importance as a producer for tobacco and cotton placed her in a strong and enviable position. She could afford an overseer, which lessened the strain of the day-to-day management of her huge plantation. These factors combined to place her at the top of the social, class, and racial hierarchy. The fact that Ada Bacot was a widow did not dampen her power and influence as an important planter in South Carolina, even in the antebellum era. Rachel O'Connor lived in West Feliciana Parish, Louisiana. Her husband died in 1815, and for the next thirty-one years, Rachel successfully managed the family plantation, producing in excess of 150 bales of cotton per year, in addition to corn, potatoes, and other essentials.[35] As a single woman she faced many obstacles such as obtaining vital credit and having to deal with the jealousy from male slaveholders who lived in close proximity to her. Yet for these slaveholding women, their lives as widows were to be characterized more by their extraordinary success in managing and growing their business and plantations, than by any constraints because of their single status.

Keziah Brevard, a widow from Richland District, South Carolina, managed to meld business acumen, managerial prowess, and financial ability in a strong display of personal agency. A widow from 1844, Brevard managed three plantations, a gristmill, and two hundred slaves. By the time of her death in 1886, she had also more than doubled her holdings, which reflected her ability and business acumen.[36] Keziah Brevard's diary chronicled her experiences as a plantation mistress in the years preceding the Civil War in 1860 and 1861. She revealed the tumultuous journey that accompanied her position as a female slave owner in the South and in doing so revealed the way that she operated within a the framework of race, class, and gender prescriptions that shifted before, during, and after the war. In her honest account, she complained frequently about her slaves, much like Laura Comer. Yet at the same time she expended a great deal of time working alongside the slaves on her plantation, and they were her main source of company. There were days when frustration and fatigue clouded her perception of the slaves and their relationship to her, which led to angry outbursts such as on 30 January 1861, when Brevard fumed: "Oh our negroes, how much we have to bear with from them—have some I scarce ever get a civil word from no matter how kind and indulgent [I am] to them," she wrote on 30 January 1861.[37] Brevard had several arguments with her black driver Jim, who she claimed showed his "impudence" by testing her authority, and trying to expose her potential vulnerability, as a female slaveholder.[38]

Historian George Rable highlighted how slaveholding mistresses frequently used the words impudence and independence in reference to the behavior of black slaves. They were words that vocalized their frustration and ineptitude in understanding that slaves also had goals and aspirations of their own and that they were not *just* property.[39] Rable suggested that female slaveholders' fixations, such as Brevard's on impudence, was a direct reflection of their growing realization that power was slipping from their hands, particularly toward the end of the war when defeat appeared imminent.[40] For slave owners like Brevard the "impudence" of their slaves was a clear sign that the slaves also sensed that freedom was on the horizon. Just as white, slaveholding women had gained sufficient mastery to manage their plantations, they saw that it was being taken from them. Yet the widow Brevard's relationship to her Sand Hill slaves was complicated; Sylvia, Rosanna, Mary, Ned, Tom, and Dorcas were her main source of company; in her diary she wrote that she worked with them, baked and prepared cakes with them, and so on.[41] Though she was not deprived of white visitors, the "servants," as she referred to them, provided her daily interaction, which explains the numerous references to them throughout her diary. On the one hand she pontificated, "Negroes such trying creatures you are"; "they are not prepared for freedom, many of them set no higher value on themselves than the beasts of the fields do." However, a few weeks later she confessed in her diary, "I wish every vessel that would go to Africa to bring slaves here—could sink before they reached her soil. I would give every ct. I own on earth if it could stop the slave trade."[42] Keziah's complex emotions regarding slavery correlate with the debate in Robert Shalhope's "Race, Class, Slavery and the Antebellum Southern Mind." Shalhope points out that while there was a growing consensus in the historiographical debate about the southern mentality on slavery, two major interpretations remain. Historians such as Eugene Genovese posited that southerners, during the antebellum period and leading up to the Civil War, were proud of the institution of slavery and of their unique, southern civilization built on it. James McPherson and others have highlighted the "Cash Sellers Thesis," which is that southerners were actually guilt ridden about slavery, but so heavily reliant on it as an institution that they had to defend it as a way of life for fear of economic devastation.[43]

In Brevard's testimony we see a personal tussle between both of these interpretations. Brevard was proud of her slaves and displayed a benevolent, paternalistic attitude toward them (for example in working with them and in caring for them). Yet she talked of wanting them to "go back to Africa," hoping to somehow manage without them, yet acutely aware that her independence was secured by their servitude. This complex relationship between female master and slave was not unique to Brevard and was often seen in the relationships between single slaveholding women and their slaves. It also provides a sharp contrast to other moments when intense frustration set in, when she referred to them as "indolent" servants. Bacot and Brevard both made it clear that they wanted to be respected—and obeyed—not unlike how a male master would be, but they had a distinctly more feminine manner of achieving this aim tied to the idea of a distinct women's culture. In doing so they exhibited personalism, personal agency, and self-control. The end of the slave system also threatened the elevated status of slaveholding women as their livelihoods and whole way of life lay open to attack. In this context Brevard's reaction to her "impudent" slave seems fairly typical of white, slaveholding women. However, she also manipulated her position as a woman by adding that "it is hard for a poor, lonely female to take impudence—I have taken gross impudence hundreds of times and let it pass unpunished."[44] This reference to her femininity is used as an explanation for her slaves' disobedience and demonstrates how male and female slaveholders were perceived quite differently by slaves. Kirsten Wood discussed slaveholding widows' use of "ladyhood" and "female mastery," and all that entailed, to help them achieve productivity on the plantation, which displayed a conscious effort to use their gender to gain authority. Wood argued that widows relied on their feminine guile in conducting business affairs, successfully wielding it to their advantage in their new role as slaveholding mistresses on plantations, which underlines how they had achieved an increase in personal autonomy prior to the war in a behavior that was subversive.[45]

The evidence from these sources suggests that material resources or class and wealth were the key to overcoming the limitations of nineteenth-century gender conventions. These women were a privileged minority group in southern society, and their experiences must be interpreted as such. However, their experiences also span a broad time frame, from the early 1800s to the Civil War and beyond, which highlights certain trends of autonomy over constraint. They demonstrate that changes in women's roles were already existent in the antebellum period. These changes often emerged from an ideologically conservative backdrop, which echoes the work of Suzanne Lebsock in her study of women in Petersburg,

Virginia.[46] Lebsock described the way in which Petersburg women "experienced increasing autonomy, autonomy in the sense of freedom from the utter dependence on particular men," despite the entrenched conservatism of the area. She also revealed that in the period before the war, "fewer [white] women were married, more women found work for wages, and more married women acquired separate estates, that is, property that their husbands could not touch."[47] These observations reflect some of the findings in this study that expose how some slaveholding widows exercised considerable autonomy in managing family plantations following the death of their husbands.

There are many more cases of slaveholding widows who managed plantations and slaves, who also turned a profit. One lady who requires attention is Sarah Witherspoon McIver from Hartsville, Darlington County, in South Carolina. Sarah was widowed in 1861, but her journal began in 1854, when she was still a married woman living at home with her husband and family. Her journal chronicles her daily life and records the tragic news of her husband's death. Widowed at the age of thirty-five, McIver noted matter-of-factly that she was now "in this world without an earthly protector."[48] Her early life had not been easy; she was orphaned at the age of eight and later lost eight of her siblings, which meant she could not fall back on an extended family for help.[49] McIver did not succumb to self-pity but rose to the challenges set before her. She was a religious woman, originally a Presbyterian, who later integrated into the Baptist community, and her faith, as for many southern women, kept her strong. The change in her personal circumstances and renewed status as a femme sole in the eyes of the law meant that she operated as a free and independent woman, which gave her considerable flexibility in managing her large estate, which consisted of a fair sized plantation, slaves, and a larger plantation that her husband had been in the process of purchasing. McIver proved that she was capable of upholding her status as a true southern woman, as a widow with two daughters, and with a foster niece to raise.[50] Later described as "a remarkable woman" by her grandson, Robert Coker, her life story certainly bears testament to this fact. Caroline Foy Foscue was likewise widowed around the same time as Sarah McIver in 1849 and became the head of household and mistress of Trent Bridge plantation (later Pollocksville) in Jones County, North Carolina. At the time of her husband's death, Caroline was only twenty-nine years old and was left to manage the plantation and the family finances, in addition to raising a family of three: Henry, Mariana, and Christiana. According to the inventory, Caroline left the family plantation, and the slaves with it, during the Civil War and headed for the interior for safety, a self-directed action that again displayed considerable foresight and personal agency.

As early as the antebellum period single women quickly realized they were able to rely on their own initiative. Catherine Smith Stone took over the management of her late husband's plantation in South Carolina when he died in 1844. Catherine was forty-nine years old and had five daughters, Martha, Regina, Jane, Susan, and Catharine, aged between twelve and twenty years old, to support. She learned to act independently and to trust her own judgments, with minimal intervention, as her husband's family proved to be of little use and relied more on her, as she provided them with additional support in a reversal of gender roles. Catherine was self-assertive and decisive in ensuring her economic survival—she worked as a housekeeper to earn extra money and moved in with her eldest daughter in the late 1850s, again demonstrating financial savvy. Her relatives Ambrose and Matilda Stone in Alabama on more than one occasion turned to *her* for money, imploring in their letters to her to help provide for them, and promising to return it when they could. This again reveals how single women were able to manage their own financial and practical affairs, but also aid others in their hours of need, which challenged traditional notions of female vulnerability and dependence in the antebellum period.[51]

It is illuminating to consider that in the mid-1850s, when ideals of southern white womanhood were supposedly at their apex, the reality of single women's lives reveals that the traditional conventions of womanhood were beginning to be subtly worn away. Widowhood remained a difficult and testing time for many southern women—practically and emotionally—but these case studies reveal how some slaveholding women were able to overcome financial, social, and cultural constraints, which they labored under in their daily lives, to foster considerable strength and independence in their lives as single women. That said, single women also turned to others for advice on how best to manage a plantation, if the support and help was available, and would seek advice on crop selection, harvesting, slave management, and financial matters. Ruth Hairston's first husband, Peter Wilson, passed away in 1813, and she was left to manage Berry Hill, a sizeable plantation in Virginia. Ruth turned to her father for advice and support on how best to manage the plantation. "I want you to rite me what I must do for I want to go altogether by your directions in everything," she wrote, imploring him, "Dear papa rite me every opportunity you have so that I may [know] how to manage for the best."[52] Evidently Ruth learned fast, and when her father passed away in 1832, he entrusted the bulk of his lands to her. In 1837 Ruth married for a second time, to Robert Hairston, a tobacco planter from Henry County, Virginia.[53] Her second marriage was fraught with problems, as Ruth was left alone for months, when Robert moved to Mississippi to attend to his plantations (Bend, Black Flat, Choctaw Springs, Moore's Bluff, and Nashville), as well as to conduct a sexual relationship with his slave mistress. When he died in 1852, a controversy broke out when he left his property to a slave child. Meanwhile Ruth was left with nothing.[54] This case highlights the vulnerability of some widows, and their precarious dependence on the exact terms of their husbands' wills, a situation that steadily improved with the advent of the Married Women's Property Acts by midcentury.

By the time of the Civil War and well into the postwar period, women's working roles further expanded as single women increasingly went out to work for wages. Initially motivated by a conservative ethos to help contribute to their families who had been affected by the material devastation brought by war, these women helped to ease the financial loss that accompanied war and its aftermath. In planter-class households the expansion of women's work was regularly discussed as young ladies talked of doing more manual work, or partaking in household labor that their slaves had previously done. Consider the case of Frances Devereux Polk, whose husband, Leonidas Polk, died at the end of the war. Frances was determined to be self-supporting and refused to be dependent on her son's goodwill, in spite of her single status as a widow. In a letter to her daughter Frances Skipton, she wrote, "I do not think it right to be dependent on my sons while I can do something and therefore my dear child I have resolved to open a school in New Orleans."[55]

Frances Polk demonstrated considerable spirit in her endeavor to open a school and to remain independent throughout her widowhood. Although her plans did not come to fruition, she did support herself by teaching at the Columbia Female Institute, and in doing so she highlighted how the war had escalated the range of opportunities open to single women. Frances Polk evidently worried about her financial difficulties, and she regularly spoke to her daughter regarding her ambition to be self-sufficient. During her time working at Columbia Female Institute in 1867–68, she shared her ongoing concerns regarding school and money. In April 1868 Frances fretted, "I am not now employed as a teacher, I am only waiting until I can make some definite arrangements for my future but now there is nothing definite, so I just go on trying each day to do the duty which that day brings."[56] In doing so she revealed the burgeoning of opportunities open to single women in the Reconstruction era. She had an acute antenna regarding financial matters, even though she had not long been a widow, and she frequently detailed the cost of running a school in her personal correspondence with her daughter. In February 1869 she noted, "My school, or rather Susan's gets on very well—we have twenty-five pupils, they give an income of a little over $160 per month—the expenses are 45 the month—but we are making repudiation and I am not afraid of failure—we are preparing to take a larger house in fall."[57] Her self-belief was evidently well placed, because in November that same year, the number of day scholars rose to thirty-two, in addition to three boarders.[58]

In the postwar period, Octavia Wyche Otey, the widow of William Madison Otey, a cotton planter of Meridianville, Alabama, and Yazoo County in Mississippi, was similarly determined to manage alone, even though her newfound responsibilities were hard to bear. In Octavia's diary that she kept from 1849 to 1888, she openly discussed the heavy burden of running Green Lawn plantation, "as a woman with six children to raise (all under the age of fifteen) as she tried to negotiate with freed slaves in the context of Reconstruction. She emitted a sense of vulnerability, of standing alone in the world without a male protector, and in her grief and desperation she often reached out to God, from whom she hoped to find peace, solace, and protection. In March 1871 she confessed, "We had no one to take charge of us, to feel that we could call upon, so I asked my heavenly Father to take care of us."[59] Clearly Otey equated her personal insecurity with the absence of an earthly male patriarch or protector, which she keenly missed, particularly during her altercations with freed slaves who challenged her female authority. In January 1871 she observed: "Everything here seems to be going through a radical change" in reference to the alterations in the labor force, now that the slaves were freedmen.[60] Octavia felt exposed in widowhood, beset with anxiety regarding her daily responsibilities and mounting financial pressures, and she seemed to dwell on them in an unhealthy way that cast her in a different light to women like Ada Bacot, Keziah Brevard, and Sarah McIver, who seemed more capable of overcoming the challenges set in front of them.

The postwar period resulted in a downward spiral of wealth and financial security for Octavia Otey, and her anxieties reflect this fact. "I feel like I will go crazy if I can't get the money to pay for my debts," she admitted, adding, "It frightens me how much I owe; I wonder if I can live through them."[61] In the period from 1868 to 1869, Octavia seemed depressed and unhappy, weighed down by her additional responsibilities as a plantation mistress, and with the problems of dealing with the freed people, as well as the mounting financial pressures. "It makes me so sad to see the month pass so rapidly by, my debts not paid, land not rented out, a heap of bad things, but yet everything might be worse" she fretted in January 1871.[62] Octavia's apprehensions clearly resonate with Catherine Edwards's comments concerning the dilemma of widowhood, that widows were queens if they had property, servants, and crops, but would struggle if they did not. Octavia *had* property, but this did not mean that she was wealthy, and she found that she struggled on a daily basis because her wealth was tied up in her assets, rather than being cash. For her any benefits of personal agency derived from running a plantation were negated by the toil and responsibility of such a momentous task, which she found exhausting. This was compounded by her lack of confidence and her perceived lack of training, knowledge, or expertise in running a plantation. In the postwar years, her problems must have escalated, as additional challenges arose connected to emancipation, with slaves literally walking free from the plantations.[63] The planter women managing them were faced with the pertinent issue of who to employ to carry out the work, which often resulted in them taking on an increased share of the household tasks themselves, which challenged and revised old notions of southern womanhood. The change to material wealth for some southern women like Otey inevitably led to an alteration in their working roles, especially if they were single. The reality of the postwar world and in women's working roles within it was at times an unwanted burden and a responsibility that caused some women considerable anxiety, particularly if they were not cushioned by wealth.[64]

Widows like Otey persevered and survived the postwar period and made it through harrowing financial times. Extensive information appears about her children, her financial and legal affairs, and the day-to-day running of the plantation. She recorded many of the daily anxieties that she felt as a plantation widow residing in Alabama in the postwar years.[65] Octavia continued to live and operate Green Lawn plantation until her death in 1891. Her story is not unique—many other slaveholding widows struggled in the postwar era. They found that their independence from men was a double-edged sword as it forced them to become more autonomous but often meant laboring under difficult personal circumstances. These women also suffered from a shift in status caused by military defeat and the loss of their workforce, which had resulted in the emancipation of more than four million slaves.[66] As Carter argued, "These women had ventured boldly into new roles" by building on their experiences of work in the antebellum South, but this did not mean that their new tasks were always easy.[67]

Many plantation mistresses struggled to understand how their good and faithful slaves could show defiance in the postwar years, and this challenged their own newfound authority as female slaveholders. Anne Jennings Wise Hobson of Eastland in Goochland County, Virginia, was the widow of Frederick Plumer Hobson, who died in April 1868. Even before her husband's death, toward the end of the Civil War, she spoke of the way that her working role was slowly expanding on her Virginia plantation. She had to train a new cook, care for sick slaves, and educate her children and the Negroes.[68] In her diary she referred to the trouble she had with some of her slaves, and her desire to work alone. Clearly a religious woman, Anne showed mixed emotions on the subject of slavery.[69] In the postwar period she talked of an "exodus" of former slaves leaving the surrounding area, all lured by the promise of freedom further north after the South's bitter defeat in the war.[70] "I have long thought it best for the white race to be free from the incubus of slavery," she noted on 30 April 1865. In reality she also felt disappointed that many of her slave family chose to leave the plantation. As she noted only Anne, Eliza, Fannie, and her children remained on the Hobson plantation.[71] She glossed over her obvious disappointment and claimed: "If we stay here we will hire labour, I have no fear of getting on and I feel a kind of relief to be so easily freed of the responsibility of caring for them [the slaves] in these times." However, Anne quickly qualified this by commenting, "I am less convinced than ever that it is best for them to be free, and I feel great pity for the race but God knows that I have always felt that whenever He willed that we should give up I should not regret to part with them. With right management, I believe that in the end we will be better off. I trust country, family, life, honor, all the past, present, [and] future to God."[72]

Historian James McPherson points to the "guiltomania" of some southerners —the idea that they were economically reliant on slavery but nevertheless felt guilty about their involvement in the institution of slavery.[73] Ultimately white, southern slaveholders, such as Hobson, Brevard, Bacot, and Witherspoon, understood that their elite position within the southern hierarchy was bound to the institution of slavery, but they may still have harbored some guilt in the part they played in helping to replicate racial hierarchies. As Hobson discovered she was far more reliant on her hired help than she would ever like to admit. In the postwar years, when the health of her husband, Frederick Hobson, declined, Anne suddenly felt the mounting pressure of her growing responsibilities. "I shall have my hands more than full with no assistance with housekeeping, teaching and sewing, and last but by no means least the baby," she mused in 1868.[74] "My husband is very, very delicate. To our human eye he is certainly declining, wasting day by day," she confided in her diary, adding, "My whole life is a pleading appeal for my Husband's life!"[75] His death on 30 May 1868 left Anne as a "lone widow with a bleeding desolate heart," which was further intensified by her daughter's death five months later, after being administered a lethal dose of tartar emetio. This resulted in extended melancholic episodes that made it even harder for her to manage the daily responsibilities of plantation life. Anne's case demonstrates that postwar independence was not always easy. Yet more often than not, slaveholding women managed even in the most difficult circumstances.

Melancholy was a mindset that hindered some slaveholding women in their daily lives; others overcame it. Ada Bacot's ability to triumph over life's difficulties is an example of how mental fortitude was a powerful weapon in overturning adversity. In her midthirties, Bacot found herself in troubling personal circumstances; a bereaved and childless widow living on a large plantation surrounded by black slaves.[76] The futility of her altered role evidently weighed heavily on Bacot's shoulders at first. "I live merely to exist. I never feel lonely but I take no interest in anything, everything I do is mechanical. Nothing gives me pleasure, I go about like one who one has but a stated time to live," she wrote shortly after the loss of her husband and young children.[77] Bacot was a religious woman, who loved her home state of South Carolina, but missed her husband and children terribly, and felt alienated by the cold treatment her sister-in-law exhibited toward her. Unable or unwilling to share a home with such a woman, Bacot eventually felt forced to live alone on her late husband's plantation, where her daily life became dominated by her concerns about family life and the tensions involved in slave management. Nonetheless at this point Bacot made a choice to reverse the tragedies of her early life, and to boldly step outside her designated sphere of the plantation, and to get involved in war work in Virginia. This kind of self-directed action fulfills the requirements of personal agency as the "capacity of individuals to shape the world in which they live."[78] That is exactly what Bacot did, in taking charge of her life and moving it in the direction of her choosing. No longer referring to her constant weariness, headaches, and personal misery, Bacot's diary entries are suddenly filled with joyful enthusiasm at the prospect of starting a new life in Virginia. In October 1861 she wrote, "How shall I discribe the events of this delightful day. . . . I am at last almost sure of my trip to Virginia. . . . I can't discribe my feelings I am so thankful to go, God has heard my prayer."[79] Bacot was a woman of enormous faith; during her time in Charlottesville, Virginia, she attended church regularly, and the same religious ethos was imprinted in her work. Her religious calling merged with her patriotism and gave her the strength to change her life and overcome the most harrowing of personal tragedies, comforted by the knowledge that "thy will be done." In this regard Bacot worked within the limitations of gender models and looked to God to sanctify the work she did, which inadvertently led to a blossoming of personal autonomy. It is with this renewed sense of purpose that Ada Bacot moved forward from the unhappy experiences at Arnmore to embrace a new life in Virginia, which significantly altered the course of her personal and professional life.[80]

Nursing

Ada Bacot was not alone in her pursuit of war work as a nurse. Approximately thirty-two hundred women were formally employed as nurses during the Civil War.[81] While nurturing and caring roles were compatible with traditional ideals of southern womanhood, the expansion of these roles into a more public arena courted some controversy. Ada Bacot's class position as a slaveholding female meant that she was more likely to encounter some opposition regarding the propriety of war work as a nurse, as some southerners perceived it as a challenge to traditional gender models by expanding nurturing roles outside of the home. "Refined, modest ladies, said the critics, had no business caring for strange men and certainly not rough, crude soldiers from all walks of life."[82] Yet women who nursed, or who wanted to nurse, got around this obstacle by emphasizing the temporary nature of their expanded sphere in wartime. Phoebe Yates Pember, a well-known widow and nurse in the Civil War, boldly stated her support of female nurses during the war, declaring that they must "soar beyond conventional modesty" and care for their soldiers in wartime. Pember suggested that the exceptional circumstances borne of wartime were a viable reason why southern women should be permitted to step outside of their allotted sphere of home and family in support of their country. She stressed that the feminine virtues of piety, purity, submissiveness, and domesticity held in such high regard by southerners could be put to good use in wartime by allowing women to nurse. Pember argued that the unique conditions of war permitted a temporary remodeling of southern womanhood in order to support the Confederacy and the men who were fighting and dying for its survival.[83] This dovetailed with a stress on voluntarism in the

South, which was another way of expressing the "temporary" nature of women's new or expanded wartime roles.[84] However, Clinton argued, "temporary changes often had permanent impact," which is reflected in women's working roles in the postwar period.[85]

It is important to emphasize the basis on which southern women expanded their working roles in wartime. As Pember argued eloquently, women's traditional roles in the household and family could be used as an effective springboard to aid the war effort. Women had a natural capacity for relieving the suffering of others, and this placed single women, particularly widows and spinsters without children, in an ideal position to transfer their skills from the private to the public arena.[86] She claimed it was a natural step for women to use their sweet empathic natures in caring for soldiers and further argued that it was evidence of women fulfilling the calling for single blessedness by being useful to their family and to their wider community. Pember therefore spoke out in defense of women's virtue and argued that it was necessary for women in their role as nurses to "become hard and gross" in their capacity to function as competent nurses in the Civil War. She argued that to ensure absolute efficiency, women must be prepared to extend their caregiving roles from inside to outside of the family. She maintained that far from sullying a woman's good nature, it purified her. In her account of life in Richmond, Pember wrote on the subject of nursing, "If the ordeal does not chasten and purify her nature, if the contemplation of suffering and endurance does not make her wiser and better, and if the daily fire through which she passes does not draw from her nature the sweet fragrance of benevolence, charity and love,—then indeed a hospital has been no fit place for her."[87] By demonstrating their remarkable resilience, hardworking attitude, and level-headed work ethic, women like Pember eventually drew admiration from southern society by fulfilling their calling for single blessedness.[88] Far from being a drain or a burden to their families and wider community, single women frequently proved that they fulfilled the requirements of single blessedness and demonstrated that they were being "useful" and doing "good" for others in the most adverse circumstances.

Likewise Kate Cumming, a single woman from Mobile, Alabama, of about thirty when the war broke out, was determined to overcome the initial negativity surrounding wartime nursing. She admitted that "there is a good deal of trouble about the ladies in some of the hospitals of this department. Our friends have advised us to go home, as they say it is not considered respectable to go into one."[89] Yet Cumming overcame this initial stigma, determined to do her bit for the cause. Upon reflection she admitted, "I confess I wavered about the propriety of it [nursing] but when I remembered the suffering I had witnessed, and the relief I had given, my mind was made up to go into one [of the hospitals] if allowed to do so."[90] Kate also referred to a higher calling, to a religious protector [God], who she claimed cast ultimate approval over her actions. She drew strength from her belief that she was doing the will of God and wrote in her journal on 7 September 1862, "Christians should not mind what the world says [as they are] striving to do their duty to their God," in much the same way as Bacot felt comforted by her relationship with God, whom perhaps she saw as he "ultimate" patriarch.[91]

These women did not stand alone in encouraging other southern women to nurse, but they were particularly outspoken in voicing their opinions. As Cumming observed, "Soldiers fight for the battles of our country, and the least we can do is to cherish them in their helplessness, and bind up their wounds, all *true* women will do it, who love their country."[92] Effectively she reasoned that southern women, who were reluctant in coming forward to nurse, were shirking their duties as women. Providing a "ministering spirit at the couch of the sick" she claimed was women's special province. It was an extension of the Cult of True Womanhood, which stated that it was acceptable to care for men within the domestic sphere of home and family. Indeed Barbara Welter observed, "nursing the sick, particularly sick males, not only made a woman feel useful and accomplished, but increased her influence" within the family.[93] Women therefore had to prove that their roles within the family and domestic setting could be expanded to help care for sick soldiers in wartime. Kate Cumming highlighted the importance of women fulfilling this much-needed new role and argued that it was simply a broadening out of their traditional gender roles. As a result the Civil War helped to significantly alter old perceptions of unmarried women and accelerated the pace of social change in single women's lives by extending their sphere.

Hospital work was arduous and exhausting, especially for the southern matrons. In her first post at Tishomingo Hospital, a former hotel in Corinth, Mississippi, Cumming joined a party of over forty women who had ventured into Corinth after the Battle of Shiloh in April 1862.[94] These women joined together and formed part of a small but growing minority of women who were committed to nursing as a means of demonstrating their dedicated support to the cause. Cumming reported the "sad scenes" she met upon her arrival on 11 April 1862, the "men and boys mutilated in every imaginable way," their bodies littering the hall, gallery, and small rooms.[95] Undoubtedly the single women who joined as nurses showed tremendous bravery by stepping outside of their protected domain of home and family into a place where the odor of death seeped into every crevice of the hospital wards. She noted, "The foul air from the mass of human beings at first made me giddy and sick, but I soon got over it."[96] Kate's matter of fact portrayal of the horrors of the hospital wards undercut certain tenets of the Cult of True Womanhood that portrayed women as the weaker, inferior, vulnerable, dependent, and more delicate sex. Her stoicism and bravery were reflected throughout the pages of her diary and challenged traditional gender models that portrayed women as needy and frail. She subverted notions of passive femininity in her detailed descriptions of her work in the hospital wards. "We have to walk, and when we have to give the men anything, kneel, in blood and water; but we think nothing of it," she wrote.[97] "It is useless to say the surgeons will not allow us [to nurse]; we have our rights, and if asserted properly will get them. This is our right and ours alone," she mused defiantly, imbued with a warrior like spirit.[98]

Cumming was clearly not inhibited by her single status or by her class position, which in theory barred her from certain types of work because of her supposed need for protection. A particularly illuminating example was Cumming's harrowing account of the amputation bay on 24 April 1862, an area that was cornered off at the end of the ward. It was a place that she generally avoided but at times was compelled to pass—"the sight I there beheld made me shudder and sick at heart. A stream of blood ran from the table into a tub into which the [soldier's] arm [fell]."[99] It represented one of the many harrowing duties that female nurses performed in wartime. These duties included managing and supervising the hospital wards or hospital departments, sitting with soldiers, writing letters for patients to send to their loved ones, attending to the deathbeds, cooking, and sewing.[100] At the beginning of the war, women tended to be a few steps removed from "direct patient care" (as in the case of Ada Bacot when she initially worked as a housekeeper at Maupin House), because their class and social position acted as a barrier preventing them from more interactive care, supposedly to safeguard their delicacy and honor.[101] Yet as the war intensified, the role of female nurses intensified in parallel with it.

Phoebe Yates Pember, a widow from South Carolina, presided as matron of Chimborazo Hospital in Richmond from 1862 to 1865.[102] Pember had been born into a wealthy Jewish family in Charleston, South Carolina, on 18 August 1823. Her father was Jacob Clavius Levy, her mother, Fanny Yates, a native of England. Prior to the Civil War, Phoebe married Thomas Pember of Boston and in doing so fulfilled her duty as a wife and proper southern lady. Soon after their marriage, Thomas contracted tuberculosis, and in spite of a move south to aid his recovery, he died in Aiken, South Carolina, on 9 July 1861, leaving his wife a widow at the age of thirty-six. At first it must have been hard for Pember, unaccustomed to life as a widow on the eve of war. With her husband gone, and her role and status altered, Pember moved to Richmond and offered her services as a nurse, in an area where she perceived the need to be greatest.[103] First she worked in Chimborazo, a large hospital located in the besieged capital of Richmond.[104] It had opened in 1862 and consisted of 150 wards, grouped into five divisions, and Pember was chief matron over the second division. At the time it was the largest military hospital in the world and treated over seventy-six thousand patients over the course of the war. When Pember first started working there she encountered "considerable opposition" as a single woman entering into what was perceived to be a male profession. Bell Wiley noted the reaction of one of the ward surgeons, who told his friend "*one of them had come*," in reference to Phoebe *and* to her gender.[105] Pember, undeterred by such prejudice, quickly demonstrated that she had nerves of steel and "ignored the opposition based on prejudice and pitched into the more tangible obstacles with zest and determination that accomplished wonders."[106]

Single, southern matrons faced a raft of different problems that had to be overcome on a daily basis—solutions therefore required considerable fortitude and personal agency. In Pember's case her workload was initially focused on ensuring there were adequate provisions for patients' care and special diets and also that whiskey was dispensed correctly. Pember showed herself to be a "brisk and brilliant matron" who had "a will of steel" that enabled her to overcome many of the constraints of her gender.[107] Throughout her diary there are several examples of Pember going beyond the call of duty and of the requirements of her station. Like many Confederate nurses, Pember wrote letters on behalf of patients to their loved ones. She also worked industriously to attend to patients' needs. On one occasion, after the battle of Fredericksburg, she went to special lengths to help an eighteen-year-old soldier, who lay wounded and dying in a hospital bed, by finding his friend Perry, who had marched alongside him during battle. After making enquiries at other hospitals, the two friends were reunited and the soldier died in the comfort of Perry's arms.[108] As Wiley pointed out, Pember's resolute nature enabled her to continue working at the hospital throughout the Civil War; while others had tried and failed, she triumphed, proving that single white women were far from the "weaker sex" but instead could be strong and capable women showing agency and self-control in the most perilous circumstances.

The recruitment of women to work as assistants in hospitals was a difficult task. Hospital work was challenging—the hours were long, the pay low, and the conditions grim. The hospitals themselves were a mix of paid physicians and nurses, working alongside a small army of volunteers. Women who nursed often did so for altruistic reasons, in the hope of making a difference to the war effort, or to help care for the men who had fallen in fighting to preserve their way of life. George Rable detailed the staff and pay structure in hospitals and how this was laid out in Congress in 1862. These included the following: two chief matrons per hospital earning $40 per month to supervise the soldiers' diets, two assistant matrons earning $35 per month to supervise the laundry, two matrons in each ward earning $30 per month to care for bedding, to feed soldiers, and to administer medicine, plus additional nurses and cooks earning $25 per month.[109] The chief matrons earned the most, but still this was not much, being in the region of $40–45 per month. The matrons were mostly widows and spinsters (without the commitment of children). Phoebe Pember wrote to her sister in November 1862, giving her details about working conditions in Confederate hospitals: "I am to have board and lodging in the Hospital and at a boarding house adjacent and forty dollars a month, which will clothe me. I have entire charge of my department, seeing that everything is cleanly, orderly and all prescriptions of physicians given in proper time, food properly prepared and so on."[110] These observations are in line with the information on pay and duties given by Congress.[111] Pember admitted that her salary was so low that she supplemented her income by regularly writing at night for magazines, or copywriting for the department, in order to make a decent wage. However, she did not complain about her low wages and confessed, "I am perfectly happy, have more than sufficient (means) for my small wants, and thrown upon myself for occupation attend more thoroughly to my duties than I possibly could in other circumstances."[112] For her, and for many slaveholding or elite women in a similar position, the satisfaction that accompanied her station was the chief motivation to nurse, as opposed to fiscal gain. Yet, in the same way that plantation mistresses became more accustomed to the different tasks required of them in plantation management during the war, Confederate nurses also came to understand the demands of their wartime roles, which stood at odds with their image as vulnerable and dependent women.

Within the hospital hierarchy, widows and spinsters typically took on the more senior roles as matrons, especially if they were from a propertied background. Over time this helped them to foster a heightened self-awareness and a sense of personal agency as they struggled to overcome daily problems associated with hospital management. As the war unexpectedly wore on, with little sign of a swift conclusion, an increasing number of women were relied on to help, and in doing so they came to be valued. However, Pember also highlighted the racial and class differentiation that existed within the hospital structure. In *A Disappointing Experiment* she discussed the recruitment of a hospital assistant: "My choice hesitated between ladies of education and position, who I knew would aid me (but be less keen on supervision and authority) to the common class of respectable servants, who were more amenable to authority."[113] This injection of class again underscores the difference social standing made to the work allocation in hospitals, and the type of work that was deemed acceptable to different classes of southern women. While some planter-class women were prepared to get involved in a wide variety of tasks, others would complain about the propriety of certain jobs that they were given, as they considered them unsuitable for their class or gender. As an illustration of this, when Pember asked a North Carolinian woman to assist her in a hospital task, her response was that she "was not going anywhere in a place where a man sat up on his bed in his shirt."[114]

Nevertheless in general the war led to the broadening of new opportunities for single, southern women to actively demonstrate their calling to embrace a life of single blessedness. This included wealthy, white, slaveholding widows who freely gave of their time and energy, to help the cause, which resulted in a broad validation of their efforts as fulfillment of the tenets of single blessedness. Wealthy widows like Pember repeatedly demonstrated their resourcefulness throughout the war. In April 1863, following a battle on Drewry's Bluff, Pember displayed considerable agency and ingenuity in her response to the lack of provisions and staff in the hospital, by using blankets on the floor as makeshift beds for soldiers. She toiled throughout the night "armed with lint, bandages, castile soap and a basin of warm water" moving from bed to bed, bathing fractured limbs" and tending to the sick as well as reading comforting words from the Bible to the sick and dying, and writing touching letters to family and sweethearts to inform them of the fate of their loved ones.[115]

The warmth of female sympathy was a valuable commodity in wartime. It replicated traditional gender roles, while at the same time gently revising them. Female nurses worked tirelessly in the care of Confederate soldiers. Pember worked as a nurse for over four years before finally she confessed, "necessity compelled me to leave my hospital" in 1864.[116] She admitted, "It had been like tearing body and soul apart. . . . I had never been separated but one day in nearly four years."[117] Pember's personal story reiterates how elite white women fulfilled the calling of single blessedness in their care of soldiers during the war. Pember's dedication was so great that she did not take a single day's break in four years, despite the fact that it was taking a serious toll on her mental and physical health. She had literally sacrificed herself for the sake of the Confederacy and in doing so slowly gained recognition for her tireless devotion to the cause. The war therefore blurred the boundaries between married and single, in what has been referred to as a cultural reassessment of singleness.[118]

Mrs. Ella Newsom was a childless widow from Memphis, who again originated from a wealthy, aristocratic background. When her husband, Dr. Frank Newsom, died, Ella Newsom was left a wealthy woman, but she decided to invest her inherited wealth in buying medical provisions that would be of benefit to the Confederate soldiers during the Civil War. Newsom distributed the supplies herself, judging where the need was greatest before distributing supplies, and in doing so displaying altruism and self-agency. Like Pember and Cumming, Newsom has become an icon for her "heroic and unselfish devotion to the cause," which included traveling to numerous hospitals across the Confederacy to distribute medical supplies, which ties in with the fulfillment of single blessedness.[119] Ella Newsom demonstrated that she was a charitable woman driven by her service to others, rather than by her own needs. She was given the "entire charge of a hospital" at Bowling Green, Kentucky, as a reflection of her capability, and by February 1862 she had moved to Nashville, where she reorganized Howard High School into a hospital for the sick and wounded. In each facility she visited, she demonstrated her dedication, "remarkable executive ability," and blossoming independent spirit as a single, white, southern woman.[120] Newsom was later referred to as "the Florence Nightingale of the South," in public recognition of her huge personal contribution, visiting numerous hospitals during the Civil War and acting as a visiting angel, distributing supplies and organizing them so as to ensure efficiency—a responsible job for a southern lady. She recognized the crucial role that southern women occupied during the war and demonstrated that she had the personal capacity to make the best of her personal circumstances.

In the *Daily Florida Citizen* in 1894, a similar tribute celebrated the achievements of Mary Martha Reid, a widow from Florida who nursed in the Civil War. The newspaper described Reid as a "peerless character," and a woman who provided "splendid services" to the Confederate soldiers during the war.[121] A letter from George T. Maxwell praised Reid's "disposition, character and invaluable services during the war" and heralded her as a "well-rounded and symmetrical character" that many soldiers saluted for her hard work and personal sacrifices made for them during the war.[122] Widows such as Reid, Pember, and Bacot were rewarded for their outstanding efforts during wartime and were highly regarded for their dedication, usefulness, and capability in aiding the cause. Class, age, and marital status were key factors in determining the potential suitability of women to nurse in wartime. Hence, as widows, Mary Martha Reid, Phoebe Pember, and Ada Bacot were well placed to contribute their services as Confederate nurses.

Twenty-five-year-old Augusta Jane Evans, an unmarried novelist from Mobile, Alabama, was also keen to offer her services as a nurse in Marietta, Georgia, persuaded by her friend Mrs. Ella Newsom.[123] However, Evans met with considerable opposition from her family and was initially dissuaded from taking up the post she had applied for because of her family's opposition to it.[124] Evans explained in a letter to Ella Newsom on 28 October 1863 that her age and status (at the time she was young and single) acted as barriers that made it difficult to take up the post. Evans admitted sheepishly, "I shall not be able to join you in Marietta as I expected when I applied to you for a position. The truth simply is, that my family is so opposed to my doing so, <u>especially my brothers</u>, that I have been forced to give up the scheme. I was and am <u>still</u>, very anxious to go into hospitals and selected Marietta because you were there. But when the boys learned of my application, they opposed it so strenuously, and urged me so earnestly to abandon the idea, that I feel unwilling to take the step which they disapprove so vehemently. . . . I feel that the work is a noble one, and I long to be at your side, working with you."[125] Evans's age and status as a young, unmarried woman proved to be early obstacles, which were both less of a problem in the case of more mature widows, who perhaps faced less opposition to initially taking on nursing roles. Augusta Evans later returned to her calling to nurse in the war, and she found the experience so profound that it inspired her much popularized wartime novel *Macaria*, which did so much to improve the perception and visibility of single women in wartime. In *Macaria*, the novel's central character, Irene, is a single woman who talks about her calling to become a nurse in Richmond and in so doing dedicates herself to a life of single blessedness. She reinforces the idea that the "the call [to nurse] is imperative. Mother's and wives are, in most instances, kept at home; but I have nothing to bind me here. I have no ties to prevent me from giving my services in the only way in which I can aid the cause for which my father died. I feel it a sacred duty."[126]

Augusta Jane Evans created characters that challenged the mores of archetypical domestic fiction and frequently placed single women at the heart of her narrative, reaffirming the centrality of the Cult of Single Blessedness. At times she depicted married women as incomplete in their conjugal roles, which helped to erode popular notions of what constituted the ideal woman.[127] Through her writing she proved that she was both resourceful and autonomous, reflected in her willingness to approach certain taboos (such as female singleness) and in the stories that she published so successfully. In doing so Evans stressed the importance of "womanly usefulness" for women who were single. Similar arguments have been put forward in Murray's work on Louisa May Alcott. Murray suggested that Alcott, a domestic novelist from the North, who penned novels such as *Behind a Mask* and *Little Women*, was making an important statement about female singleness. Like Evans, Alcott developed a number of strong female characters, often single women, who lie at the heart of the novels. For example Jo March in *Little Women* was a bright, ambitious individual who clearly understood that in order to be accepted in nineteenth-century America she must be seen to adhere to the ideals of "true womanhood" and to the Cult of Domesticity. Consequently Jo performed or "mimicked" the part of the ideal woman and in doing so gained social acceptance, thus avoiding the marginalization associated with spinsterhood. Evans's heroines did much the same, fusing social acceptability with a degree of autonomous behavior. Evans mirrors the same behavior in her own life, by claiming that she started writing for altruistic reasons rather than a personal desire to win fame and fortune.[128]

Fiction aside single, southern women shared in a drive to offer their time and services to the war effort, perhaps buoyed on by the change in perception toward female nurses. Emma Mordecai, a mature, never-married woman from a well-respected Jewish family in North Carolina, offered her services as a nurse in 1864. Emma was disturbed by the devastating picture given by her relative Rose, who described "our brave men, now more prostrate and helpless than infants, and the urgent need there was of help at the hospital determined me to go in and lend my mite towards alleviating their sufferings." She recognized, "I am grateful to be strong enough to help nurse," and in doing so she highlighted the gap between the model of true womanhood (that saw women as delicate and weak) and the reality of the strong and capable southern woman who was committed to do her part to support the war effort. Emma Mordecai described herself as physically fit juxtaposed to the weakness of the male soldiers.[129] As a woman of fifty-two she more easily gained access into the profession that tended to stigmatize younger unmarried women, who were sometimes perceived as a potential threat and disruptive element in the hospital. Even women who were unable to sign up and nurse owing to commitments at home had a growing respect for those who did. Emma Mordecai's sister Ellen, an ageing single woman from North Carolina, felt constrained by her responsibilities at home and confessed in a letter to her brother George Mordecai in September 1862, "If I had no home duties I should most willingly be detailed one [a nursing assignment] and go and do a woman's part in ameliorating the sufferings of the wounded at Manassas."[130]

These examples make it clear that unmarried women were increasingly willing to transplant their prewar skills as nurturers in the domestic setting to the more public arena of nursing on the front line in wartime. While not all women were prepared to expand their traditional gender roles outside of the home, increasing numbers were, which revised and challenged old notions of femininity. Consequently women temporarily revised and expanded their working roles owing to the exigencies of wartime and gained respect and admiration for doing so. These changes, which some claimed were temporary, often became more permanent in the postwar era, which helped revise and expand the boundaries of southern womanhood, which included a cultural reassessment of female singleness. This led to greater autonomy for single women. These women helped to challenge the idea that women compromised their delicacy and femininity by working outside the home. Thus, in the course of time, these changes contributed to a growing acceptance of women as nurses, as their role could be justified as an extension of their traditional role as caregivers within the home and family.

Teaching

Teaching was another vocation that had its roots embedded in the home and family. In the prewar setting it was yet to develop into an established vocation for women in the public sphere. Yet single women often spoke of the ways in which they helped care for brothers and sisters, nieces or nephews, or gave Bible readings to the slaves as part of their daily routine within the domestic setting. Plantation mistresses cared for the physical, mental, and spiritual well-being of their slaves long before the firing of the guns at Fort Sumter. Anne Jennings Wise Hobson noted in her diary that she had taught two classes of slave children in the morning and met with the older bonds people in the afternoon. In 1864 she described her usual morning routine, which included "reading the scriptures and prayers," "attending to household matters," and "teaching some of the colored children before breakfast and my own little ones."[131] Teaching the slaves involved reading from the Bible and prayers: religious instruction intended to civilize black slaves and converted them to Christianity. It was part of a woman's traditional role on the plantation, and it was considered appropriate behavior for upper-class women.

Before the war few elite women taught in an official capacity, although they often worked tirelessly in helping to educate children (and sometimes slaves) within the private setting of home and family. As elite women came from wealthy families, they seldom had the financial motivation to work outside the home (before the war at least), and they were usually discouraged from doing so by their families. In North Carolina it is estimated that only 7 percent of women were teachers in 1860, which rose to 50 percent by 1865.[132] The war, therefore, seems to have again acted as a catalyst in expanding women's traditional roles as nurturers and educators in the home, and it made their roles more acceptable and widespread in the Civil War and postwar eras. The war highlighted trends that were already afoot in the antebellum years and accelerated the pace of social change in single women's lives by expanding the rigid ideologies surrounding true womanhood. Even in the early 1800s some cases exist where single women were already well established in their role as teachers, though these were relatively uncommon. Consider the example of Rachel Mordecai, a young, unmarried woman from North Carolina. Rachel's father owned a boarding school for girls, and he was clearly driven by his desire to show that his school operated by "the highest standards of pedagogical excellence and moral respectability."[133] As part of this plan, he decided to use his daughter, Rachel, as a "walking advertisement" for what could be achieved in the education of refined young ladies, which seems revolutionary for his time and place.[134] In the context of the early 1800s this seems an unusual decision on his part, considering the early nineteenth-century view that "learned women risked being seen as asexual and unfeminine," thus placing his daughter outside of the framework of appropriate gender conventions and openly challenging them. Rachel was made a partner in the school and helped to teach and manage the administrative responsibilities that came with running a school as her father believed she had the "ability to shape the female character and intellect in the girls who attended the school," which reflects his liberal philosophy on southern womanhood.[135] Conversely perhaps her father simply used her to reenergize his flagship school for girls, without fully considering the personal cost this could have on Rachel's reputation, as "genteel women did not, as a rule, take on paid work."[136] Yet Rachel stepped outside of her designated sphere and risked criticism from the outside world. Rachel understood that by aiding her father she was jeopardizing her reputation but pursued the vocation nonetheless. Rachel's case, while unique, demonstrates that some women taught even in the early 1800s, if only to conform to the patriarch's wishes, which was in many ways an alternative form of power and control. Fortunately for Rachel she discovered enormous self-satisfaction and fulfillment in her work, which culminated in a sense of growing independence.

These isolated cases gradually became more prevalent in the late antebellum period. In 1859 Anna Clayton, a young, single woman from North Carolina, spoke with obvious pride in connection to her work as a teacher. She described teaching as a "noble, high toned occupation" and added that her work melded with her single status made her "feel quite free at this time."[137] Anna Elizabeth Holt similarly worked as a governess and teacher from the late 1850s to mid-1860s. By contrast Holt was far less effusive about her role. In May 1859 she commented, "little did I think two years ago that I should be a teacher, and that to a family I knew nothing about. . . . I have been here three months and though my duties are not arduous for I have only two regular scholars. . . . I know the responsibility is great."[138] That responsibility at times weighted heavily on her. Holt admitted her pupils were often "hard to manage," leading her to question her ability as a teacher. "I am altogether unsuited to the task of controlling [the pupils]. . . . I have long seen that I lack the essential qualifications of a teacher."[139] Holt also questioned her single status and longed for a male protector. In April 1860 she bemoaned, "Oh! I wish I was married. Alas miserable wretch I am."[140] However, on her twenty-fifth birthday she reasoned that if she "was doomed to the sisterhood through life" (as twenty-five was rather old to still be single) then her "care should be to gain by a good example and upright conduct a more worthy and honorable character," achieved through teaching.[141] In spite of her volition to teach, Holt regularly faltered, and she frequently revealed an uncertainty in her abilities as a teacher and her concerns that the occupation would adequately sustain her independence. On 18 May 1859 she acknowledged, "I know and feel my weakness and dependence and [realize] that my best resolves are worth nothing and my greatest efforts are worthless without the assistance of his Holy Spirit."[142] Holt's language of dependence—looking up to God to "assist" her, and worrying that she would fall short in her endeavors as a teacher, does not detract from the fact that she was attempting to be self-sufficient, and to manage on her own by continuing to teach in the prewar era.

The initial motivation that led single women into teaching was varied. A significant number of women were galvanized by economic necessity that intensified in the Civil War period and in its aftermath. The vagaries of war significantly altered the economic landscape of the Confederacy and propelled women into work outside of the home in an effort to contribute to the domestic economy. The conservative ethos that pushed women into teaching in the Civil War and postwar eras led to a reassessment and broadening of working roles outside of the home and resulted in an increase in personal autonomy for women.[143] As the superintendent of the public instruction in Alabama revealed in 1833, "members of the most elegant and cultivated families in the State are engaged in teaching," which reflects a growing trend that began long before the war.[144]

A particularly harrowing story of a woman driven by economic need was the case of Mary Elliott Johnstone. Mary was the wife of rice planter, Andrew Johnstone, who owned property at Annandale, near Georgetown, South Carolina. He also owned a house in Beaumont at Flat Rock, North Carolina. The couple had six children, in addition to a son from Andrew Johnstone's first marriage. In June 1864 a terrible tragedy befell the Johnstone family when five Tories, or Confederate deserters, murdered Andrew. He "survived but an hour," and the shocking attack was made worse when Johnstone's eldest son, Elliott, took revenge on the killers and "seized a gun, and fired his father's murderer."[145] Elliott's retaliation meant that the entire family were put at risk, which forced them to abandon their home in Flat Rock and start a new life in Greenville, North Carolina. Plunged into economic hardship, and with a growing family to feed, Mary Johnstone's life had been destroyed and her wealth suddenly depleted. Family members offered them shelter, but she refused to be dependent on them: "Our household of nine whites with spoiled servants I could not impose anywhere," she wrote to her sister in October 1864.[146] As an aside it is interesting that Mary described herself as poor but in the same breath admitted to having a number of servants until the end of the war, by which time she took on many of the household chores herself, which reflected her fall in status wrought by misfortune and war.[147] By 1865 her large household slowly disentangled, her son had joined the Confederate army, and two of her daughters lodged elsewhere, with a woman in Baltimore. In her fight to keep her family together, Mary took a job as a teacher in Baltimore at the Edgeworth School for Young Ladies. Chiefly motivated by her desire to provide for her children, and with nobody but herself to rely on, she relied on herself and threw herself into her new job, reporting that her new duties had "gone very well indeed"—she gained satisfaction from her new role, reciting prayers to the children and caring for the sick.[148] Victoria Ott noted that as more and more women went out to work in order to contribute to the household economy, they started "to rely less on the hierarchical relations of the slaveholding family and assert instead a sense of independence," which dovetails with the evidence in this study.[149]

Women's teaching gathered momentum during the Civil War years. For some it was a source of liberation, for others simply an additional hardship to be endured in the context of a brutal, hard war and its aftermath. Few women openly challenged the social mores of the time, but nonetheless by taking on teaching roles outside of the home, even in the context of wartime, they were expanding and reshaping their gender roles. For Josephine Varner, a young unmarried woman living in Indian Spring, Georgia, the reality of war was at first a bitter disappointment, as she had hoped that the coming of war might spark new opportunities to expand and improve herself, by studying in preparation for future employment at the war's end. As she noted: "In the beginning of this war I thought what a golden opportunity it would be in the absence of our friends to improve myself reading and studying. I hoped that when the troubles were over to be ready for teaching, but now I am farther from attaining my object [than] ever, I have nearly lost all control over my mind," she wrote, adding, "My life now is perfectly useless. I neither benefit myself nor anyone else."[150] Josephine, like many unmarried upper-class women, had a deep-seated desire to prove that she was useful. Her story therefore embodies the initial despondency felt by many southern women at the start of the war, who felt uncertain of what their new role was to be in the absence of the men folk.[151] For Josephine Varner the Civil War signaled an initial crisis of identity and a feeling of dashed hopes for the future, and as the war dragged on, she sat mourning friends lost, ambitions thwarted.

The social constraints of her position as an upper-class white woman seemed insurmountable at first, and she perceived herself as hemmed in by her social class and gender. It was a feeling that soon passed, and it was replaced instead with a renewed vigor and sense that she had a range of options open to her; one of these options was teaching. By February 1863 Josephine's personal journal took on a different tone, as she felt emboldened in realizing her dream of finding a useful occupation as a teacher. She noted, "So far, I have enjoyed my little school very much. I love the children already, which makes me more patient and then they are bright and sprightly which makes it a pleasure to teach them. How long I shall be here I have not the remotest idea but so long as I can be useful and I am not needed at home and can keep my health, I shall stay."[152] Josephine's pleasure in her newfound employment and the satisfaction that she achieved from fulfilling a role that was considered "useful" to the wider community dovetails with the growing popularity of the Cult of Single Blessedness. Unmarried women from middle-to upper-class white families demonstrated that they were also true women, despite their failure to marry. This suggests that rigid ideologies surrounding "true womanhood" were breaking down in the South before, during, and after the Civil War, and that alternative models of femininity were gaining popularity. Barbara Welter posited that nineteenth-century women's gift annuals, which were widely circulated and read by women, were actively working to remove old stigmas attached to the unmarried woman. "Their stories showed maiden ladies as unselfish ministers to the sick, teachers of the young, or moral preceptors with their pens, beloved of their entire village."[153]

This shifting opinion on the role of single women was beneficial for women like Josephine. It enabled her to immerse herself in teaching without the fear of reprisal, or being accused of challenging the existing status quo. Paradoxically it also presented an opportunity for single women to be more independent, and to establish a life for themselves that did not include marriage and motherhood. In a telling confession, Josephine confided in her journal her plans to continue teaching: "I shall stay just as long as I wish, it may be wicked, it may be weak, but I greatly enjoy being mistress of my own movements, if I am to steer my own boat through life, God grant that I may do it cheerfully, as I feel that I can now."[154] The contrast in Josephine's attitude before, during, and after the Civil War is striking in that she clearly equates teaching with a rise of self-esteem and with it, a burgeoning sense of autonomy.

Across the South single women from wealthy white families expressed an interest in being useful in the public arena, particularly in the outbreak of war. Julia

Tutwiler, an unmarried twenty-year-old white woman from Tuscaloosa, Alabama, was initially dispirited at the outbreak of war as she had expressed an interest in nursing, but her father had refused her request, perhaps dissuaded by her naïveté and youth. Instead he commandeered her to help in his school for the duration of the war, and she had to forfeit boarding school in Philadelphia and return home in order to do so.[155] Julia recalled how crestfallen she had been when she had returned home, even though in retrospect she came to appreciate the value gained in her work at the school. In a letter to her sister Ida written much later, in 1872, she admitted, "the responsibility of helping father, and the necessary work in preparing the recitations brought with it some little order and system into my labors. Those three years [of teaching during the Civil War] I gained a great deal."[156] The early experiences of working as a teacher in her father's school helped to shape Julia's future ideas on educational reform and led to a fulfilling and satisfying career as a teacher, educational reformer, and women's rights activist. In her career she demonstrated that she was not only useful, but also independent. Work therefore represented a broadening of opportunities for single women that continued in the postwar era. If we consider Barbara Welter's argument, then great reformers like Julia had almost "absolved" themselves "from the necessity of marriage" by virtue of their good works as single women, which were "so extraordinary that [a woman] did not need the security or status of being a wife."[157] Unmarried women strove to do their part and fulfill their role as "useful" single women, but they also helped expand and revise female roles. As Censer pointed out, "their very existence posited a role for women outside of the family and expanded the possibilities of female education, autonomy, and authority."[158] Family still remained of extreme importance to unmarried women, and the initial stimulus to work was often born out of a commitment to provide for their family.

Mary Harth, widow of Dr. John Harth from Lexington County, South Carolina, was motivated to find work as a teacher in the postwar years in a quest to support her four children (Corrie, Ella, Willie, and Alice) following on from her husband's death. Simultaneously Mary was desperately trying to rectify a financial transaction she had made in the war years concerning the sale of her slaves in 1861 that left her financially exposed and vulnerable. Mary had accepted $1,100 from a Mrs. Watson for the sale of the slaves, which was considerably less than they were worth, but she claimed she had been promised the remaining $3,400 in Confederate bonds, which proved worthless after the war. Mary's failure to receive the money left her financially exposed and demonstrated her lack of business acumen as a widow. Despite her desperate appeals to Mrs. Watson, who she hoped must be "honor bound to make the debt good," Mary soon realized that she must find an alternative solution to help solve her mounting financial problems.[159] Mary described herself as on the "brinks of despair," unable to afford a home or a satisfactory standard of living, in lieu of the debts owed to her. Therefore she couched her request for money in the language of female dependency; replicating traditional gender models in the hope of gaining financial security from it: "Turn your heart to the unprotected widow and fatherless children," she wrote in November 1865. "Do me justice and pay a poor woman her debt"; but it was to no avail.[160] Keen to find an alternative solution to her predicament, and realizing that the debt would not be paid, Mary demonstrated her stoicism and resourcefulness by actively seeking employment. She wrote a letter to the proprietor of an old schoolhouse, previously owned by her late aunt. Having heard that a position needed to be filled, Mary exhibited initiative and recommended herself for the vacant position to teach freedmen.[161] In doing so she stepped outside of her role as a female dependent and exerted self-direction, in a last-ditch effort to keep home and family together.

According to Anne Firor Scott, teaching "absorbed the largest number of upper-class single women in search of employment" in the war years and during Reconstruction.[162] It was a vocation that had quickly gained respect and popularity and was less demanding than some other types of work. It also paralleled women's traditional roles as caregivers and nurturers in helping to raise the next generation, linking to the idea that "the mother heart beats in all women." Significant numbers of single, southern women turned to teaching in the war years and in doing so highlighted their commitment to single blessedness. Mary Susan Ker, an unmarried woman from a planter-class family in Mississippi, began teaching after the war to help support her family, who had been financially devastated by the Civil War.[163] Throughout her life Mary took several jobs, both as a governess, and later as a teacher, and she worked at a number of schools including Public School No. 28 in Adams County, Mississippi, in 1874.[164] Her work had a degree of flexibility that enabled her to care for her (adopted) children while facilitating her independence, although only just. By her own admission, Mary was not a natural teacher, and she easily felt frustrated with the children, regularly bemoaning her "black Mondays."[165] Yet, when the opportunity arose for her to give up teaching and live as a dependent on her brother, she rejected his offer without hesitation, which suggests she valued the independence that working provided her.[166] Mary often complained of being poor, but her circumstances were only relative to her earlier life, growing up in a wealthy, slaveholding family. Teaching wages were low for female teachers, and remuneration varied from state to state, from $24 per month in Carolina and Alabama, to $34 dollars per month in Florida.[167] Mary was not paid well, and she constantly referred to the difficulties she had in making ends meet. For example, in the run-up to Christmas she found the lack of money a pressing concern: "Christmas is a sad time for me always, got my November check cashed, sent $25 to Natchez, paid the dentist, have no money to buy Christmas

Mary Susan Ker's fourth-grade class, 1905. Courtesy of the Southern Historical Collection, Wilson Library, University of North Carolina, Chapel Hill.

presents for the children and nothing to live on till next pay day." But at the same time she managed to travel widely, even taking an extended trip to Europe.[168] She was "a tower of strength," recalled Pierce Butler in his book *The Unhurried Years: Memories of the Old Natchez Region.*[169]

Mary Ker's story also illuminates the difficult fit between the ideal of true womanhood and the changing reality of women's lives in the Civil War era. The ideal of true womanhood increasingly did not fit, and it therefore had to become more accommodating, or it would shatter altogether. "Real women often felt that they did not live up to the ideal of true womanhood. Some of them blamed themselves, some challenged the standard, [and] some tried to keep the virtues and enlarge the scope of womanhood," which was the case for single women.[170] Mary Ker's life demonstrates a combination of all the above: she was a woman who never married and as such hovered on the periphery of true womanhood (since marriage and motherhood were key components of the ideal). Yet conversely she showed a maternal instinct and practical resourcefulness, in her role as the maiden aunt.[171] She challenged the negative stereotype of the dependent, single woman by helping to support her family in the postwar period, which demonstrated her capacity for embracing social change.

Teaching therefore provided single women with a limited independence: a small wage, a route to self-fulfillment, and an increased self-esteem. Sarah Walthall Rosier, though not from a wealthy, slaveholding family, illustrates this point. Sarah grew up in Christiansburg, Virginia. She was a lover of music and literature and spent most of her life as a teacher in the South, as well as in New York. Sarah was a complex, emotional woman, who spoke openly of the benefits and constraints of her life as a teacher. She valued the benefits of hard work and the security that she hoped it would bring to herself and family: "I am trying hard to earn a reputation that will enable me to command necessary comforts in my old age if God spares me," Sarah wrote with a distinct air of independence.[172] However, she also recognized the hardships that came of working as a single woman, managing a large music department in the late 1860s. "It is not an easy task you know, and in fact in these days when the young ladies music is so exhibitional, it gives a teacher considerable anxiety and engrosses nearly the whole time to make ready for receptions."[173] Yet, despite the hard work, and injustices of a woman's salary, she talked with passion and enthusiasm about her work. "I always find teaching in a school so absorbing. I have, I suppose, some unnecessary pride about my pupil's progress, and work very hard to make this apparent, which you know is difficult to do with the average talent and application."[174] Members of the music department limited her workload owing to her "delicate nature" as a woman, which she found frustrating, but she also talked about feeling unsexed because of her profession.[175] Sarah was a woman who aspired to gain perfection in her work. Inevitably this resulted in moments of anxiety, concerning the nature of her work and the propriety of conducting her profession as a woman. In January 1870, seized with self-doubt, she wrote to her friend Fitz, her old music teacher, and later her husband. "With my natural gifts and opportunities, I think I should have been wiser, to make for myself a home, and take a place among the good society I could have commanded, than to devote myself to the independent life of teaching. In other words I think I ought to have married. I think the probability is that I will never marry now, and I much fear I shall not be so contented as an old maid as I expected to be."[176]

She reflected in much the same way that Grace Elmore Brown had upon the realization that the independence that she had so hankered for was not quite as liberating as she had imagined it to be.[177] Her words are reminiscent of Laura Comer's initial disillusionment in widowhood, when she had dreamed for so long about the freedom singleness would bring her and how she expected it would be. The everyday reality of independence meant providing for oneself, with all the anxieties that it entailed (rent to pay, low wages). In Sarah Rosier's words it made "music teaching [in] these hard times [post war] a precarious dependence."[178] Teaching might have been a precarious dependence for women in the postwar era; but it nonetheless represented a broadening of opportunities and a route to enhanced autonomy. Women had long been responsible for the care and education of their children and of their slave families. Single women had also played a key role as family helpmeets, maiden aunts, and caregivers to the slaves. In this context teaching was a natural extension of a woman's traditional role, but it also led to self-fulfillment, broader opportunities, and the blossoming of personal independence that had a liberating effect on women in the postwar South.

Summary

It is clear that the expansion of single women's working roles had begun in the Old South. While planter class women were seldom gainfully employed prior to the Civil War, they had clearly established their burgeoning role within the family and domestic setting. From this starting point, a small number of single women had begun to tentatively venture beyond the home and family, when they were required to contribute to the household economy. From this conservative basis, single women opened up a doorway to greater opportunity, which was accelerated by war and its aftermath. As Cornelia Phillips Spencer wrote in "The Young Ladies' Column," in 1870, "Girls who are growing up at the present day ought not to compare themselves with those of even twenty years ago. Every year is adding to their opportunities and advantages. Door after door is being flung open to them, and the question must be . . . which shall I enter. . . . With the strongest conservative principles it is impossible to believe that they continue to move in the same narrow ruts as heretofore."[179] The blossoming of new opportunities for women was linked to the respect and admiration that they had gained during wartime. For women who were single, this reflected the growing popularity of the Cult of Single Blessedness. Paradoxically the fact that unmarried women responded so positively to the demands of war demonstrated their motivation to do "good" in their duty, to the family, and to the Confederacy.

In fulfilling their feminine roles as plantation managers, nurses, and teachers, single women upheld but also challenged gender prescriptions. They upheld them by taking on roles that had their origins firmly rooted in the home and family— nurturing or educational roles—yet they also indirectly challenged them by temporarily amending their character in order to carry out their roles competently. Phoebe Yates Pember spoke of the need to be "hard and gross" in order to be an effective Confederate war nurse. Slaveholding females described the difficult balance they faced in maintaining their ladyhood and managing their slaves. Likewise women who taught discussed the challenges of working in a classroom and the need to develop an authoritative voice in managing students. As Emory Thomas argued, "In terms of roles and models, Confederate women took a giant step away from the romantic ideal of the Southern Belle. . . . The model Confederate female was a red eyed nurse with the unkempt hair or a war widow who succeeded as head of her household by force of will."[180] As a result these women helped to alter preconceived notions of singlehood by demonstrating quite publicly that wealthy, unmarried white women of a certain class could also be self-reliant, brave, and autonomous but still "women."[181] Consequently plantation mistresses, nurses and teachers show a definite correlation between women's working roles and a flowering of personal autonomy.

Chapter 4   FEMALE FRIENDSHIP

A lice Baldy, a middle-aged schoolteacher from Griffin, Georgia, often daydreamed about her desire to set up a home and school with her much loved friend Josephine Varner.[1] Her ultimate goal was to live with her sisters *and* with Josie in a sororal group, and to share in the running of their own school, which would enable them to support their families while sharing a home together. Her "isolated dream" spilled onto the pages in several of her letters to Josephine Varner and in doing so revealed much about the romantic friendships that some women in the nineteenth century shared.[2] "I want so much to get our school underway—yours and Mary J's and mine—Amanda and Mary J would keep domestic affairs straight—and you and I could manage quite a number of children. I look forward to that as the happiness in store for me."[3]

Alice Baldy's life had not been easy—her father died in 1856 when she was twenty-one years old; two of her brothers were dead, her sister Mary J was losing her sight, and her mother's health was rapidly failing.[4] To make matters worse, the family had financial difficulties, after losing much of its wealth in the years following their father's death, which propelled Alice into the workplace as a teacher in order to support her family. This must have been especially hard for Alice as she had grown up in a wealthy plantation-class family in Burke's County, Georgia. By the time the Civil War began, Alice was already twenty-five years old, still unmarried, with a family who suddenly relied on her work as a teacher and the income that she provided. It is set within this challenging backdrop that the friendship between Alice and Josephine Varner was cultivated and sustained in excess of two decades. Having first met several years earlier at La Grange College, the pair seem to have a lot in common; they had each lost their father, they were single, and they taught for a living (although Miss Joe later became the proprietress of the family hotel, the Varner House). Both women maintained close bonds with their families, but they also recognized the importance of friendship in their daily lives: "the love of my friends is a world of comfort to me," Joe confessed in her journal in December 1866.[5] "Indeed I commit a daily sin in longing to see them and not being contended with my lot in life."[6] The dissatisfaction that bubbled underneath the surface of Miss Joe's diary entries reveals a latent frustration with not being able to do more in life, perhaps constrained by her gender. It was in this vein that Joe reflected in February 1867 how "friends make the charm of life to me," while admitting, "I have such rebellious feelings."[7] Joe rarely vocalized these feelings of discontentment in public but buried them in her diary. It is feasible that she discussed such matters in her letters to Alice Baldy, but as the letters have been destroyed, it is difficult to say with any degree of certainly what secrets were hidden inside them.

The friendship shared between these two mature women warrants attention, not only in its own right, but as a means of providing a deeper insight into the form and function of female friendship in the nineteenth-century American South. The nature and longevity of their friendship went far beyond the short-lived "crush" commonly associated with girlhood or the transitionary stage of youth particularly apparent in all-girls' boarding schools.[8] The Baldy and Varner friendship while established in youth endured for several years, well into adulthood, until the women were in their forties, when the letters either stopped or have since been lost or destroyed. Either way their friendship represented a long-lasting and passionate attachment that stands out because both women never married. In the letters that remain from Alice Baldy to Joe Varner it is clear that the primary goal, for Alice at least, was for them to establish a permanent home together. Their relationship was evidently infused with a strong physical chemistry, and several of Alice's letters refer to their tender embraces and physical connection: "laying your cheek on mine" and her longing to "kiss" Josephine's lips, mimicking the language of heterosexual love.[9] The effusive outpouring of emotion in Alice's letters to Joe forms a stark contrast to the frigid detachment of heterosexual love that existed between men and women at that time. Alice implores, "I will never love [another] human being more than I do you—I want you every day to sew and read and talk with me—every night I want you with me that I may wake you with a kiss—that I may always make you happy and that you would always love me. Will you always love me Josie, even when I am old? Will you promise to be with me as much as you can, as long as I live? Let us promise to each other to be as much together as we possibly can as long as we both live."[10] Their relationship was passionate by nature; Alice's words ooze sensuality; she even admitted in a letter to Joe, "Do you know that if you touch me, or speak to me there is not a nerve or fibre in my body that does not respond with a thrill of delight," thus accentuating the physical nature of her attraction. While we do not have a written response from Joe (as she made Alice destroy the letters), the fact that Joe kept Alice's letters for all her years suggests that the relationship was important to her.[11]

Ultimately Alice's longed-for dream of sharing a permanent home with Joe never reached fruition, yet the fact that she hoped that it would raises key points about the form and function of female friendship in the American South, as well as the changing nature of female friendship as the century progressed. Female sexuality has been a relatively taboo topic until recent years, and until the late nineteenth century, female asexuality—or female passionlessness—was considered the norm. According to this definition, women were devoid of carnal desire, hence the labeling of them as asexual.[12] Women were instructed to be chaste and pure—hence any outpouring of female affection between women was considered harmless, and even seen as an ideal training ground for marriage for single women. Friendships were encouraged to develop within a framework of a "women's culture" that existed in the antebellum South.[13] From this conservative ethos, men and women were taught to operate in their separate spheres in their daily lives, and women were encouraged to form close and loving bonds with each other. These bonds began with the family and kin but also extended beyond it, to include friendship between women.

Changes in women's lives were further accelerated by the Civil War, which acted as a catalyst that provided single women with more opportunities to prove that they were useful to southern society, particularly in paid work. This led to a heightened autonomy for single women, which also led to the possibility of single women setting up more permanent homes together.[14] Yet it would seem that as the friendships between single women began to mature beyond conventional limitations, and as women also gained more opportunity to expand their roles in the public arena of work, they started to threaten the southern hegemony, who in turn questioned the true "nature" of female friendships, viewing them as potentially subversive. Historian Pippa Holloway argued, "Opportunities for female economic independence provided the means necessary for the development of lesbianism."[15] Elizabeth Knowlton also questioned the nature of female friendship and labeled Alice Baldy a "lesbian." Her opinion is based on a definition by Blanche Wiesen Cook that "a woman who wishes to nurture and support her female beloved and create a living environment in which to work independently" could be evidence for homoeroticism.[16] Even though nineteenth-century observers would not have understood such modern-day terms, they increasingly shared a concern about female sexuality and questioned the orthodox view that women were sexless. The rise of sexology, and the belief that women were sexual beings with carnal desires, therefore had an impact on the way romantic friendships were perceived and understood in later nineteenth-century society.

Single women were able to exercise considerable autonomy in their friendships with other women, but only within clearly designated limits. If they overstepped the invisible boundaries, or if the nature of their friendship came into question, then women discovered the confines of their personal autonomy. Perhaps this is ultimately what caused the relationship between Alice Baldy and Josephine Varner to burn out—the realization that establishing a permanent home together lay beyond the realms of what was acceptable in nineteenth-century southern society. There are three overarching questions in reference to female friendship and the single woman before, during, and after the Civil War: the social context of how and why they developed, the function and form that these relationships took, and what they tell us about constraint and agency in single women's lives.

The Development of Female Friendship

According to Aristotle, "A friend is a single soul dwelling in two bodies."[17] Georgian Mary Telfair concurred that friendship was as "an entire communications of thoughts, wishes, interests and pleasures, being undivided; a mutual esteem which comes with a pleasing sweetness of conversation and terminates in a desire to make each other happy."[18] Josephine Varner admitted, "Friends were the charm of life." It is clear, therefore, that friendship was an integral part of a southern woman's life, as it provided a level playing field for communication, mutual understanding, support, and mutual affection between women. In the antebellum period, female friendships were accepted and encouraged if they operated within certain boundaries; women had to understand that family came first and that their friendships should not interfere with this rigid hierarchy. For women who were single these ties to other women were especially important. Even though they were not married, single women were expected to fulfill very specific role assignments in the southern family as caregivers, helpmeets, surrogate mothers, or maiden aunts.[19] From these roles women often gained considerable kudos and inadvertently a degree of autonomy. Unlike married women, who gained automatic recognition in southern society through marriage, single women had to carve out an alternative identity for themselves by proving that they were active contributors to the home, family, and community. In light of this, women actively sought approval from others—especially friends—in order to bolster their own reputations as unmarried women devoted to a life of single blessedness, which heightened their social persona and in turn enhanced their level of personal autonomy. The avenue of female friendship represented another way in which unmarried women could gain recognition for their contribution to society. Furthermore it was an opportunity to feel the closeness and warmth of a personal relationship that lay outside of the family, particularly in an age that frowned on physical closeness with men.

The Victorian age believed women were "passionless," and in this context women were able to conduct intense and loving friendships with the same sex because they were perceived as devoid of sexual desire or "sexless."[20] The same conduct with men was strictly forbidden, as men, unlike women, were charged with carnal passion, which made male and female interactions fraught with danger, which discouraged some women from having heterosexual relationships at all. Women were repeatedly warned off public displays of affection with men, and they were encouraged to be shy and reserved in their relationships with the opposite sex, in order to avoid disrepute. They were taught to guard fiercely their reputations with men by withholding affection, which was tightly interwoven with their race and class as well-to-do southern white women. By withholding their affections from men, women were openly demonstrating that they were "passionless" and therefore "true" women. Carroll Smith-Rosenberg argued that the separate spheres ideology led to the development of a distinctive female culture and a subtle form of personal agency, albeit within tightly controlled boundaries.[21] Women's historians continue to contest if this was a sign of agency or constraint for women. Either way the existence of a thriving women's culture enabled unmarried women to find fulfillment—and to flourish—in their relationships with the same sex.

There has been much debate among women's historians who have been exploring female friendships since the 1970s and analyzing the possibility and implications of a shared women's culture. Pioneering scholars such as Carroll Smith-Rosenberg argued that a "rigid gender-role differentiation within the family, between and within society as a whole" resulted in "the emotional segregation of men and women" that started in childhood in strong ties between mother and daughter.[22] Smith-Rosenberg's work focuses on the North, yet her research base includes letters and diaries written by women in the Upper South. In the North the separate spheres ideology was possibly a backlash to the forces of change that were sweeping through the country; a conservative reaction to the market revolution, and the rapid urbanization and industrialization of American society and culture that resulted in the physical and emotional divide of the sexes. By saying that "true women" belonged in the private sphere of home and family, men used women as an anchor of stability amid turbulent and changing times. In the South, however, the ideology of separate spheres was tied to notions of paternalism, chivalry, and honor, which some have argued were becoming redundant by 1850.[23] The drive for industrialization and urbanization while less apparent in the South did not detract from the fact that both North and South were motivated by a conservative ethos, at least when it came to defining gender prescriptions.[24] The North and South were in many respects distinct regions before, during, and after the war, yet they upheld the same dictum concerning women's roles. The role of women in the North was linked to economic change, yet in the South the construction of the southern lady was conversely tied to the maintenance and protection of a slaveholding society. It was part of a conservative worldview that made the experiences of southern women unique.[25] As Pippa Holloway argued, "As long as southern ladies could be placed on pedestals of purity, white men could be assured of legitimate heirs."[26]

Race, class, and gender were inextricably intertwined in southern society, and slaveholding women therefore had a unique role to play in upholding the southern, white hegemony—and with it the institution of slavery. The cultural construction of the "Cult of True Womanhood" therefore fused with very specific southern ideals of class and race. The net result meant that men and women occupied different spheres, or social spaces, and women's role was designated as the guardians of the home and as the repositories of moral virtue. Women were told to accept their roles, and in doing so fulfill their duty as true women, raising the next generation, and restoring moral order amid turbulent times.[27] The so-called separate spheres ideology maintained a social framework that kept women contained within the domestic sphere of home and family, and granted men the freedom to explore and dominate the public domain, which was particularly pronounced in the South. Slaveholding women were encouraged to fulfill the role of the southern lady, which involved living within tightly defined parameters of the home and family with limited social contact with men. For planter-class women who remained single, it posed a considerable challenge in all areas as they were expected to demonstrate that they upheld the tenets of true womanhood, even though they remained single. The conservative ethos that separated the sexes also encouraged women to spend increasing amounts of time in each other's company, with mothers, daughters, aunts, cousins, and nieces, but also between friends. This led to the formation of a unique female-centered world from which single women were able to nurture autonomous female friendships.[28]

For single women without a husband or a family of their own to protect them (and this also extended to widowhood), their ties to other women were especially important. The close bonds that women forged with their own sex provided a special place for them to be themselves. In their relationships with other women, they discovered an arena in which they could exercise considerable freedom of thought, desire, and action. In the antebellum period, female friendships were accepted and encouraged, as they were considered to be harmless if they existed within certain boundaries. For example women had to understand that family came first and that their friendships could not interfere with this rigid hierarchy. In light of this, women actively sought approval from others in order to bolster their own reputations as unmarried women living a life devoted to single blessedness, which elevated their social persona, and in turn, enhanced their level of personal autonomy. Female friendship represented another way in which unmarried women garnered recognition for their contribution to society. Furthermore it was an opportunity to feel the closeness and warmth of a personal relationship that lay outside of the family. Often women continued to show that they were respectful of the tight gender conventions that controlled them, if only as a means to enhancing their personal autonomy. Romantic friendship between women was largely accepted mainly because it was controlled, but nonetheless women often manipulated it to their best advantage. According to Sheila Jeffreys, it was "precisely women's lack of any possibility of an independent life which made their passionate friendships acceptable as [they were] no threat to the heterosexual structure in early nineteenth-century society."[29] Yet as soon as the opportunity for economic independence increased this was reflected in the limitations of female friendship. By the close of the century, the view that women were asexual was challenged with the rise of "sexology."[30] Women were no longer viewed as "passionless," and this revelation impinged on society's perception of what constituted a "romantic friendship." Hence women who were single were seen as potentially subversive, especially if they continued to engage in loving same-sex friendships as they rocked the status quo.[31]

Form and Function of Female Friendship

Friendship manifested itself in many different forms. Some friendships were platonic, others fiery and passionate; they could be short lived in youth or span a lifetime. Friendships often started in youth, as families grew close through the custom of extended visits, and older girls often met up again at boarding schools, where they spent a concentrated amount of time in each other's company, which encouraged friendships to grow and flourish. Girls spoke in terms of their fictive kin in verbalizing their strong ties with young women, as they considered them to be so close that they viewed them as sisters, even though they were not blood related. This was certainly the case for Mary Telfair and Mary Few, childhood friends in the early 1800s, who later boarded together at school, and then remained friends for life. Although the pair spent long periods apart (typically they met in an annual visit when Telfair visited Few in the North, and even these visits ceased during the Civil War), the friendship was kept alive by letter writing, and the pleasure and significance of the time spent together was so special that it sustained a lifelong friendship.

Mary Telfair admitted that happiness for her centered on "friendship." Despite her wealth and notoriety as a southern benefactress in Savannah, and her loving relationship with her siblings (which was reinforced by sharing a home with them), Telfair continued to place a high value on her friendships with other women—in her attachment to Few especially. Mary admitted on a number of occasions that it was her dear friend Mary Few whom she felt closest to in the world. She referred to Few as her "Siamese twin" or "second self"—a relationship she considered so strong and intense that neither time nor distance could pull it apart.[32] Mary deliberately blurred the boundaries of family and close friendship by employing the language of fictive ties in her description of her relationship with Few.[33] In doing so she elevated Few to an untouchable status by comparing their relationship to that of conjoined twins—to emphasize that their friendship was based on the closest possible physical and emotional ties. In this way Mary marked out their relationship as more intimate than any other she experienced during her lifetime. Yet Mary also recognized the limitations of her friendship with Few and was careful to locate it within the proper parameters of southern society. The pair thwarted convention by remaining single, which combined with their lifelong friendship with each other could potentially be construed as a cultural form of resistance to gender conventions, as early as the 1830s. This suggests that the process of change was already underway in the pre–Civil War period in regard to the revision or expansion of gender models.

For slaveholding women who were passionate about their female friends, little would prevent them from keeping in close contact with each other. Planter-class women relied on writing and receiving letters to keep friendships alive when physically separated by time and place. To receive a letter from a close friend was an important demonstration of their friend's affection, as well as a sign of reassurance that they were being thought of regularly. Mary Telfair anxiously awaited Mary Few's letters and often grew ill tempered if she had not heard from her. Mary described herself as "very dependent" on Few for "intellectual nourishment" and said that she was the only "cure for the heartache" that she felt when she had not heard from her.[34] In a letter written to Mary Few in March 1829, Telfair wrote self-depreciatingly: "You are the laborer, for one of your letters are worth half a dozen of mine. . . . Yet I with all my dullness 'thick upon my head' attempt to answer your letter."[35] Telfair was not alone in seeking frequent reassurance that she worthy of her friend's attention. Alice Baldy frequently sought reassurance from her friend Joe Varner that her love was long lasting: "Will you promise to be with me as much as you can, as long as I live? Let us promise to each other to be as much together as we possibly can as long as we both live."[36]

Letter writing also offered an excellent opportunity to openly communicate on a wide range of issues, particularly in regard to remaining single. Mary Jones Taylor wrote regularly to her friend Mary Sharp Jones of Liberty County, Georgia. The pair had been friends since childhood, and they had attended a seminary for young ladies in Philadelphia together. Even though Jones had moved from Georgia when her father took up a new post as secretary of the Board of Domestic Missions of the Presbyterian Church in Philadelphia, the girls had maintained contact through letter writing until the start of the Civil War, when Mary Taylor would have been in her late twenties. For an extended period of time, the pair proved to be close confidantes, until their friendship slowly died out after Mary Jones married.[37] Mary Taylor noted to Jones in September 1858, "I am more devoted than ever to spinsterhood," adding jovially, "Did you ever hear of one who bore the illustrious cognomen of Mary Jones who was not a blessing to society at large."[38] Another young woman from Virginia wrote to her friend Frances Bernard, begging her to remain single. "Let me live and die in single blessedness," she vowed; "I can imagine no state more miserable than to be joined for life to one who has not affection and confidence."[39] Frances clearly outlined her views on marrying only for love or else her preference to remain single. This concurs with the wider historical discourse on the rise of companionate marriage, or marriage for love, and the decision that southern women increasingly made to delay marriage or reject it altogether, if they did not find a suitable mate.[40] Sarah Morgan, a young, nineteen-year-old from Baton Rouge (and later New Orleans), Louisiana, abhorred the idea of marriage and boldly confessed to Captain Huger that "women who look to marriage as the sole end and object in life are those who think less of its duties; while those who see its responsibilities, and feel its solemnity, are those who considered it by no means the only purpose in life," which no doubt included herself. She added, "If women only considered for one minute all of the awful responsibilities that hang on that solemn I will" they might be slower to rush into matrimony.[41] Morgan and women like her recognized that marriage was an important decision and not one to be rushed into, and when she eventually did marry she was in her thirties.[42]

Women often modeled their friendships on sororal ties. The comfort, solace, and good feeling derived from a close friendship replicated that of family, and unmarried women cherished the warmth of a dearly loved friend in much the same way that they appreciated a close sister. Women often translated this affection by adopting the language of "fictive kin" and referred to close female friends in familial terms, such as "sister," particularly in their letters and journals.[43] There were two main reasons for this. First, it tied into the idea of an explicitly female-centered world, in which men and women occupied such distinct social spaces that it encouraged women to forge close bonds not only with female relatives but also with female friends, that is, women who they saw as "sisters of the heart." By adopting familial terms, women fostered and reinforced the idea of a distinctive women's culture that was in keeping with their strong ties of affection. Second, "sister" was a safe, platonic term; it conveyed closeness and longevity, without passion. It transmitted a sense of belonging that was as natural and as prized as blood ties, and it also stressed its longevity and permanence in women's lives. A sister, after all, was a lifelong companion and a blood tie that could never be broken. In close female friendships, it therefore seemed like an appropriate term for conveying the depth and endurance of a treasured friendship.

Conversely female kin (or blood relations) employed the language of friendship in addressing each other in their correspondence as an extended term of affection. Sisters and cousins often referred to one another as "friends," and non-kin emulated familial bonds, thereby creating fictive kin networks. In writing to Eliza DeRosset, her cousin Miss Moore complained, "Never my dear cousin plead the exhaustion of my patience as an excuse for your laziness—for surely friends who love as we do can find enough to fill one small sheet of paper?"[44] A small number of women took on a specific gender role within their same-sex friendship. Lizzie Grove, a young woman living with her family in Missouri, wrote frequently to her close friend and cousin Laura Brumback. Rather than employing sororal terms, Lizzie went a stage further and donned the language of heterosexual love, referring to Laura as "my dearest husband" in their private correspondence.[45] Likewise Alice Baldy's letters to Josephine echo an almost masculine persona, and a desire to look after her sweetheart, which evoke a reversal of gender roles in their correspondence. In 1870 she wrote: "I love you and I want to take care of you—I would do it if I could, and save you contact with anything rough, or harsh," almost as if she were fulfilling the role of the husband and Joe fulfilling the role of the dependent wife who needed protecting, which was a deliberate subversion of her own gender.[46]

South Carolinian single lady Hannah Wylie wrote regularly to her married sister, Mary Mobley. She made candid observations on the institution of marriage, with particular reference to weddings that she or her sisters attended. After attending a friend's wedding in May 1865, she noted, "Katherine looked beautiful, what a contrast to her choice," making it plain that marriage was an undesirable state for her, unless it was a companionate one. By emphasizing how poor Katherine's choice was, she insinuated that she had settled for second best, which was far worse, in her opinion, than remaining single.[47] Eliza Travers Lewis also confabulated with her cousin Eliza Holladay on her "exceeding liking" of a life devoted to single blessedness.[48] The fact that these unmarried women were so frank and outspoken in their letters demonstrates a confidence and ease in their own beliefs, and also in their discourse with other women. As Amy Wink observed, writing was an expression of personal agency for nineteenth-century women and was thus "a moment of action and agency despite the culture that encourages passivity"in the South and beyond.[49] Therefore women harnessed their passion for letter writing in an effort to cultivate and sustain close ties with loved ones that included parents, siblings, cousins, but also female friends. They were physical manifestations of their heartfelt affection for another woman and an important means of communication that helped maintain friendship, even when friends lived many miles apart. Anna Moore expressed the comfort she received when she opened a letter from her cousin, Magdalen Mary DeRosset. "Thanks to you for your kindness, I feel grateful for your affection and value it more than you can imagine. Every letter from you my beloved cousin makes me love you more and more. All those who wish to keep the flame of friendship bright and burning possess an effectual antedate against its becoming extinct by means of lazy intercourse."[50] These sentiments resonate with Mary Telfair's confession that she would rather "employ a rusty nail as a pen" than "forego the pleasure of confabulating" with Mary Few.[51]

Friendship such as theirs provided women with the forum in which to safely express their most intimate thoughts and desires, without fear of rebuke. Furthermore it offered unmarried women an outlet to share in the various ways in which they were making themselves useful to their families and it offered them a chance for encouragement and praise. While women's journals were a safe place for women to establish their identities, letter writing provided further scope for them to test out the boundaries imposed on them by society. There was a strong sense that single women wanted to prove that they were actively contributing to society or that they were useful, almost as if to dispel any preconceived notions that they were redundant women and a drain on their family and society. Therefore women's letters and diaries often spoke at length about how busy they were or how useful they had been. It was also an opportunity for elite white women to use their skill of literacy to show "women's agency in the midst of social constraint" by having their voice heard by a sympathizing friend.[52] This theme of usefulness is crucial. It reverberated throughout women's letters and diaries almost as if it were a badge of honor through which they might gain recognition and inadvertently enhance personal agency. Mary Telfair mused that she wanted to be "amicable and if I can, a useful old maid."[53] Ellen Mordecai spoke of "making herself useful" during her stay with relatives in Richmond, Virginia, in 1817, and Sally Hill praised Virginia Holladay for her "usefulness" in the family: "You must have your hands full with the babies—I am sure I could not make myself so useful."[54] These women merged words of support with praise and recognition, as well as speaking candidly about their desire to be reunited with their friends again soon.[55] In addition to proving that they were useful, women were also keen to prove that they were virtuous, busy, and fulfilled. Domestic novelist Augusta Jane Evans wrote to her friend Rachel Lyons detailing how busy she was. "You have no idea how many claims I have on my time and attention. My correspondence is absolutely formidable and you would pity me if you knew the number of unanswered letters staring at me in the face to write."[56] She spoke of being "constantly engaged" writing newspaper articles, and attending to familial duties (which is again illuminating considering she is single).[57] On one occasion Augusta talks of taking "charge" of her sisters, Carrie and Sarah. She helped them with their studies and devoted time and patience listening to them read on their history and philosophy course that required "at least half a day" of her time. During the war she supervised them single-handedly for two weeks again underlining how useful she was to the family unit.[58]

Eliza DeRosset wrote to her unmarried sister Magdalen Mary, professing that "if I do not write for often dear Mag, you must not, by any means attribute it to indifference or want of affections"; "I have really so many correspondents and so little time to devote to that that I fear some, who do not know me may accuse me of forgetfulness."[59] Likewise the ageing Miss Ker penned in her diary, "school or other work all day long, no time to myself, no privacy."[60]

Josephine Varner measured her own self-worth by how successful or busy she had been, or by how much she had read, worked, or corresponded with family or friends.[61] When a friend, particularly a close friend or kindred spirit, recognized those achievements by writing about them in the affirmative in their letters, it generated a feeling of external affirmation and a sense of well-being (in line with the Cult of Single Blessedness); it also led to an enhancement of personal agency.[62] Augusta Jane Evans in spite of her many responsibilities—writing, home, and family—clearly felt comfortable in telling her friend about the pressures of her daily life and admitted openly to her friend Rachel, "It helps me marvelously to know that you do remember and love me so kindly."[63] Likewise Mary Telfair wrote in rapturous delight upon receiving news from Few, as she wanted confirmation "that you still loved me."[64]

Friendship, then, was a complicated business that often traversed the boundaries between familial and nonfamilial affection. The language of sisterhood laces in and out of the writings of American women in the eighteenth and nineteenth centuries and highlights the loving bonds shared between kin and nonkin. Female friendships weaved themselves into the fabric of everyday life, and from an early age "mothers and daughters, aunts and nieces, cousins and female friends often hugged and kissed" in public without risking subverting the social or moral order.[65] Girls learnt that physical displays of affection, such as hand holding, embracing, and giving each other small tokens of their love, was a casually accepted part of southern society, with no sexual undertones. That said, the conventions and expectations that were accepted in youth were different from those that governed adult friendships.[66] Drew Gilpin Faust argued that girls understood relationships with other women within a framework of language customarily associated with heterosexual love. Such language, words or deeds were not considered deviant (until the end of the century) but supposedly represented "a sensitivity and authenticity of feeling celebrated in this sentimental mid-Victorian era as appropriate to true friendship as much as true love."[67]

In school, particularly in female seminaries, girls fashioned exclusive relationships with a roommate, bedfellow, or sweetheart. They chose pet names for each other (for example Mary Ker was referred to as "Molly") and shared rooms and beds, took walks together, and gave each other little gifts or wrote notes and letters to one another, which reinforced the cliques they had formed.[68] Girls talked of being "in love" or having "a crush" on a fellow pupil, and if that pupil had left the school they spoke of the difficulty of being "torn" apart.[69] The types of intense friendships often experienced by girls at boarding school "delineated a female centered sphere" rather than a preparatory stage for anything more permanent in terms of a physically intimate female friendship.[70] As Holloway pointed out, this began to shift at the turn of the century, reflected in the changing patterns of marriage, reproduction, sexual practices, and socialization, which heralded in new ideas and possibilities in female friendship.[71]

Occasionally pupils targeted their affections on a female teacher who they looked up to admiringly as a positive role model for their future lives.[72] Their strong attachments were considered a normal part of growing up and also a useful training ground in preparation for marriage, which inevitably followed for the majority of women. Historian Melinda Buza discussed the way "same-gender networks" prepared "men and women for the companionability and commitment of marriage but also served as a forum for reservations about the other gender."[73] Even when intense female friendships died out, important lessons were learned that helped girls and women consider alternative gender models for their future lives. North Carolinian Anna Cameron greatly admired her music teacher during her time spent at her female seminary. "I am perfectly in love with Augusta, she is beautiful and charming," she wrote in 1863. The love affair though, was evidently one-sided, and the object of her affections, Augusta Stevenson, became engaged and later married. Yet Anna instead "translated her intense attachment for her music teacher" into a lifelong desire to remain single and "planned for an independent future" by supporting herself through her work. Her case was not unusual, and older schoolgirls also drew inspiration from their teachers and saw them as an alternative model for living a future life of single blessedness.[74]

Alice Baldy and Joe Varner's case is indicative of a desire to set up a more permanent residence with another unmarried woman, and to live as a couple in an all-female household. It moves far beyond conventional, residential living arrangements for single women, who typically lived in their families' homes and demonstrates that single women actively sought alternatives to traditional living arrangements that far surpassed sharing with an unmarried or widowed sibling.[75] This echoes Grace Elmore Brown's plan to set up an "establishment independent of everyone else," which also demonstrated personal autonomy.[76] Anya Jabour argued the main reason why female friendships between unmarried women were "allowed" to exist was that they were viewed as only temporary in nature and they had little hope of gaining any real permanency. Therefore, because their friendships were perceived as only temporary or transitory in nature, they did not pose as a threat to the existing social order. Besides, as Alice's case illustrates, single women often lacked the material resources to make their vision a permanent reality. As a result unmarried women were given limited freedom to pursue their female friendships because they were perceived as short lived, nonsexual, and without sufficient economic means to ever become permanent.[77] Yet in the postwar period, as single women's working roles expanded further, and women accumulated the material resources to turn their vision into a reality, new theories on female sexuality emerged that questioned past beliefs that women were asexual and pure in nature. These new ideas cast a shadow on female friendship between unmarried women and caused single women to conceal friendships in a way that had not been necessary previously.

In the letters and diaries of the single women in this book there can be little question that the language employed between close friends was loving, passionate, and demonstrative in tone; yet should it be interpreted differently if the women were permanently single? It is useful to consider again the nature of the correspondence between Alice Baldy and Joe Varner. While many letters remain to bear testament to Alice's feelings of romantic love for Joe, no letters exist from Joe Varner to Alice, as Joe insisted Alice burn them. Josephine seemed nervous that anybody other than herself and Alice should see her letters, and she seemed forever anxious to keep the nature of their relationship shielded from the public glare, to such an extent that she made Alice burn them. The reason why Joe felt the need to destroy any tangible evidence of the relationship she had shared with Alice Baldy suggests that she was fearful of the reaction she might encounter should the content be made public, and she was therefore keen to protect herself from public scrutiny, which she succeeded in doing, as she was revered by all those who knew her or by those who had heard of her.

These letters, from the 1870s, were written at a time when notions of female asexuality started to come into question and physical displays of affection between women suddenly came into question. This was in tandem with a new wave of medical thinking and new ideas regarding female sexuality. It coincided with the increased economic independence of single women, who gained independence through wider opportunities at work. Previously held notions of female passionlessness became unhinged by new philosophies and medical interpretations—sexology—that claimed women had the potential to be sexually active in their relationships with each other.[78] This rebranding of romantic friendships between women as socially deviant caused unmarried women to retreat and to hide their relationships from the lens of public scrutiny. It was almost as though, after the war, women had adopted a new identity, and as they showed themselves to be more capable in and out of the public arena, they were considered more of a threat to the social order. Women started to hide their most intimate thoughts, which included love letters to other women. This perhaps accounts for Josephine's insistence that Alice destroy the letters she wrote to her. It is hardly surprising in this context that Josephine felt uncomfortable about her written declarations of love for another woman, either because she feared that they would be misconstrued, or perhaps because they revealed erotic desires that even she was unsure of, should they become public. This reveals the dichotomy between the private and public worlds that women inhabited, and the way in which established cultural ideals attempted to constrain single women's autonomy well into the late nineteenth century. Alice Baldy discovered the constraints of her status as an unmarried woman when she tried to turn her dream of sharing a permanent home with Josephine Varner into a reality. By attempting to do so, she threatened the patriarchal structure of southern society and subverted the conventional definitions of southern womanhood.

Simply put, female friendship, particularly in the form of "romantic friendship," was accepted on a temporary basis up until the 1870s, if it fell within acceptable social parameters of southern society. If, however, it clearly challenged the existing structures of southern society, or failed to operate within its conservative framework, then it was immediately perceived as a threat, which gave rise to new ideas and interpretations of femininity. Alice discovered this to her peril when she found she was unable to set up a home with Joe because it was blocked by a number of obstacles: some personal, others financial, or familial. Ultimately in

Alice's case the benefits of single blessedness proved to be a double-edged sword, in that it allowed her considerable autonomy in some areas of her life but severely restricted her in others. For example, in order for her to demonstrate that she was devoted to a life of single blessedness, she had to demonstrate that family was her first priority to win her respect and a good reputation. However in achieving this, she sacrificed her long-term desires because her birth family became a constraint that held her back from achieving her goals. It ties in with Lee Chambers-Schiller's argument regarding single women in the American Northeast that family helped define single women's roles but it also hindered them from fulfilling more long-term personal ambitions, because of the heavy demands often made on them.[79] This was true for Alice, who from the age of twenty-one shouldered considerable responsibility within the family, owing to her mother's and siblings' ill health and the death of her father in 1856.[80] In this context Alice was stuck in the predicament of having to prove her usefulness to her family, and quash her private desires for an alternative life. The notion of friendships having permanency was clearly important in single women's lives and paralleled the blood ties between sisters, which blurred the boundaries between familial and nonfamilial ties.

Female friendship was also a vital source of emotional and practical support for women who were unhappily married or widowed. Not all marriages conformed to the companionate ideal, and many women spoke of their high hopes for marriage contrasted to the disappointing reality of married life. Laura Beecher Comer was one such woman. Born in New Haven, Connecticut, in 1817, she moved south after the death of her first husband, Mr. Hayes. In 1848 she married James Comer, a cotton planter in Alabama, and the couple settled in rural Georgia. In her diary she recalled the early days of her marriage to James, and the lonely reality of living "alone with him year after year" thereafter.[81] For Laura it was a life she endured but rarely enjoyed. Her expectations of marriage and the desire to have a family of her own remained permanently unfulfilled, and she regularly confided in her diary her feelings of isolation and repressed anger. "I cannot, nor will not spend all these precious days of my life, following after and watching Negroes. It is a terrible life!" Laura confessed in her journal in 1862. "Who can appreciate or understand anything about such a life—but a woman who marries a Bachelor; who has lived with his Negroes as equals, at bed and board!"[82] Laura's daily life was far removed from the companionate marriage that some women enjoyed. She made clear in her diary that the man she had married failed to provide for her and referred to him as "barbarous" in nature.[83] She spoke of feeling undermined as a woman living among the slaves, who she noted her husband treated "as [her] equals," rather than elevating her to a higher position within the plantation hierarchy, as a woman of her race and class would have expected to be. Comer was deeply disillusioned with marriage, and she found it an insult to her femininity that her husband failed to provide her with protection, provision, and respect. It was within this context that Comer sought the love, support, and acceptance from her friendships with other women, which was sorely lacking in her relationship with her husband. On occasions she also complained about her friendships, but overall, the letters from her close friends helped to sustain her.

Laura Comer valued the fact that her friends "understood and appreciated her."[84] She felt a closeness and warmth in her relationship with female friends who openly shared their "heart, love and affection," with her.[85] Laura regularly bemoaned the harsh treatment she received from her husband, but after his death she initially appeared paralyzed by the additional responsibilities that came with managing the plantation: attending to ditches, ploughs, and crops; caring for slaves; and balancing the accounts.[86] In 1867 Laura dedicated a long section in her diary to the estate being "settled" following her husband's death; she noted, "I am released from courts. My debts are paid. My plantation business is comparatively off my hands and this home place I shall soon, (God so willing) have put in repair and leave it with the gentleman in my family and a housekeeper."[87] Yet at first life didn't seem to get much easier for Laura Comer. The intervention of the war, and the mass exodus of slaves from their plantations as they won their freedom, added to her daily woes. "I must sell my plantation, for I long to be free from cares and of the vain and insolent freedman."[88] Finally in November 1872 she acted on her firm belief that "I have been a slave to my business affairs for too long. I have taken care of others and neglected myself—it is high time I should attend to myself," and she traveled north to visit family in New York and Connecticut, before voyaging on to Europe.[89] Two decades later, in January 1899, by this stage an old woman, Comer reflected on her life and on the friendship of one particular friend, Lilla. The "flame of friendship is well burnt on the altar of my heart," she wrote in regard to her friend Lilla, whom she knew and loved deeply, describing her letters as "more precious than gold to me."[90] Laura Comer discovered a sense of well-being from her female friendship, which clearly helped her to endure an unhappy marriage, and later to cope alone during her widowhood.[91]

These close and loving friendships between southern women were highly prized. They came in various different forms and had several important functions. They gave women a sense of self-fulfillment and a chance to be heard, and a safe place to share their honest opinions on marriage versus spinsterhood. It was an opportunity to let someone else know how useful or how valued they were to others, which kept women connected even though they may have lived miles apart. This highlights the need for an external affirmation to feel worthy and appreciated in a society where single women could potentially feel undervalued or unappreciated. Single women often formed collectives or female "networks" especially in urban areas where they lived in closer proximity to one another, which increased the feasibility and frequency of meeting up in person more regularly. The loving and supportive network of kin and nonkin was essential for building confidence and self-identity in single women. Many single women had a wide circle of female friends. Mary Ker from Natchez, Mississippi, valued her female friendships and devoted time and energy in keeping up a prolific and detailed correspondence with many women over her lifetime, including Lou Connor, Amelia Choppin, and Lou Butler. Mary was well respected by her friends. One friend described her as "my very particular friend," and another as "my much loved Mary."[92] In Mary's case she did not rely on one individual friendship to sustain her, and she developed a large social network of other like-minded women who lived in the Mississippi region, rather like a proverbial magpie, taking what she needed from different friendships. A friend and widow concerned for Mary's poor health later in life encouraged Mary to consider boarding with her: "I want you to come and live with me," implored Mrs. Reid in March 1880. "If I am successful in getting my business arranged to suit me I shall have plenty for us both and if I do not you can teach and get 35 dollars a month here and your company would be the greatest imaginable comfort to me."[93] It was an offer that Mary never took up, and yet it demonstrates the comradery and networks that built up between single women. Mary's correspondents were virtually all women, with the exception of family, and many of them kept up a rich and detailed correspondence with Mary for over sixty years, proving how much they valued Mary as both a friend and confidante.[94]

Likewise Mary Telfair, the never-married spinster from Savannah, Georgia, belonged to a tight-knit circle of female friends, the majority of whom were single and from wealthy slaveholding families in the seaboard area. Friends in her circle included Anne Clay, Sarah Cecil, and Catherine Hunter. In Mary Telfair's letters to Mary Few, the pair discussed the individual merits of various friends; the majority were permanently single, although a minority did eventually go on to marry. It is clear from Telfair's critique of each individual that some women were more highly esteemed than others in the group. Anne Clay was "very much admired" owing to her "dignity, grace, intelligence and vivacity"; Catherine Hunter was "satirical," Sarah Campbell was "amiable, pious and benevolent," and Mrs. Bryan "fascinating."[95] Telfair described a "coterie" of like-minded women who met weekly to enjoy oyster suppers, needlework, light reading, and stimulating conversation.[96] Hers was a vibrant picture of a strong and well-connected support network of unmarried women who lived in Savannah, enjoying the advantages that city living brought to them in their position as wealthy but unattached single women. Christine Carter noted that these networks tended to be more prolific in the urban centers of the antebellum South, with evidence of elite, slaveholding women flourishing as members of a wider community in cities such as Charleston and Savannah. This was presumably because such networks were easier to maintain in more cosmopolitan, urban centers as opposed to more isolated, rural areas, where it was harder for women to meet up regularly.[97] Women in rural areas tended to have family and friends stay for extended visits, whereas friends in urban areas could meet up regularly for shorter periods of time. Networks probably developed a little later in rural areas or were simply maintained in different ways—mostly by regular correspondence and extended visits, rather than regular meetings. Virginian Eliza Holladay, for example, lived with her four unmarried sisters at Prospect Hill plantation Spotsylvania County. The four sisters spoke of the joy that visits from family and friends brought them, referring to the latter's visits as a "delightful intercourse" that helped to "renew" "friendship and love" for each other when distance kept them apart, which was fairly typical in the antebellum and post–Civil War eras.[98] These visits kept single women connected, thus enabling them to withstand the test of time that was essential for maintaining close bonds.

War and Its Aftermath

With the build up to secession, war, and its aftermath, letter writing continued to be an active forum in which single women could express and debate their most intimate thoughts, feelings, or desires. The Wylie sisters frequently talked politics in their letters, swapped opinions on political lectures they had attended, and made it plain what their political views were. The sisters went against the tide of prosecession feeling within their own family and also in their state of South Carolina. Hannah stated that slavery was "a dirty business," even though her father was himself a slaveholder.[99] She talked about political figures, the Mexican War, the annexation of Texas, and, of course, the Civil War.[100] Susan Wylie admitted in September 1847 that she wished herself a man, so that she could do battle and make an imprint on the world. "Though it appears hard, I would rather be a man and risk all [than] be the weak and insignificant creature that I am and must die without a name."[101] Letters kept women connected when they were apart and allowed a degree of freedom of expression (albeit within the strictures of Victorian letter-writing conventions) that unveiled the true spirit of women like Susan and Hannah Wylie. The opinionated, impassioned, and forthright views expressed, particularly by Hannah Wylie, come across strongly in their letters. These women were outspoken and fearless in voicing their opinions, even if they caused offence. Yet this forms a stark contrast to how they were remembered in their obituaries; Susan Wylie was noted for being "in the meridian of woman-hood," in the midst of a life of usefulness."[102] A woman's outspokenness might well have been accepted within her family and in her close friendships, but in the public arena it was not. Ultimately Wylie's public persona was effectively controlled by the dominant patriarchy of the South.

In the private forum of their personal correspondence with like-minded single women, women were at their most honest. They expressed opinions on numerous topics, including the impending secession and the coming of war. Harriott Middleton, a well-to-do, single lady from South Carolina, revealed an active interest in politics, secession, and war. In the extended correspondence between Harriott and Susan Matilda Middleton, which is particularly well documented in the lead-up to and during the Civil War, it is obvious that Harriott is a strong secessionist. A native of South Carolina, Harriott described how the white, slaveholding women of New Orleans "vomited secession" despite being surrounded by Union troops during the war, when they were being forced to pledge an allegiance to the North "whilst surrounded by their own slaves, armed and placed as guards over them," while Susan referred to Lincoln as "vulgar."[103] Caroline Kean Davis, a single woman teaching at a school in King Williams County in Virginia, spoke of her interest in politics and wrote that she had taken time out to attend a four-day state convention in April 1861, during which she had heard "interesting and exciting debates from various members."[104] The novelist Augusta Jane Evans also spoke out in her correspondence with General P. G. T. Beauregard and Confederate congressman J. L. M. Curry regarding specific battles in the Civil War. Rebecca Sexton in her book on Evans noted that she wrote "freely and confidently" in her letters to high-ranking men, and gave them "advice concerning everything from battle plans to government politics."[105] Nonetheless she was not considered as a threat to male authority and she made it very clear that by expressing her opinion she was not intending to interfere, but simply fulfilling a "sacred duty" to assist her country during the exigencies of war. Evans took special measures to protect her reputation as a lady from the "ridicule or wrath of those who contend that women have no interest" in politics or in the battlefield.[106] For example she did not sign her name to some of the articles that she wrote, as a means of shielding her reputation from any potential abuse from those who considered her efforts too intellectual, which was a sign of masculinity. Evans defended her political discussions with Beauregard and Curry and commented that she felt "compelled to step out of her feminine role" out of a strong sense of "patriotic duty" to the South.

Evans recognized the additional freedom she accrued from her status as a successful writer. However, she remained watchful and protective of her position as a single woman from the elite class, perhaps fearing that if she overstepped gender conventions she might court unpopularity that could result in the loss of independence. Women placed a high value on being seen as "useful" and liked to be seen as doing so within their designated sphere. Therefore however "free" Evans may have seemed in her correspondence with men, in reality she was checked by the social prescriptions of womanhood that continued to control her within a designated space. Therefore her "freedom" was circumscribed in her relationships with men in a way that it was not with women. The exceptional circumstances born of war granted Evans additional freedom to overstep her normal boundaries of womanhood, which inadvertently led to larger share of female independence.[107] Yet Evans remained "reluctant to transcend the proper sphere of womanhood, and always fearful of encroaching upon the prerogatives of [her] sex," by engaging in inappropriate activities for a woman—a theme echoed in her novels and writing. Evans celebrated women's contribution to society but also noted that those contributions should be restricted to certain "noble" professions that did not draw women away from their home and family.[108] It was often in the open communication between female friends that single women tested the boundaries of womanhood, actively seeking approval for their contributions to their family, community, and beyond.

During the Civil War, ladies gift annuals and prescriptive literature praised the benefits of female friendship upholding them as pure and noble, which reiterates how close friendships between women were viewed as innocent relationships that fitted in with conventional models of womanhood. Unmarried women spoke with unbridled delight regarding their friendships with other women but were often at pains to emphasize their temporary nature. Bettie Lyell's valedictory address in Petersburg, Virginia, in 1863 wistfully reminisced that "as a band of sisters many and joyous have been the hours we have spent together [at college], and it may be, that the future has no gift in store to recompense us for their loss," now that the special time in their lives was over. Bettie vocalized a common truth that many southern women accepted as fact, that the friendships that girls enjoyed in their youth was different from those experienced later in life when they became wives and mothers, with responsibilities of their own. The stage of girlhood or adolescence was seen as a transitory phase that girls would usually grow out of as they reached maturity, and as such the stage was considered as a good preparation for marriage. As Martha Vicinus argued in reference to female friendship in nineteenth-century England, "An intense female friendship was an important step in growing up; it was also a valuable alternative to flirtations with the opposite sex."[109] These so-called homoerotic friendships of a girl's youth were generally accepted, even encouraged, "as long as they did not risk the balance between authority and self-control that characterized girls' schools.... Homoerotic friendships were an important means to maturity."[110] Yet by the late 1800s this perception of female friendship altered, and close emotional and physical relationships between women became replaced by a generalized suspicion toward intense or "romantic" friendships that were labeled "deviant." This coalesced with the rise of sexology and new medical opinions that began to question female asexuality.

The Civil War therefore acted as a catalyst and shone a bright light on the number of women who were now single (owing to widowhood or nonmarriage). With 260,000 Confederate men dead, and many more injured or disabled, increasing numbers of southern women faced life alone as single women. These women often found themselves in altered economic, demographic, and social circumstances, which meant they had to expand their sphere in order to adapt to the new realities of their everyday lives that reflected the new social order that surrounded them.[111] Drew Gilpin Faust argued, "young and unmarried women often turned to one another not just for companionship but for the passion and feeling more generally associated with heterosexual attachments," owing to the dearth of men, which led to a reinterpretation of gender conventions and challenged previous held notions that women were passionless.[112] In this way the war can be interpreted as acting as a catalyst for accelerating a change of opinion on how female friendships were perceived. It stimulated existing trends that were underway in the antebellum period by covertly confronting and challenging gender conventions in the form of more passionate—or sexual—female attachments.[113]

As new opportunities (and challenges) for single women began to open up that reflected the altered social scene, particularly in paid work, women's chance of achieving greater independence and permanency in their long-term friendships rose. This went beyond setting up homes with other female family members (typically with other unmarried sisters or cousins) and instead focused on female-only residences that included sharing a home with close friends. After all it was not uncommon for widows and spinsters within the same family to live together. The Holladay sisters shared a home together throughout their lives; Mary Telfair lived with her widowed sister Margaret, and Susan and Harriet Wylie, two unmarried sisters from South Carolina, shared a home. In the Mordecai family, widows, spinsters, and married couples lived together, pooling resources and supporting each other in everyday life.[114] This became particularly pronounced in the post-war period, as the war highlighted female singleness in an unprecedented way. With many more southern women facing altered living arrangements owing to widowhood or permanent spinsterhood, a change in residential living patterns represented an increasing threat to the existing social order. As a result "defeat and post-war conditions in the South undermined the patriarchy," and some southern women criticized men for their failure to provide for them, or to protect them from the brutalities of war.[115] As a result, during Reconstruction and moving into the late nineteenth century, women's friendships were interpreted within an altered framework that mirrored their increased personal agency in other areas of their lives. This ties in with Joe Varner's request that Alice Baldy burn the love letters she had written to her for fear that they would be interpreted in a negative light. This additional pressure did not result in the decline of same-sex friendships between unmarried women—many simply went underground and hid their friendships from the outside world.

There were many literary devices that single women used to cloak their passionate desires for each other in their letters and in the conduct of their same-sex friendships—in school, in adulthood, and in society. In the antebellum period some women had already done this, to an extent, but in the post–Civil War era it came into sharper focus in order to protect women from possible criticism, or accusations of subversion. Superficially it would seem that single women directly benefited from the notion that women were passionless, for the first half of the nineteenth century at least. It enabled them to nurture close and loving same-sex friendships albeit within clearly defined limits without any accusations that they were being sexually deviant, since they were perceived as having no sexual desires. The question arises as to whether these passionate female friendships had a sexual dimension, and if and why that should matter. Feminist historians in the past have "cautioned" us against looking for "lesbians" in the eighteenth and nineteenth centuries, fearful of imposing twenty-first century ideas on the past. Historians such as Lillian Faderman have argued convincingly that same-sex love and romantic friendship between women was widely endorsed by contemporaries. They were accepted as a transitional stage in girls' lives that did not challenge the status quo and therefore were not feared.[116]

Yet surely sexuality has a central place in the context of nineteenth-century female friendship. For if female asexuality had come into question, then female sexuality, or sexual desire became a heightened possibility—which made intense and physically close romantic friendship between women a real potential threat. It is worth highlighting at this point the infamous trial of Alice Mitchell, a single white female from Memphis, Tennessee, who murdered her female lover in 1892 when their planned elopement [as a couple] was aborted. Even though the Mitchell case falls outside of the time frame of this book, it remains an important example that illustrates the tension and passion that some romantic friendships could generate between female friends in southern society. The case came at a time when scientific models of sexuality were being raised. Historian Lisa Duggen argued race, gender, and sexuality fused together to create "a particular set of concerns and interpretations of white womanhood, and racial issues were embedded in this trial."[117] In the final analysis, the court deemed Alice Mitchell "insane," so stirred up were they over the prospect of lesbianism. Trials such as this raise the possibility that other women, especially single white females, were engaging in sexual practices in the South.

After all, by the late 1870s, elite white women's lives had begun to change more dramatically, with new opportunities developing outside of the family unit (such as paid work). The war had helped to accelerate the rate of change in their public and private lives, and it was at this stage that female friendship started to come under closer scrutiny. The friendship between unmarried women started to be perceived as a threat to the social order, in a way that they had not been previously. As Lillian Faderman argued, "Love between women had been encouraged and tolerated for centuries—but now that women had the possibility of economic independence, such love became potentially threatening to the social order. What if women would seek independence, cut men out of their lives?"[118] As a result the "love between women was metamorphosed into a freakishness," which dovetailed with new interpretations on female sexuality that no longer assumed that the love between women was nonsexual.[119]

Summary

Female friendship between single women developed out of a distinctive female culture in the antebellum South. These friendships were accepted and enjoyed by single women in a myriad of different forms—from long-distance letter writing, or annual visits, to more frequent meetings with a close friend, or group of friends, in the form of a single women's network. Unhappily married women, or women who were alone owing to widowhood, also drew great strength from their friendships with other women, as the case of Laura Comer attests to. Research indicates that women prized their female friends and even dreamed of setting up a more permanent home with them, if it was economically viable. Female friendship often mirrored sororal bonds and at times even surpassed them, such as in the case of Mary Telfair, who described her friend Mary Few as her "Siamese twin." Female family (sisters, cousins) also blurred the boundaries between kin and non-kin by referring to their much loved sisters and cousins as "their dearest friend," reinforcing the overlap between friends and family. In the antebellum period women exercised considerable freedom in their same-sex friendships owing to the fact that they were regarded as nonsexual. Thus from a conservative basis, women achieved a limited degree of autonomy and independence in their relationships outside of marriage. The war further expanded women's roles in terms of their place in the public sphere. It highlighted single blessedness in a way that further promoted alternative gender models for southern women, and made nonmarriage a blessing rather than a curse.

Regardless of the nature of female friendship, it is clear that single women felt a sense of ease in their friendships with other like-minded women. They felt comfortable in disclosing their private thoughts on numerous topics such as marriage, singleness, family, and personal aspirations. This was because a close friend could bolster self-esteem and validate a single woman's sense of usefulness, which coalesced with the rise of the Cult of Single Blessedness, which measured an unmarried woman's worth by the contributions that she made to her family and community.[120] The war accelerated the rate of social change and painted female singleness in a more positive light. However, it also underlined the growing autonomy of single women, which had an adverse effect on the way in which female friendship was understood. By the late 1870s female friendship was no longer viewed as a "temporary" state, or a benign relationship that could be conducted alongside marriage. With the rise of sexology and medical science, romantic friendship between women—especially single women who never married —came under greater scrutiny as women gained economic power, their same-sex relationships threatened the social order of the South, because of their potential to become more permanent. As the nature of female friendship came into question in the postwar period, unmarried women became more cautious of openly declaring their love for other women and moved cautiously within the gender conventions prescribed to them in order to preserve their growing autonomy.

Chapter 5   LAW, PROPERTY, AND THE
SINGLE WOMAN

Mary Reid, a slaveholding mistress from Halifax County, North Carolina, filed a divorce petition to the General Assembly of the state of
North Carolina in 1832. Having suffered what can only be described
as a horrific catalogue of marital abuse, Mary finally turned to the courts for protection.[1] The petitioner argued that her husband, Elias Reid, married her for her
property, which included "a very large personal estate consisting mostly of slaves,"
and the petitioner claimed that he cared little for her well-being or happiness.[2]
He had "banished" her "from the house and placed her at his Negro quarters"—
insulting her status as a lady by making her live among "Negroes" and "depriving
her of all the conveniences," of life, including adequate food provision—the most
basic of human requirements.[3] As a result of Elias Reid's failure to offer protection
and provision for his wife, Mary felt she was granted special dispensation to challenge his authority by seeking the higher protection of the law. As a southern lady,
her plight was complicated by her class, race, and social position, which meant that
her elevated status was dependent on submission to her husband's will. In a patriarchal society, in which she occupied a privileged social status compared to lower-
class white people and black people, women like Mary Reid had a reputation and
a stake in the system to protect by remaining married.[4] Up until the Civil War,
planter-class women understood that the relative advantages of their class were
tied to slavery and to their veneer of ladyhood.[5] However, as Mary Reid's case illustrates, there were occasions when married women were compelled to step outside
of their subordinate role in order to protect themselves, when their husbands had
failed them. They were required, in certain circumstances, to reject the authority of
their husbands in favor of the overarching patriarchy of the court in the hope of the
protection that it might offer them. By invoking the higher authority of the courts
women demonstrated their need for protection and provision in the absence of
a male protector, while at the same time exhibiting female agency in putting forward the request. Similar patterns can be traced in a variety of other petitions filed
by slaveholding women who were single or who petitioned for a return to their status as femme sole. This included setting up separate estates, rights to inheritance,
widows' requests for their dower share, or women (widows in particular) seeking
the courts' permission to sell land or slaves following a husband's death.

The petitions form part of the Race, Slavery and Free Blacks Petitions taken from southern legislatures in the period 1777–1867. Most of the petitions examined in this discussion fall in the period 1820–70, and a sizeable number are weighted in the antebellum and Civil War period, which helps to underline how the process of legal change was underway in the first half of the nineteenth century.[6] Important alterations to the law led to the broadening of the grounds for divorce, and to fairer property settlements for widows in the antebellum, Civil War, and Reconstruction eras.[7] Historians such as Jane Turner Censer argued that the nineteenth century saw the liberalization of divorce laws for southern women, which paralleled the social, economic, and political changes during the Civil War and postwar eras.[8] Evidence suggests that the broadening of divorce laws, rather than being a sign of liberalization that favored women, were in fact motivated by a conservative impulse to protect women and favor men who wanted to divorce their wives.[9] Similarly, the Married Women's Property Acts, which allowed married women to retain property in marriage in the form of a separate estate, were driven by a conservative ethos to safeguard the property of wealthy, slaveholding families, but also to protect women.

Legal Status

A woman's legal status was defined as either a "femme sole" or "femme covert." A femme sole was the legal term for a single woman and included women who were permanently single, widowed, or divorced. When a woman married, she became "a femme covert and a husband possessed a dependent wife."[10] The word "covert" literally means to be covered, and when a woman married her legal identity was covered by her husband and she lost any separate legal identity. Marriage, in theory, was a contract between a man and a woman, in which a woman forfeited her legal identity and her rights in exchange for the cover and protection of her husband, rendering her dependent on him in all respects. In reality "marriage negated a woman's powers to make contracts, or own and dispose of property in her own right; to write wills, or to engage in any form of business, or to testify and demand the obedience and guardianship of her children."[11] Marriage, then, equated to a loss of power for women, in a way that singleness did not. The law also gave men control over family finances, full custody of the children, and even the right and responsibility of governing wives' behavior "by physical force if necessary," which complicated petitions filed by wives who pleaded for divorce on grounds of cruelty as their situations were interpreted so broadly by judges from state to state.[12]

A single woman, or femme sole, had a distinct legal identity and certain rights enshrined in law that married women did not. A "single woman's legal status was for the most part, indistinguishable from the legal status of many men. A single woman could contract, own, dispose, write wills, engage in most forms of business, testify, [and] demand the obedience and the guardianship of her children."[13]

This put her in a unique and, in theory, potentially powerful position that was quite contrary to the "redundant" myth often attached to single women, and the suggestions they had failed in their pursuit of true womanhood and were a drain on their birth families. Simply put, single women retained their rights and identity under the law, whereas a married woman forfeited hers when she entered into the marital union. Given this context single women could be perceived as a potential threat to the rigid social order of southern society for their failure to comply with the expectations of nineteenth-century southern womanhood, inculcated also in the fact that they retained their legal independence. According to the Cult of True Womanhood, marriage and motherhood were essential markers of the nineteenth-century feminine ideal.[14] Through it women gained social respectability and, in theory, provision, purpose, and protection. Yet in reality marriage, rather than guaranteeing protection and provision for women, actually placed it in the safekeeping of a husband's hands and entrusted him to act in a wife's best interest. As Hendrik Hartog noted, "By marriage, a host of property rights, obligations, losses, gains, immunities, exemptions, remedies, and duties had come into one's life," and a wife had to rely on her good judgment in accepting a proposal of marriage and hope that it had been the right one.[15] Clearly there was a real dichotomy when it came to marriage because women exchanged legal autonomy for social respect. All southern women operated within a framework of gender conventions that curtailed their behavior in the nineteenth-century South. However, some women were also able to manipulate their class privilege in manifesting feminine or ladylike behavior in order to gain the sympathy of the courts. This tied in with education, standards of literacy, and a conscious awareness of the southern legal system, with all its inherent bias. Anya Jabour's work on young women in the Old South reflects on how women acted as "quiet revolutionaries . . . in waging a form of ideological—if safely invisible—warfare" by both accepting, but also quietly rejecting, the ideological constraints that threatened to destabilize their elevated race and class position in the southern hierarchy.[16]

Companionate marriage steadily rose over the course of the nineteenth century. In wealthy planter families, where keeping money within extended families was customary, marriage between cousins was common, yet the currents of change remained apparent. Wealthy southern families were often instructive in persuading their daughters on suitable marital partners, thus ensuring their wealth and social standing were not compromised at the top of the social hierarchy. However, parents increasingly recognized that wealth and assets were not enough to make a happy union. With the dawning of the nineteenth century, a new consensus started to build that saw marriage as a union that could, and increasingly should, be for love, hence the term "companionate marriage"—a marriage built on companionship and love.[17] Paradoxically the advantages of a single life were emphasized more strongly as ideals of companionate marriage became more prominent—a single life was preferable to a bad marriage. Historian Suzanne Lebsock argued that the rise in companionate marriage enhanced women's status in domestic life, by providing women with "greater power, greater autonomy, and a strong, even equal voice, in family affairs," a thought echoed by historians, such as Carl Degler.[18] Yet, even though companionate marriage was the "ideal," it was not always widespread, and it remained frequently challenged by ingrained social, political, economic, and legal attitudes that were slow to die out.[19] Expectations of marriage were heightened, which prompted disappointment for men and women who felt that their raised expectations had not been met. Social historians have also developed their own interpretation of divorce, informed by the concept of companionate marriage. Their argument maintains that changing expectations in marriage (and the high hopes of finding a suitable love match) led to inevitable disappointments if and when marriages failed, coupled with a greater willingness to dissolve what was perceived as a "flawed marriage."[20] The companionate marriage ideal made women "start to complain of men's adultery and men of women's desertion," which is strongly reflected in the divorce petitions examined here.[21] In other words the rise in the expectations of marriage led women to become more confrontational—or at least more vocal—in their expectations of the marital union. Men perceived opinionated women, who were willing to exert themselves, to be exhibiting subversive behavior that fell outside of the realms of "true womanhood," thus creating friction in marriages that were not built on the solid foundations of companionship and love. As the century progressed, the liberalization of divorce laws started to reflect the increasing demand for companionate marriage and the growing belief that women (and men) deserved to be happy in their marriages. This led to an increasing number of (men and) women starting to file for divorce if and when their needs or expectations of marriage were not fulfilled. These requests were also increasingly granted.[22]

Divorce

There were many reasons why men and women petitioned the court for a divorce. The outcome of the petitions varied enormously according to when the petitions were submitted, where (that is, which state they were submitted in), and by whom (the social class of the petitioner). The process of obtaining a divorce was still fraught with hazard in the nineteenth century, and cases regularly hinged on *upholding conventional views about femininity*: the need for female protection; a woman's vulnerability to cruelty; and the necessity of financial independence for her own sake and for her children's welfare, in the face of neglect, drunkenness, or cruelty. In early nineteenth-century law, the only grounds for divorce were having a shared ancestry or blood relation, insanity (which was difficult to prove), impotence at the time of marriage, and bigamy. As the century progressed, the majority of the southern states also decreed "adultery, cruelty, and desertion" to be causes for divorce, but the courts' interpretation of what constituted cruelty in particular varied tremendously from state to state.[23] This is reflected in the wide range of divorce petitions filed by white, southern women from state to state and in the reaction they received from the courts. It would seem that a woman's chances of having a divorce petition granted hinged on a number of different factors including: which state she filed her divorce petition in, what her race and social class were, and last, and quite importantly, if she had demonstrated that she was an upstanding woman or "true woman" in the eyes of the community. In order to gain the sympathy of the courts, slaveholding women petitioning for a divorce had to demonstrate that they had fulfilled the tenets of true womanhood in their marriage. They had to show that they had done everything in their power to make a marriage work, including turning a blind eye to minor indiscretions or annoyances from their husbands, if they were to be granted a divorce and returned to their single status. It was vital that women act with ladylike decorum in order to gain the approval of the legislative body, which had a clear class dimension attached to it, which included showing they were faultless in almost every way.[24] Additionally they had to prove that their husband had failed in his duty to provide protection and provision for his wife (and family).

There were two main categories of divorce, a bed-and-board divorce, or "mensa et thoro," and a complete, or total, divorce. The former to all intents and purposes was a legal separation, but within a continuing marriage. It is important to remember, as Norma Basch pointed out, that for "all of the nineteenth and much of the twentieth century" divorce only "provided relief for the wronged or innocent spouse," and it was granted only on very specific grounds. Therefore when filing a divorce petition it was vital that women could identify and validate acceptable reasons for having their appeal granted.[25] This was obviously far easier for well-educated, literate white women from the middle or upper class who were more able to manipulate their position as "true women," demonstrating what Jabour referred to as "a prudent awareness of the balance of power."[26] Norma Basch described divorce as "the gambit of the desperate," because it was the final avenue open to women who found themselves in extreme or desperate circumstances.[27] When a woman was threatened with loss of property or financial devastation, or if she felt that she was in grave personal danger, she was compelled to take drastic action. Some women reached out to their family or to the local community for help; others appealed to the legislative body to validate and then act on their claims; some women did both. Basch argued that divorce had little to do with the desire for female autonomy but argued that women who sought divorce had generally exhausted any other options available to them. Divorce embodied a final attempt to have their voice heard, and to have their concerns validated in the court of law. The chief motivation was protection, provision, and personal survival.[28]

Julia Patterson complained that the "cruel, harsh and inhuman" manner and frequent "intoxication" with liquor of her husband, George Patterson, rendered her vulnerable and defenseless in his "care." She explained to the courts how she had once taken refuge with her mother, "in order that she might be provided with the necessities of life," which echoes Mary Reid's exact words in her petition to divorce her husband, Elias Reid, some thirty years earlier. Unlike Mary Reid, Julia Patterson was lured back to the marital home, and she attempted to make the marriage work for a second time; shortly thereafter she fled for good and petitioned the court for a divorce and relief from her husband, in February 1865.[29] When a petition was granted it restored a woman's legal status as a femme sole and it resulted in the reinstatement of certain rights and qualifications. In doing so it allowed single women to provide for themselves because the court had intervened to protect them. This included women who were widowed and subsequently remarried, such as Rachel Miller, who petitioned for a divorce from her second husband, Isaac Miller, in March 1866. Having endured five years of abusive behavior from him, she finally petitioned the court for a divorce, noting that a year earlier, her husband had "struck her a violent blow in the breast" and "shoved her down on the floor hurting her very much."[30] Rachel found herself in a vulnerable position, with five young children from her previous marriage, still to raise. Rachel asked the court for a divorce and alimony, fully aware that she had relinquished all her property to Isaac upon their marriage. According to the petition this included a "sizeable estate including horses, cattle, hogs, sheep, a wagon, buggy, a large amount of furniture and 8 slaves."[31] The court clearly favored her case, and her petition was granted on 28 May 1866, a little under three months after it was filed.[32]

There are numerous cases of white, southern women petitioning for a divorce from their husbands, often citing the need for protection. Margaret Selina Oliver, a slaveholding widow from Lowndes County, Alabama, found herself in such a position. Having shown considerable personal agency in accepting the role of coadministrator of the estate of her first husband, John McGill, which included over fifty slaves, and a "large real and personal estate consisting of lands and slaves and other personal property to a large amount," Margaret Oliver's situation soon became more complicated.[33] After Margaret's subsequent marriage to second husband, Creed Oliver, the administration of the property fell into his hands. For Margaret this was a mixed blessing; handing over power and control of an estate to her second husband placed her in a vulnerable and dependent position. Consider then how disappointed Margaret must have been, and how vulnerable she must have felt, when her second marriage started to turn sour. Remarriage was fraught with pitfalls, legally, economically, and personally, and a second (or subsequent) marriage had serious legal and economic consequences for a woman and her dependents unless she had taken precautionary measures to safeguard her property in a trust or separate estate. Margaret recalled with regret "the cruel and barbarous treatment" that Creed Oliver began exhibiting toward her. He threw "open knives" with "great force and violence" and even threatened her life with a "loaded pistol" on one occasion.[34] Fearing that her safety (as well as her property) was in jeopardy, Margaret galvanized into action and appealed to the court for its protection. The urgency of Margaret's personal circumstances propelled her to make public what would otherwise be a private family matter.[35] Her case illustrates how women filing for a divorce were often propelled by their desire for "protection" from a villainous husband who had failed to provide the provision and the protection promised to her in marriage, and in Margaret's case the appeal was granted. This was extremely important, as a granted petition effectively restored a woman's status as a femme sole, and it resulted in the reinstatement of certain rights and qualifications. In doing so it allowed single women to provide for themselves because the court had intervened to protect them.

Margaret Oliver's plight therefore resonates with the cases of other planter-class women for whom divorce was overwhelmingly about upholding traditional gender conventions in marriage, for both men *and* women. As slaveholding women from the highest echelons of southern society, their expectations of marriage and motherhood were tied to the protection and provision ideals promised to them in their coverture in exchange for their legal anonymity and sexual subordination. Margaret Oliver was not alone; numerous cases illustrate this point. Sarah Mason from Franklin County, Virginia, petitioned for a divorce from her husband, Nathan Mason, in 1863 following "violent" and "abusive" episodes from said husband, including "frequently beating and choking her" in addition to his "adulterous or illicit intercourse" with other women. Sarah's petition to the court stressed two key points: her femininity and her right to "reasonable maintenance" based on the fact that she had brought six slaves and a tract of land into their marriage. The petitioner stated plainly, "it is a duty which she owes to herself, and to the dignity of her sex . . . to sever the existing relation between them," and she appealed to the court to grant her "a dissolution of marriage and reasonable maintenance."[36] The most interesting part of Sarah Mason's divorce petition is in the exact wording chosen in writing her plea; she described it "as a duty" to seek a divorce from her husband, as well as a necessity to uphold "the dignity of her sex."[37] In doing so she highlighted the manner in which female petitioners often evoked the sympathy of the court by stressing their femininity, which lay in jeopardy and which needed protecting by the courts. This is tightly interwoven with their race and class position as slaveholding women, who were considered the embodiment of southern femininity, in stark contrast to poorer white people and enslaved black women, who were considered as lying outside of the parameters of femininity.

Likewise Mary Terry from Goochland County, Virginia, stressed in her petition to the court in 1850 that her personal conduct throughout her fifteen-year marriage to her husband, William Terry, had been exemplary and that she had acted as "a dutiful and affectionate wife."[38] Mary clearly understood the importance of couching her request for divorce in the language of benevolence and duty, and she was keen to prove that she was not in any way to blame for her husband abandoning herself and children, to instead live in adultery with a "Negro" woman.[39] In the closing lines of Mary Terry's petition, she took pains to emphasize "the extraordinary conduct of her said husband," which had "not been brought about by any neglect of duty or affection on her part."[40] The wording of Mary Terry's petition was once again typical of most divorce petitions filed by female plaintiffs at the time. Women not only had to show that their husbands were at fault and why; but they also had to prove that *they* were the innocent victims of that abuse, if they were to regain their status as a femme sole.[41] These cases demonstrate that divorce was a hazardous area for married women, and their success or failure in navigating the legal system often hinged on their understanding of, and ability to manipulate, the legal system to their advantage, which could then provide a route to enhanced personal autonomy.

However, the law "offered limited use in seeking relief from overbearing husbands precisely because the law so favored the authority of the husband over the wife," which reflected the patriarchal society of the nineteenth-century South.[42] For example in Texas Sarah Black told a similar story of marital discord and abuse. She sought a divorce and alimony from her husband, James Black, in Brazoria County. She had caught him "in the act of having illicit sexual intercourse" with two of his slaves, a "mulatto" woman named Susan and "a Negro woman named Ann or Annie" in 1855. When she confronted him, he threatened her with "a damned good whipping or cowhiding," presumably for what he considered to be an outspoken and unladylike outburst. He told her "he would give it [the whipping] to her unless she minded her own business." Sarah recalled the profane language used by her husband, reporting that he had called her "a god damned bitch."[43] He also instructed the slaves on his plantation to disobey her orders, further undermining and demeaning her status. She reported feeling threatened, surrounded by recalcitrant slaves, who chanted at her, calling her a liar, which belittled her to such a degree that she felt her status was as low as a "Negro" enslaved on the plantation, again revealing the interplay of race, class, and gender positions in nineteenth-century southern society. The overseer told her that he had been "given orders not to punish any of the servants at her request," which eroded her authority further still.[44] Yet in spite of this catalogue of indiscretions Sarah Black's petition was unsuccessful, and her case was dismissed by the courts. Although it is difficult to substantiate, it is possible that the court were unconvinced that Sarah had acted with sufficient ladylike decorum. Since she had remonstrated against her husband, and challenged his authority, the court may have decided that she had actually provoked the physical attack he made on her and therefore was undeserving of the court's protection.[45]

The results of the petitions are not always clear: some appeals were partially granted, others were referred on, and no final results are recorded for others. Jane Brown, from Guilford County, North Carolina, suffered a catalogue of physical and mental abuse over the course of her twenty-nine-year marriage to Hayley Brown. Her husband had "beaten her with a stick" and insulted her honor by sleeping with a white woman, who he later eloped with (which also brings up a whole raft of new questions about the white woman's conduct and why Hayley Brown was willing to run off with her, as she clearly thwarted any conventions of femininity). Brown was "a man of large estate" consisting of "valuable lands, stock, horses, mules, cash, notes, bonds, and twelve or thirteen slaves," which propelled his wife into an appeal to the court. Jane, fearful that her husband might flee the state and sell their property, which included their slaves, appealed to the court for a divorce and alimony. Her request was partially granted, which led to a degree of financial security, and with it a route to enhanced personal autonomy.[46] Other women were significantly less fortunate in claiming to the courts for protection or support, even though their stories were marked by extreme violence and cruelty. The reasons why these individual petitions were denied (or in some cases only partially granted) again requires further investigation, as they reveal a great deal about the southern mindset and prescriptions of femininity.

Martha Smith Green from Williamson County, Tennessee, had her divorce petition rejected in 1829 in spite of what she described as "violent" physical abuse that was so horrific that she "carried the marks . . . on her body for twenty weeks."[47] Desperate to seek protection from her husband's malicious conduct and fearing for her life, Martha attempted to escape, sneaking out of their plantation home, cloaked in the cover of darkness, and fled to her father's house in search of safety. Martha did not escape from the plantation home unnoticed. Her husband "pursued" her with "Negroes and dogs," until he caught her and dragged her back to the plantation home in a "violent" manner.[48] That night's terrifying events acted as a catalyst that sparked a long period of ill health for Martha that became so serious that she almost died. Nevertheless it was only under considerable duress that Thomas Green (her husband) finally relented and had her removed to her father's house for recuperation and medical care, so keen was he to exhibit his patriarchal authority over her in a clear display of gender roles. This demonstrates how slave-holding women's position in the southern hierarchy—regardless of their privilege and class—was ultimately tied to their subordinate status to male authority. The intervention of Martha's father and the pressure that he exerted on Green as a rival figure of male authority resulted in Martha being granted temporary relief from a violent and abusive marriage. Nonetheless in the end Martha's divorce petition to the court was ultimately rejected, proving that in her case at least, even the forced arbitration of her father had limited power in changing the long-term decision of the courts, in whether or not to extend its protection toward her, and grant her a divorce, which it did not. Thus Martha's personal autonomy remained checked by the power and authority of the southern judiciary. There are a number of possible reasons why her petition was rejected. As a wealthy planter, her husband may have exercised a considerable amount of influence in the county, which afforded him preferential treatment in court. Also in spite of Mary's emphasis of her own lady-like and dutiful conduct, she did admit that she had "remonstrated" against her husband, simultaneously claiming that she had been "dutiful" and "affectionate" in her conduct. Therefore her behavior may have negated any claims that she was the innocent party. The case states that Thomas Green had "knocked her back" in response to her "remonstrations" to his accusations that she was too familiar with other gentleman.[49] Therefore the case of Martha Green illustrates an important point. Elite women seeking a divorce would fare better if they demonstrated an ongoing adherence to traditional gender conventions within marriage. It helped the court decide if a woman was indeed worthy of its protection, which ultimately led to a favorable divorce settlement or outcome.[50]

In a similar case Mary Hookins from Anderson County, Tennessee, had her divorce petition rejected by the courts some fifteen years later, in 1846, again in the state of Tennessee. In her petition she described the gradual deterioration of her husband's conduct toward her (like so many other similar petitions lodged within a broad chronological timeframe), which began as verbal abuse but quickly developed into violence, adultery, and desertion. As in the case of Martha Green, Hookins admitted that she had "remonstrated" against her husband's conduct. In reference to his adultery, she reflected, "when your petitioner greatly remonstrated against his conduct, so far from apologizing for his acts, he picked up a poker and flourished it over her head, knocked down her cupboard, broke down her table, furniture and cups and saucers into a thousand pieces."[51] When he whipped her for "no good reason" she again objected, to which he remarked, "He would whip her every day of her life if he wanted to."[52] This aggressive display of masculinity, typically associated with the punishment of slaves, rather than southern wives, reiterates a manifestation of male power, and with it the inherent expectation of female subordination. However bad the situation, southern wives were not expected to remonstrate but instead were expected to show quiet submission in line with prescribed models of femininity. These cases highlight the manner in which the court sympathized with middle-class and upper-class women who conformed to traditional models of southern womanhood. If women proved that they were pure, submissive, needy, and dependent, they were rewarded with the court's protection. Any sign that a woman protested against her husband, or challenged his authority in any small way, could be interpreted as unladylike or subversive behavior. This in turn warranted physical chastisement from her husband, from which she deserved no protection from the courts, much less a divorce that threatened the patriarchal order.

Therefore women often constructed their divorce petitions in such a way so as to gain the sympathy of the courts, and in doing so they maximized their chances of their petitions being passed, thus regaining them their single status.[53] The evidence suggests that this remained the case as late as 1855, and even though the courts' interpretation of what constituted "cruelty" inside marriage was slowly altering, these changes were patchy and varied considerably from state to state. For example women who filed for divorce in Alabama, North Carolina, Tennessee, or Louisiana on the grounds of cruelty had an increased chance of their petition being granted than in other states. This also reflected the courts' desire to protect innocent victims against *excessive* cruelty or personal abuse in a society that vested so much power into the hands of men. The legislative body therefore aimed to protect "wronged wives" rather more than to provide women with an enhanced level of personal autonomy.[54] As a result women who voluntarily sought a divorce had to prove (without any shadow of doubt) that they had lived an upstanding, good, and moral life as a southern wife. Women often wanted to protect themselves from personal indignities or false accusations that could potentially tarnish their good character. This again reflected the importance of nineteenth-century gender conventions, which were particularly marked in the petitions of women from the elite class. This was connected to their status as southern ladies and the added pressure to continually prove that they were upholding the tenets of true womanhood in a manner that was absent from the petitions of lower-class white men and women.

In the divorce petitions filed by poorer white men, the overwhelming reason cited by men seeking a divorce from their wives was the accusation of sexual infidelity. Women were reported to have indulged in extramarital sexual liaisons (often with black men) resulting in the birth of a "mulatto" child. These cases had a clear class bias and only rarely surfaced for the elite classes.[55] Norfleet Perry appealed to the court of Tennessee as early as 1819, complaining that his wife, Rachael, had "delivered of a mulatto child," six months into their marriage.[56] In Haywood County, North Carolina, John Chambers, a lower-class white man, requested an annulment of his marriage to Riney O'Neal. His divorce petition claimed that his wife "about two weeks after marriage . . . was charged with having delivered of a mulatto child," which he declared he previously knew nothing about.[57] Thomas Culpepper filed a similar divorce petition in December 1835, in light of his wife's actions that had "polluted the marriage bed" by her "engaging in carnal intercourse" with "black men."[58] It was at the court's discretion to interpret cases such as John Chambers's and Thomas Culpepper's and to disentangle fact from fiction. However, what we do know by reading through the petitions was that there were far more accusations of sexual infidelity that resulted in the birth of "mulatto children" filed by the lower class than from middle-to-upper-class white men, which suggests that ideas about female sexuality were also driven by class (and race) ideals.

This strong race and class bias is of uppermost importance when evaluating the divorce petitions of slaveholding white people. As previously discussed, the protection of a woman's "virtue" was of considerable importance to planter-class women (in marriage, widowhood, or nonmarriage) as it was connected to the embodiment of gender roles, and dominant prescriptions of femininity dictated to them by the society in which they lived. Slaveholding families naturally had a larger proportion of property, and therefore it should come as no surprise that the majority of the petitions regarding property came from the elite class. Elite, slaveholding women had a greater investment (in property) to protect in appealing to the courts for help. By examining the various petitions, it is apparent that the courts rarely extended their protection to poorer white women, as they were not considered worthy of the support of the courts in the same way as wealthy white women were. In the antebellum era, a strong class and race bias perceived lower-class white women and black people as having a far lower threshold to behave as true women and conversely a far higher one when it came to dealing with personal offences. Elite women by contrast were considered far more "delicate" and "refined" in their conduct and nature, creatures that could easily be troubled or affected by verbal insults and personal indignities targeted at them.[59] Judge George Goldthwaite of the Alabama Supreme Court in 1855 spoke with reference to personal indignities and stated that, "Between persons of education, refinement, and delicacy, the slightest blow in anger might be cruelty; while between persons of a different character and walk in life, blows might occasionally pass without marring to any great extent their conjugal relations or materially interfering with their happiness. We can lay down no certain rule, as to what violence will amount to cruelty, when it does not affect life, limb or health. Each case must depend on its own particular circumstances."[60] Judge Goldthwaite was referring to what Jane Turner Censer termed "relativism."[61] Relativism was imperative to the way in which southern legislatures dealt with divorce petitions of southern women and with regard to other areas of disparity such as race.

As many of these divorce cases have demonstrated, the concept of cruelty was broad and variable in how it was perceived and interpreted by the courts, which varied considerably from state to state, supporting the claim that the broadening of divorce law in the South was an uneven and patchy process. For example in antebellum Georgia common law was followed to the letter. The code read, "In this state the husband is the head of the family, and the wife is subject to him," which made it much harder for women to obtain a divorce if they resided there.[62] This is reflected in the court petitions, which reveal the ways in which Georgian women were subject to more extreme legal demands than women in many of their sister states. The process of legal reform was slow and measured in Georgia; it was not until Reconstruction that changes occurred.[63] By contrast in Alabama the statute of 1820 requiring "cruelty to endanger life" was modified by 1832 "to cruel and barbarous and inhuman treatment."[64] In Texas an additional clause concerning cruelty was passed in 1841 that permitted divorce on grounds of "excesses, cruel treatment, or outrages towards the other [person]" and if "such ill treatment is of such a nature, as to lend their being together insupportable."[65] It helped to dilute traditional interpretations of what previously constituted as cruelty. In Florida, again, it was much easier to obtain a divorce on grounds of cruelty. Eliza Patterson had her petition passed granting her a divorce from her husband, Alexander Patterson, in Monroe County, Florida, in December 1836 because of his "cruel and inhuman treatment" and "criminal connection" with a slave girl.[66] Clearly the state in which a petitioner resided played an important part in determining if the divorce petition was passed. Carl Degler argued that the new emphasis on cruelty (and the broadening of the grounds for divorce) was a reflection of a growth in female autonomy. Degler posited that women were demanding their rights for protection under the doctrine of separate spheres.[67] In other words women manipulated the conservative ethos of the South (and of the courts) and used their dependent status to their advantage, claiming that they had a right to do so because of their husbands' failure to protect them. Therefore from conservative soil sprang more radical social change for single women. For slaveholding women, who were considered to be the personification of femininity, their right to male protection was far more pressing than the appeals of black women or lower-class white women. Slaveholding women often had greater success in their appeals to the court, which mirrored their elevated social status, and the evidence in the court petitions reflects this fact.

As the nineteenth century progressed, women (and men) began to file for divorce on an expanding list of personal grievances. In the late antebellum period, for women this included a raft of "unreasonable behavior" such as drunkenness, cruelty, and neglect to provide, which reflected the broadening of divorce laws from state to state.[68] By the end of the antebellum period, North Carolina, Tennessee, Arkansas, and Texas all granted divorces on grounds of cruelty without physical violence, which previously had not been a key constituent for divorce. As these cases demonstrate, the liberalization of divorce laws was a step forward for women living in intolerable circumstances. It offered them a measure of relief if they were able to prove that their cases aligned with very specific guidelines. As increasing numbers of southern women filed for a divorce, fresh interpretations on the common law came about. While women still operated within certain legal limitations, their scope was slowly widening, and women seized the opportunity to have their voices heard, which granted them additional rights and freedom within the law and in relation to property. Similarly, following the Civil War, men started to cite wives' "failure to live up to the idea of the submissive subordinate" as reasons for divorce, which reflects the heightened social shifts in the construction of gender in the Civil War and postwar periods.[69] As women's lives were reshaped in wartime, women began to foster alternative ideas on marriage, which is perhaps reflected in their reticence to conform to gender roles, particularly if they were married to men who clearly were unwilling to live up to theirs. Victoria Bynum suggested that divorce favored men in the case of North Carolina, which again highlights the patchy, uneven transformations in divorce law.[70]

In the postwar period, men and women became less constrained by their separate spheres, and both parties were more willing to air their grievances in the event of an unhappy marriage. This is also indicative of the social shifts in men and women's roles in the Reconstruction era. By the late 1860s, men complained of cruelty from their wives as grounds for divorce, which included wives who spoke to them too harshly (or in an unfeminine manner), or who lost their temper, throwing objects at them. Degler estimates that there were almost 13,680 divorce petitions filed on the grounds of cruelty in the five-year period from 1901 to 1906, which suggests that women were actively rejecting the prescriptions of femininity that had dominated their lives in the early nineteenth century. By rejecting these notions of passive womanhood, and voluntarily seeking a divorce, women were making a statement that broke free from the constraints of the past.[71] While some elite, slaveholding women still attempted to prop up a failed southern hierarchy, by returning to their prewar roles, which had temporarily shifted in line with the vagaries so war, others continued to be influenced by ideals of companionate marriage. Reconstruction may well have been an era marked by a return to old values in the South in order to reassert control over freed slaves and white women.[72] Yet even in the context of heightened conservatism, southern women's roles still continued to change, though the process remained uneven from state to state. In Arkansas, Mississippi, and Florida more lenient terms were introduced that dealt with cruelty, and in Arkansas and Florida a woman could be granted a divorce if her husband had abandoned her for as little as a year, compared to five in Virginia.[73] In Mississippi adultery and desertion were also considered worthy of an "absolute" divorce, but "cruelty" was still a bed-and-board offence until later in the nineteenth century.[74] In Arkansas, Florida, Georgia, Louisiana, or Mississippi, "drunkenness" was another validated cause for divorce.

In spite of the uneven reforms in divorce, the trend was clear that it was generally becoming easier for a woman to obtain a divorce that freed her from an unhappy marriage. According to Degler two-thirds of divorces were granted to women in 1860, which indicates that the postwar years led to a burgeoning in the rights of women, and an avenue to enhanced personal autonomy.[75] From 1872 to 1876, "some 63 percent of all divorces granted to women were for grounds that implied inadequate familial behavior by husbands. The general grounds were cruelty, desertion, drunkenness and neglect to provide."[76] For example Winney Jeter complained in a divorce petition to the chancery courts of Alabama in 1844 that "her husband failed to protect her"; Virginian Sally Ballinger accused her husband of "forgetting his duties," as he was so consumed with drinking and infidelity.[77] On 29 April 1864 Elizabeth Rea also filed for a divorce and alimony from her husband, who she claimed was "much addicted to intoxication."[78] In some states, being convicted of a felony also represented adequate grounds for a divorce. Therefore an awareness of the legal system and the prerequisites for divorce was important, as it directly affected a petitioner's chances of his or her appeal being granted. Different clauses existed that gave justices powers to grant divorces for "any other just cause," and these clauses were again very much open to interpretation, which meant that women wanting a dissolution of marriage often trod on unsteady ground. This was particularly true in relation to the cruelty and indignity clauses.[79] By the end of the antebellum period, North Carolina, Tennessee, Arkansas, and Texas all granted divorces on grounds of cruelty without physical violence (that is, mental cruelty), which had not previously been the case. As these cases demonstrate, the liberalization of divorce laws was a step forward for women living in intolerable circumstances. It offered them a measure of relief, if they were able to prove their cases aligned within very specific guidelines.

As increasing numbers of southern women filed for a divorce, new interpretations on common law came about. While women still operated within certain legal limitations, their scope was slowly widening, and women seized the opportunity to have their voices heard, which granted them additional rights and freedom within the law and in relation to property. This evidence contributes to a broadening picture of divorce in the nineteenth-century south. It demonstrates the way in which planter-class women were able to manipulate their status as ladies as a means to achieving a divorce.[80] Two key themes emerge from the divorce petitions—the need for protection and for provision, especially when women had children to support and provide for. As Degler argued, women were less concerned about male infidelity and were often willing to overlook these shortcomings, particularly if their husband promised to change his ways. This can be seen in the case of Gatsey Stevenson from Lenoir County in North Carolina. Gatsey had returned to her "wayward," "drunken," and "adulterous" husband following twelve to eighteen months' separation, during which time she lived with her four children at her father's house.[81] She described how she was "doomed to disappointment" for when she was eventually persuaded to return to the marital home, her husband let her down once again. He had "wasted" their property, which included her "filial portion" brought to him in marriage. This consisted of "a valuable stock, and a plantation at the time of the value of $1000 or $2000."[82] It was at this point, when the issue of family provision and the protection of property came into sharp focus, that Gatsey was far less forgiving, and she forged ahead with her petition, publically airing her grievances in the public setting of the court, which included an appeal to return to her legal status as femme sole, in an effort to care for and protect herself and children. Her case resonates with slaveholding women in similar predicaments and underlines the reluctance of many women to leave the marital union, until they felt forced to do so, because of the urgency of their personal circumstances.

In the postwar period divorce became more accessible and hence more widespread, which led to an opportunity for increased female autonomy in the public sphere. This highlights the shift in the nature of marriage but also, just as crucially, a change in men's and women's perceptions of what constituted acceptable gender roles. In the postwar period, the South may well have attempted to return to the conservatism of its past, in the way that some men and women (particularly from the old elites) tried to reassert gender roles. The courts reflect this in some respects, such as in their preferential treatment to elite women who had fulfilled the ideal of true womanhood but who had been let down by their husbands. The era of Reconstruction was also marked by the slow but steady liberalization of divorce laws, which may well have sprung from conservative roots but which nonetheless enabled women an easier route to divorce and therefore a voluntary return to their femme sole status.

Property

Women also required alimony and the protection of their property. In 1861 Hannah Crawford filed a petition for a divorce from her husband, Jesse Crawford. Despite a marriage spanning over fifty years, Hannah claimed that she had lived unhappily for the last twenty years because of her husband's "personal abuse and violent manner" and sought a "fair and equal division" of their "handsome estate" of land and slaves. In the Crawford case, they managed to make "a division and partition of [their] property without the intervention of the court."[83] Many others did not. In Talladega County, Alabama, in 1861, Margaret Merritt requested the courts to remove her estranged husband as trustee of her slave property or from "intermeddling" with her property after she had filed for a divorce and alimony.[84] Still feeling constrained by her husband's interference in her financial affairs, Merritt was willing to take her complaint to a higher body. Finally, in 1868, a full seven years after her request was lodged, her plea was eventually granted. Why the plea took so long to reach a conclusion is open to speculation, and yet what her case demonstrates is that the protection of property was just as important to slaveholding women as a return to their femme sole status. Without it they were stripped of their ability to remain self-sufficient, rendering a divorce useless.

Women also complained about their husbands' initial motivations to marry them. Lucy Norman from Henry County, Virginia, filed for a divorce on 20

December 1848. After a brief spell of marital happiness, the Norman marriage quickly unraveled in line with her husband's "dissipated habits," "violence" and "adultery," which culminated in him deserting Lucy for another woman. Yet Lucy Norman had more to protect than simply her good name. She was at pains to emphasize how much her husband had gained as a result of their marriage, including his ownership of "a large estate with lands and negroes," that she had provided in 1844.[85] Norman and women like her therefore showed considerable autonomy in seeking compensation for property lost to dishonest or villainous husbands in the process of seeking a divorce. Similar tales of men tricking women into marriage for monetary gain are legion. Polly Reid from North Carolina claimed her husband married her for her property in 1832.[86] Similarly Virginian Mary Lawson sought a divorce from her husband, Fabius Lawson, in January 1840.[87] In the statement she made to the court, Mary claimed that Fabius had deprived her of all her money and never "conferred upon me a cent."[88] She also made it plain that he married her for her property and consequently "deprived me of a portion of that which was my own property and I am now left without adequate means of support."[89] Wealthy women were still at risk because in spite of the rise in companionate marriages, some men continued to harbor more selfish motivations for marriage, namely gaining property. Fathers could protect their daughters' welfare by protecting their property in the form of a separate estate, which again had a strong race and class bias attached to it.

Ruth Balderee was one such woman, residing in South Carolina. One of the most recalcitrant states in the South, historians have noted that it was "virtually impossible" to obtain a divorce there. South Carolina was a staunchly conservative, slaveholding state that placed a high value on marriage, and therefore those in power did everything they could to protect the marital union and were extremely reluctant to dissolve marriage under any circumstances.[90] The highest concentration of wealthy, planter-class families came from the southern seaboard states. They were the arbiters of power and wealth in the region and as such were well represented in politics and the legislative system. South Carolina was particularly strict regarding its divorce laws, and it was not until 1868 that it "granted a divorce with the right to remarry"; however, it did accommodate wives some relief from "intolerable" marriages. In an 1822 statute, women were provided with a bed-and-board divorce in cases of "intolerable ill temper" or adulterous behavior from either of the parties, which was a huge step forward.[91] However, as Ruth Balderee discovered, there were other ways that a woman could hold on to family property. One of these was signing a prenuptial agreement, or ring-fencing property in what was commonly referred to as a separate estate, which is exactly what Ruth did. Prior to her marriage in 1819, Ruth and her fiancé, Sterling Balderee, signed a contract granting her control of a separate estate. The question of what motivated Ruth Balderee to take such an action seems self-evident as she was in possession of a large number of properties and slaves and had a vested interest in protecting them. Sterling Balderee, her fiancé, was "financially destitute" and had little, if any, property of his own, yet he was still willing to allow his wife-to-be, Ruth, to retain her land and slaves. He must have anticipated that by doing this he was actually protecting the property from falling into the hands of creditors, who would have seized it had it been passed into his hands. Like many men who allowed their wives (or future wives) to set up a separate estate, there was almost always an ulterior motive, in preventing property falling into the hands of creditors, which it would almost certainly have done in Sterling Balderee's case.[92]

In the economic crisis of the 1830s, men became increasingly concerned about losing their own property and therefore set up separate estates, called equitable trusts, for women, in the hope of saving their own property, without any foresight into the long-term ramifications of their spurious actions.[93] As it so happened, it was also a prudent decision on Ruth Balderee's behalf, as it sheltered her from financial destitution in the future, when her marriage started to unravel. When Sterling's behavior became "vulgar" and he started to beat and whip his wife, she had some economic recourse, and she left the family home and filed for a divorce. Ruth was an autonomous woman who was propelled by her husband's extreme behavior to fall back on his promise of a separate estate. Sterling had clearly given little consideration to his earlier agreement of granting his fiancé a separate estate, which later resulted in her request for the return of her property and twenty-four slaves, which was partially granted by the court.[94] The separate estate had several different functions. In the eyes of the law it safeguarded men and women from economic ruin. In the 1830s women even began to trade their dower rights to secure separate estates for themselves, a point that will be explained more fully later on. Separate estates were also a means of keeping wealth or property in the family and effectively ring-fencing it from unscrupulous husbands. The creation of separate estates benefited wealthy families as it "increased the odds that legacies would pass intact from one generation to the next," rather than being lost or squandered at the hands of "unreliable men."[95]

The passing of the Married Women's Property Acts, the most important of which was in 1848, and the gradual erosion of coverture meant single women benefited from property protection, whether they were never married or if they had become single again at some stage in their life course.[96] The separate estate could also be useful to widows, particularly if they were considering remarriage, for they were loath to forfeit the terms of their inheritance or jeopardize any property held in trust for their children. Therefore the separate estate offered them some protection. The area of property provision and protection was of vital importance to all women, not only to those who married. After all, at some stage of their lives, all women were single: it was the natural trajectory that formed part of their lives as young women, and many of those women who married later regained their femme sole status through widowhood or divorce. "Most women probably moved through the full spectrum from spinster to wife to widow throughout their life course," and at some stage the issue of property would be an issue to each and every one of them.[97]

There were many different forms of property protection. In the postwar period the number of never-married women who had a separate estate rose dramatically. "In the past spinster daughters could expect for no more than a provision of a home with an inheriting sibling in a will."[98] By 1850 a new pattern was emerging whereby never-married daughters began to benefit from family inheritance as past qualifications were removed concerning a woman's marital status and whether or not she would be left anything in a father or sibling's will. Jane Turner Censer argued that "the typical child in old elite Upper South families could expect a share of the patrimony relatively similar to that of a sibling," which was a huge step forward for unmarried women.[99] It also demonstrated a growing acceptance in the family and in society in general toward the single woman. She was not simply provided for, but she was counted as an individual with her own legal identity and rights, which were not swept aside by social condemnation or disapproval. Margaret and Mildred Cameron, the two unmarried daughters of the banker and planter Duncan Cameron of Orange County in North Carolina, provide a good illustration of this point. Duncan Cameron died in 1856, and in his will he ensured appropriate provision for all his children. His son, Paul Cameron, received the largest legacy, and he took "Fairntosh plantation in Orange County, North Carolina and the lands and the slaves in Greene County, Alabama."[100] The remainder of his slaves were divided between his four children, Paul, Margaret, Mildred (who were both single), and Thomas who was mentally disabled and received his share in trust. The two girls jointly inherited Cameron's house near Raleigh and its hundreds of acres of land, and Mildred received the Brick House plantation in her own right. Cameron knew that his eldest daughter, Margaret (and helpmeet for Mildred), was likely to marry her long-term suitor, George Mordecai, and therefore he ensured that the provision for Mildred was especially generous. This example clearly shows that unmarried women were not necessarily disadvantaged if they chose to remain single for life in the nineteenth-century South, and also within the southern family by midcentury.[101]

The Cameron family were no anomaly—in the postwar South there was a growing tendency to bequeath property and land to unmarried daughters. Mildred Marshall inherited land in 1868 even though at the time of her mother's death she was forty-four and unlikely to ever marry. The Holladay sisters from Spotsylvania County in Virginia were also beneficiaries of their late father's will. They were granted permission to remain living in the family home, and they each received $4,000 while their "five surviving brothers received land."[102] Clearly women's relationship to property and the law was "influenced by changing social values as well as the increasing importance of equity jurisprudence and the passage of new statutes that encroached on the common law tradition."[103] This helped alter perceptions of single women, as there was a growing acceptance of women on their own and how they fitted into society. The separate estate could also be beneficial to widows, particularly if they were considering remarriage, as a way of protecting both their own and their children's property from falling outside of the scope of their power and control.

Single women also received (or inherited) property from their brothers. This was particularly apparent in the Civil War period, when large numbers of men lost their lives fighting for the Confederacy. Often fathers had bequeathed land and property to their sons, who later died and passed on their property to their sisters. Isaac Avery left his lands to his two unmarried sisters, Laura and Adelaide Avery, which highlighted a growing trend of female property ownership that dovetailed the close relationships shared between siblings that also enhanced the status of single women.[104] Mary Ker from Natchez, Mississippi, devoted her life to the care of her siblings and their offspring. Contemporaries viewed Ker as a woman operating at the heart of the family, keeping the family together when financial and practical difficulties threatened to break it apart. Mary was always generous with her time and money and on one occasion even sold the family silver to help her brother establish a new business venture in the postwar period.[105] "Unmarried sisters were willing and able to aid their brothers, but sometimes they carefully balanced this, with their desire to also assist other relatives. Consequently, property for married women was often placed in trust rather than allowing it to be swallowed up by the husband's creditors."[106] By the late nineteenth century, female property owners had "become the bulwark of the propertied class, helping to bolster husbands or siblings against hard times."[107] Single women involved themselves in financial affairs, in addition to their practical contribution to the family unit, and they demonstrated their active participation in both the private and public world of the postwar economy. Amanda and Josephine Varner, an unmarried sibling pair, ran the family hotel in Indian Spring, Georgia, for half a century. When Amanda Varner died in 1915, she bequeathed all her property "both real and personal" to her sister, Josephine Varner, which amounted to everything except a small lot of land in the town of Indian Spring and "a milch cow" to her friend, Mrs. A. H. Ogletree."[108] In doing so she passed on power and autonomy to her never-married sister in a legally binding document.

Parents started to view unmarried daughters in a new light, which was reflected in the type of provision left for them, such as in the case for the Holladay sisters. This helped alter less favorable perceptions of single women. Women took their new roles seriously; they invested time and energy in writing their wills, often bearing in mind those individuals who were most deserving or needy, in what Suzanne Lebsock described as "personalism."[109] This is well illustrated in

Mary Ker's will, penned in December 1870. She averred, "I have made this disposition of my property according to my judgement and feelings combined," in determining whom she would leave her property and personal belongings' to.[110] These enhanced property rights for single women were another strong indication that single women were viewed positively by the family and community and underline the way in which they had carved out a place for themselves in southern society. For slaveholding women the acquisition of personal wealth was important because it gave them the protection needed to survive as women on their own in the nineteenth century. Single women thus benefited from a bolstered self-confidence and a degree of economic agency, as is evident in the case of Mary Ker from Mississippi. While the Civil War did not create a revolution for privileged white women in property relations, it certainly gave rise to additional opportunities for single women to exert their autonomy.

Widowhood

The term "involuntary singleness" refers particularly to widowhood—to women who were single owing to the death of their husband, which was particularly marked during the Civil War. The pertinent question is to what extent these women were expected to adhere to the same gender conventions in widowhood that they had previously striven to attain in their role as wives and mothers, and what impact it had on them if they did. In many cases widows were keen to uphold their image of "virtuous" femininity, even though their legal status as a femme sole had been reinstated. Despite the fact that widows were single for very different reasons to never-married women or divorcées, they likewise shared a commonality of experience in their outward adherence to fulfilling gender expectations as southern women. Slaveholding (and middle-to-upper-class white) women had to demonstrate that they embraced the tenets of true womanhood at every stage of their lives (as spinsters, widows, or divorcées) in order to garner social respect that could be brokered to gain a degree of personal autonomy; widowhood was no different. Three important bargaining chips were essential for widows to achieve this: the widow's dower, protection in the form of a separate estate, and the widow's inheritance.

The law of dower was a vital legal provision that all married women were entitled to. Scholars have likened it to modern-day life insurance, in that it was designed to protect and provide for a wife upon her husband's death by giving her a one-third share in her husband's estate, which varied considerably depending on class, wealth, and status.[111] The dower was intended to be an extension of the protective cover that women experienced (in theory) in marriage and ensured a minimum amount of provision for a woman should her husband die, safe from the hands of any creditors, therefore enabling her to provide for herself and children.[112] John James Park, in *A Treatise on the Law of Dower*, described the law of dower: "Technically, under common law the dower came to be defined as an estate for life—in the third part—of the land and tenements—of which the husband was solely seized either in deed or in law—at any time during the coverture—of a legal estate of inheritance—in possession—to which the issue of the wife might by possibility inherit and which the law gives—to every married woman . . . who survives her husband—to be enjoyed by such woman . . . from the death of her husband—whether she have issue by him or not—having for its object the sustenance of herself, and the nurture and education of her children, if any;—the right to which attaches upon the land immediately upon the marriage, or as soon after the husband becomes seised—and is incapable of being discharged by the husband without her concurrence."[113]

Almost all the southern states were based on English common law (Louisiana and Texas were the exceptions) that stipulated that the law of dower "meant that a widow was entitled to a life interest in one third of the land held by her husband *at any time* during the marriage."[114] In practice widows often discovered that they were limited to "a one third share of the real property held by the husband at the time *of his death*," which had significant financial repercussions for them. Most state and federal decisions handed down between the 1780s and 1850s claimed to uphold dower rights but within ever-narrowing boundaries. In other words the law (and society) created new ways of limiting a woman's independence both inside and outside of marriage.[115] Beginning in 1839 in Mississippi, states began to enact legislation overriding the restrictions associated with coverture, and the concept of coverture was gradually eroded. Yet the motivations that resulted in these legal changes were not generated by concerns for equality between the sexes, but by the desire to secure and protect men's property. Over the course of the nineteenth century the laws of coverture died out, but it was an uneven and patchy process that dovetailed with the Married Women's Property Acts in the 1830s and 1840s.

Widows sometimes willingly gave up their dower rights in order to pay off debts owed against the estate. Widows also appealed to the courts to be granted permission to hold on to personal property, usually slaves, that they believed were transportable (should they wish to move to another state) and also more profitable. When Rebecca Caven's husband, Dr. Thomas Elrath, died in December 1825, she petitioned the court, asking for them to transfer some of her husband's real estate to Benjamin Bedford (who was the administrator of the estate). It was a shrewd, calculated move on her behalf that demonstrated her clear understanding on the limitations of her dower share. She realized that in her specific circumstances it would be better to trade in her dower share for real estate that she could sell. This would enable her to clear her late husband's debts, as well as providing her with adequate provision for her to live comfortably.[116] The court favored her appeal and in doing so ensured that she remained provided for in her widowhood.

Women primarily showed themselves to be driven by their need for protection, rather than a desire for enhancing personal autonomy, when filing various petitions to the court in the first half the nineteenth century. Widows often relied heavily on their birth families for support and advice, especially in the early days of widowhood. Ruth Hairston relied on the advice of her father, and his years of experience, when she first took on the plantation at Berry Hill. She urged her father: "Dear Papa, rite me every opportunity you have so I may [know] how to manage for the best."[117] Likewise Ellen Shutt kept up a detailed correspondence with her uncle George Mordecai throughout her widowhood (and beyond) seeking his advice on financial transactions, on whether or not she should move to another state, and on the care and provision of her children.[118] Clearly widows valued the knowledge and experience of their male kin, particularly when it came to managing farms or larger plantations. They could appeal to men's wider sense of honor and patriarchal protection, thereby replicating male and female gender roles, in establishing support early on in their widowhood.

Martha Powell, a widow with six small children under the age of thirteen, and also pregnant with twins, lived on a small farm in Nottoway County, Virginia. Following her husband's death in 1829, she was left in sole charge of "a worn out" farm and eleven "negroes." Martha quickly felt overwhelmed with her additional responsibilities and petitioned the court to grant her permission to sell the farm and move closer to her brothers so that they could support her during her widowhood. As she admitted in her appeal to the court, "she was unskilled in the management of land and Negroes" and therefore sought permission to remove herself and property, sell the land and farm, and move from Virginia to Alabama, in order to be closer to her birth family, particularly her two brothers who could help her run a farm. She also noted that the farmland in Alabama was sterile and that consequently she was "unable to support herself or family" if she continued living there. By petitioning the court to allow her to sell her land and move her property (slaves) she showed forward thinking and considerable self-motivation and autonomy. However, Martha demonstrated that she continued to operate in line with established expectations of her gender (and class). Though no recorded result exists for Martha Powell's case, it is likely that her petition was granted, as she had made it clear in her petition that she was requesting the move to best support herself and children, and not for selfish motives.[119] Martha's case also benefited from the support of her brother, who wrote to the court, "You are well acquainted with the land upon which she resides, you know it is impossible for her to live upon it in comfort (if at all)." He added, "the distance from me is so great and my confinement by my public duties as such, as to render it out of my power to aid her in the management of her affairs as I wish," therefore "by removal to Alabama she will go immediately into the neighborhood of our two brothers William and Richard Leigh who are very anxious she should move," which threw considerable weight behind her case.[120] The case underscores the importance of family in many widows' lives, in extending their help and support in difficult times, or during bereavement. Yet it also underlines the limitations of a widow's new status as a femme sole, in that women still prescribed to the ideals of femininity (and to the protection that it offered) in order to live comfortably in their new life without a husband.

Widowhood could be fraught with pitfalls. In theory widows were entitled to their dower share of their deceased husband's estate. In practice women often found that ensuring that they obtain their dower share was littered with further complications. First, the business of calculating what exactly amounted to a wife's dower share, or her third share of her deceased husband's estate, was often a complex and protracted affair. In South Carolina an alternative solution was to award widows the "cash equivalent" of their dower. Yet these so-called cash dowers often failed to cover a widow's long-term expenses in bringing up a family and paying for their children's education. Even in cases where women did finally get awarded their dower share, it still might prove to be an inadequate provision for her, depending on her wealth and social status.[121] For poorer or middle-income families this was a problem, as by the time a widow received her share of the estate it often amounted to very little and certainly did not cover the expenses that came with raising and educating dependents.[122] By the Civil War, widows benefited from a change in the law that meant that they could receive their dower share before creditors claimed their due, which placed them in a much better financial position and hence increased their personal autonomy. Conversely after the war widows often discovered that their property was not worth the amount it had previously been worth, and their slave property became emancipated, causing further problems. Marena Lefevre, a widow from Pulaski County in Arkansas, noted that "six negroes valued at $5,800 were liberated and set free," by the federal army and since "she has derived no benefit from said property" requested in a petition to the court that "she may be released from all responsibility as such admix of said estate."[123] Her appeal was granted, thus reflecting how the courts were willing to accommodate widows' requests if it provided them with provision and protection.

Widowhood came with a long list of social, economic, and personal constraints, but what it did provide was legal autonomy, as wives became widows and in the process returned to their single identity of a femme sole. Unlike never-married women, widows benefited from an elevated social status connected to the fact that they had been married and had fulfilled their role as "true" southern women. They were not subject to the same pressures to remarry that never-married women were. In that sense widows had the freedom to "choose" or "reject" remarriage according to social, economic, and personal needs.[124] According to Lebsock, "the wealthier the widow, the less likely she was to remarry," and "widows generally did not remarry if they could afford to remain as they were," which echoes the point made by the rich, slaveholding widow Catherine Edwards, who stated that "widows are little Queens if they have property. . . . Poor widows . . . get husbands but those who are independent have respect enough without them."[125] Remarriage after all was fraught with uncertainties, and affluent slaveholding widows had to be mindful of this in order to protect themselves, their property, or any property left in trust for their dependents. The separate estate could therefore be useful to widows, for it offered them an opportunity to ring-fence their property from second or third husbands, therefore keeping it safe if things should go wrong. Husbands were also watchful in protecting their property in the terms set out in their will and sometimes clearly stated that a wife would forfeit any rights to his property if she remarried.

When a husband died, there were a number of possible outcomes when it came to his will: first, he could die intestate (without a will); second, he could leave his wife an inheritance as a "fee simple," which meant leaving everything to her; or third, and perhaps most common, he left his wife a "lifetime estate."[126] The distinctions between each type of legacy are very important, each bringing with it certain legal, economic, and personal ramifications that affected those left behind. Each will be dealt with in turn. Even if a husband died intestate, the widow was entitled to her dower share, worth one-third of the estate, before creditors could claim their due (which was an important change in the law just prior to the Civil War).[127] For widows who were from a lower social class, this amounted to very little, and in reality they seldom benefited from what amounted to a small fiscal reward for what could have been a lifelong marriage. Wealthy widows fared much better, with some women inheriting handsome legacies. Slaveholder William Burney died intestate in 1817, leaving his wife, Mary Burney, in a quandary. As he had left no written will, half of his estate had been left to the state of Alabama, the state in which they lived. This amounted to a sizeable portion of their estate, which Mary claimed she had helped to build up, almost from scratch. Therefore if half was escheated to the state, Mary was left at a serious disadvantage. She could have accepted the constraints of her position, but instead, in a sudden drive of determination, and fueled by her need to survive, she petitioned the court of Alabama to allow her the "other half" of her husband's estate, in order to pay his debts and to give her sufficient provision to live comfortably.[128] In doing so she exhibited considerable agency despite the constraints placed on her that could have easily prevented her from taking any action. Although no result is recorded for Mary's case, she clearly demonstrated that as early as 1820, widows were proactive in their efforts to gain the additional portion of the property that was rightfully theirs.

Miriam Porter's husband also died intestate in September 1827, leaving her to file a petition in order to be granted permission to sell perishable property belonging to the estate, including "a considerable number of slaves."[129] Although a decade separates the two cases, they both demonstrate the limitations of a widow's position and the ways in which southern women tried to overcome them. Elizabeth Saunders, a widow from Tennessee, was also left in unfamiliar circumstances when her husband passed away without leaving a written will. Elizabeth was primarily driven by economic need as the estate had been left in debt by three thousand dollars. Elizabeth approached the courts to pass a law to "authorize the administrator of the estate . . . to sell so much of the land" to enable her to clear the debts and also to provide her with adequate funds to bring up and educate her children.[130] Finally, as late as 1863, Elizabeth Latta, a widow from South Carolina, appealed to the court for its provision and protection. Her late husband, John Latta, had also died "intestate, seized and possessed of a considerable real and personal estate." Having "recently removed to this state [from Florida] to reside," the petitioner requested to be "appointed Guardian" of her minors, which included control of the land and property.[131] It is therefore clear that the theme of protection and provision runs through almost all the personal testimonies examined in here, spanning the period from the early 1800s to the 1870s. Paradoxically it was in the attempt to uphold these conservative values that women also found a route to personal autonomy.

A second option for widows was that they could be bequeathed property in their husband's will, in what was called a "fee simple," which meant that they were given absolute authority over his estate. A widow who was given an estate as a fee simple was placed in an extremely powerful and autonomous position. Fee simple estates were more common with second or third wives, who were also not the mother of their children. Colin Clark, a wealthy Halifax County planter, bequeathed his "whole property and estate of which I shall die seized or possessed of consisting of real, personal and mixed property to my beloved wife Eliza L. Clark and her heirs in fee simple forever."[132] In doing so Clark proved unequivocally that he had absolute confidence in his wife's ability to manage a large and profitable estate, and he demonstrated his belief by giving her sole responsibility to manage it. Widows, then, could inherit large amounts of property and land through the division of their husbands' estates. By taking on these opportunities, widows understood "the need for domestic authority" and challenged the "inherited idea" that "husbandless women were powerless."[133]

Slaveholding widows donned masterful roles in order for them to be taken seriously while managing large estates, conducting business affairs, and managing of slaves. It was acceptable for widows to act in this manner because if they did not they were easily dismissed as weak or ineffectual managers and could therefore be taken advantage of.[134] The inheritance patterns of widows therefore varied considerably according to several factors: "age, capabilities, and willingness to accept responsibilities, rather than simply her gender."[135] If a wife was youthful, she could be seen as lacking the experience to manage a large plantation or farm; too old and she might herself have been less able or unwilling to take on the physical hardship or added responsibility of taking on such a task. Young widows fell into the category of women most likely to remarry, which would also be a key consideration when writing a will, and husbands would put measures in place to protect their property from being lost or squandered through their wife's remarriage. In the postwar period, men began to demonstrate a growing confidence in their wives, which was reflected in the nature and content of their wills. It was partly linked to the changing nature of southern society, and to the end of slavery and to a mounting realization that widows could care for themselves, as many had already proven during the Civil War.

Women could also be left a life estate in their husband's property. This was almost akin to having the property on loan to them, in that it remained in a widow's safekeeping, but she was also limited in what she could actually do with it, in buying or selling property, moving slaves to different locations, and so on. Susanna Hamm, a slaveholding widow from Albemarle County in Virginia, inherited her husband's "entire estate" following his death in 1839. Attached to Susanna's inheritance were a number of important conditions that restricted her buying and selling land, relocating, or even writing a will. Also because it was "a lifetime estate," further stipulations stripped her of the property if for example she remarried. Furthermore she had no control over whom the estate would be passed on to when she died. Elijah Hamm had already clearly stated that "it is my will and desire that my estate be equally divided among all my children except my son," for reasons that he did not disclose.[136] Third, and perhaps most important, Susanna filed a petition to the court to enable her to sell "eight or nine hundred acres of land . . . at seven or eight dollars an acre," rather than selling the slaves as stipulated in Elijah's will. She defended her position well, maintaining that they were "family Negroes" and "could not be easily spared" because the family relied on their labors "to support and maintain the petitioner's younger children."[137] Clearly Susanna's plea fell on sympathetic ears, as a bill was drawn in support of her case. Once again the undercurrent of protection and provision runs through her heartfelt petition requesting the court's permission to remove the constraints placed on her through her husband's inheritance. Her case clearly demonstrates the ongoing restrictions placed on slaveholding women that extended from marriage into widowhood, and the way in which patriarchy exercised some control over single women's lives. In Susanna's case, as with many slaveholding widows, the newfound legal autonomy of widowhood was carefully controlled by her late husband's will, which stipulated the limits of her personal freedom.

Virginian widow Hetty Jacobs clearly believed she had no option other than to address the court to gain the right to sell her slaves (rather than land) to invest in bank stock. In her particular case, Hetty was frustrated and disillusioned by the "insolence" of some of her slaves, who failed to respect her authority as a female slaveholder; therefore she filed a petition in order to grant her permission to sell them. Yet Hetty's case in 1829 was atypical in contrast to the majority of petitions explored here, which involved slaveholding widows wanting to sell land rather than slaves that they considered to be of more long-term value. Hetty on the other hand, had a strong desire to sell some of her slaves, probably driven by the fact that they were causing her a great deal of trouble, refusing to obey her, culminating in a decision that it was better to sell them. She noted that the slaves were "insolent" and that they failed to recognize her as their female master, which left her with little choice except to sell them, so that she could reinvest the capital elsewhere. As her petition makes plain, her husband had not released sufficient funds to satisfy all demands against the estate, which forced her to be proactive in an attempt for survival.[138] The courts thus determined her fate, and Jacobs like many other single, slaveholding women, learned that even if she were free of the patriarchal control of her husband, she was still beholden to the overarching paternalism of the southern justice system that was controlled and operated by men.

Widows quickly discovered that their petitions relied heavily on the discretion of the courts, and therefore, much like the cases of women seeking divorce, widows learned to frame their petitions in a way that would gain them maximum sympathy from the judicial body. In this way widows demonstrated that they were able to manipulate the gender conventions that controlled them, returning again to the notion of them being "quiet revolutionaries."[139] Widows were expected to live up to certain prescriptions of femininity in order to get them what they wanted. They addressed the courts on a broad range of grievances; the most common focused on land and slaves. In Virginia, Texas, Mississippi, and Tennessee, widows spoke of their need to sell land in exchange for the payment of debts, or to nullify provisions in their husbands' wills that prevented them from receiving adequate support.[140]

Widows also made requests to move a minor's property. Caroline Johnson petitioned to the court to relocate a minor's personal property from Texas to South Carolina, where she now resided.[141] Widows validated their claims for removal by stressing the need to protect a dependent's property. Martha Powell wanted to relocate from Virginia to Alabama, in order to be closer to her birth family, and appealed for a law to be passed to give her permission to take her slaves with her.[142] Slaveholding widow Martha Orgain, from Surry County, filed a petition in 1843 to secure permission to move her son's property to "more fertile lands" that she claimed would benefit them both. She explained that her son had inherited "considerable property in lands, slaves, horses and cattle" and had in excess of "two hundred slaves" in Surry and James City Counties, which she described as an "exceedingly poor," "unproductive, and unhealthy" environment.[143] Martha flexed a degree of personal agency in vocalizing her request to move the slaves to a state that better suited her health and their prosperity. Martha advised that the slaves were mostly in family groups, and she wanted to keep them together, as "hiring" them out would involve splitting them up, which she felt would be disadvantageous. However, in spite of her practical knowledge of what would work best, she lacked the legal authority to ensure the course of events. As she made plain in her petition, "if she were authorized, with a portion of the profits already accrued" from the sale of the land, she would "purchase more fertile lands in a healthier part of the state for him [her minor]" and remove the slaves as well. Martha's case met with partial success, as the recorded result was that "a bill was drawn," but we know little more information than this. Martha's case thus reverberates with the experience of other slaveholding widows, who discovered that wealthy planters tended to exhibit a heightened conservatism when writing their wills for their wives, partly owing to the fact that there were more land, property, and calculable assets at stake.

This gradually altered during the Civil War and postwar years, as men's confidence in their wives' ability to manage large estates, presumably as a response to their successful management in the war years, was increasingly reflected in widows settling their husband's estates, which revealed the heightened agency of single women in property law. For example Harriett Montmollin acted as administrator of her late husband's estate in Richland District, South Carolina, in 1863. Montmollin showed considerable agency upon discovering that her husband owed over $30,000 and petitioned the court to sell the plantation and eighty-one slaves. The appeal was granted.[144] As Censer points out, husbands increasingly trusted wives to settle estates, and to divide them among their children and families. Widows of the old elite were able to exercise their own personal judgment on who would benefit from their legacies; and they often demonstrated that they felt more confident in stating their posthumous wishes than when they were alive. Widows could ensure that their daughters, close sisters, or nieces were well provided for in a manner that revealed self-action and autonomy.

Summary

In the antebellum South, the gradual process of legal reform in women's lives had already begun. In Mississippi, as early as 1839, the passing of the Married Women's Property Act led to a series of legal reforms that one by one expanded married women's property rights. The reasons that motivated these changes in law and property rights were often germinated in conservative soil, and driven by financial concerns for men regarding the best way to protect their own property from debtors. At the same time, the Married Women's Property Acts were also about the protection of women and were meant to provide them with a safety net should things go wrong; each time a new state passed a law that gave women additional rights over property in marriage, it also had important implications for single women.

At the beginning of the nineteenth century, the law of coverture had clearly defined the differences between a single and married woman, but as the century wore on, and coverture gradually died out, those differences started to become less apparent. Prior to the Civil War, married women's property laws were concerned with equity procedures; in other words they dealt with women's specific grievances in marriage or widowhood but did little to modify a husband's privileges granted to him via prior common law principles. After the Civil War laws became more concerned with altering property relations between husband and wife, which had serious repercussions for single women. This included women who were single by choice (never-married women, and for some divorcées), but also for women who were involuntarily single, such as widows. The expansion of property laws for women "ranged from the simple ability of wives to write wills with or without their husbands' consent, to granting femme sole status to abandoned women, to allowing women some control over their own wages, to establishing separate estates for women, to protecting land inherited by widows from their husbands' creditors, to allowing widows legal access to their husbands' personal estates."[145] In theory these were extremely important measures that over time gradually helped women free themselves from unhappy marital unions, in which they either were mentally or physically abused or were poorly provided for by their partners. The steady broadening of the divorce laws in the South, and especially what constituted "acceptable" grounds for divorce, were again significant measures that signaled an evolving attitude toward women's roles and status.

However, these changes were often patchy, and the actual interpretation and implementation of the law varied according to custom and beliefs of those individuals in power. The changes often occurred slowly and haltingly and for the most part were motivated by an ethos of patriarchal control, in that wives still had to prove that they were the innocent victims, confined in marital unions that failed to provide for them, thereby allowing a higher patriarchal body (of the law) to step in and take control. By the time of the Civil War, changes were already afoot as is evidenced by the Married Women's Property Acts and the gradual broadening of the divorce laws in states such as Tennessee or Alabama (with a wider interpretation of the concept of cruelty). The Civil War expedited these legal changes, as the status of single women became more acceptable, and the trends of romantic love and the companionate marriage ideal blossomed further still. Men had also experienced how their wives had coped during the war, and for some this convinced them that their wives were able managers of their plantations who could be trusted as safe keepers of their family property in the event of their death. For slaveholding women the brutalities of war had magnified the fact that men could not always protect them, and the end of race-based slavery that came crashing down at the war's end and the emancipation of the slaves also challenged the rigid definitions of southern womanhood that further eroded the gender ideals of men and women, particularly those from the slaveholding elite. Men had failed to protect their women in wartime, and by the end of the war, when the slaves walked away from the plantation, the antebellum worldview based on a racial and gendered hierarchy crumbled.

The two key themes of provision and protection run through virtually all the petitions filed by men and women examined here. Women's divorce petitions stemmed in part from the growing desire and expectation of having a more companionate marriage, and when they found that their marriage fell short of this new model, they began complaining about it. Women showed their agency in voicing discontent with adulterous husbands who drank, lied, or squandered property. As the divorce rate steadily rose by the late nineteenth century, women appeared to achieve greater success in voluntarily regaining their single status, which was mirrored by the increasingly liberal divorce laws that sprang up from state to state. Until this point female agency had been limited to women working within the constraints of nineteenth-century gender roles, which varied from state to state. If women wanted to regain their single status (through divorce), it was important that they demonstrated an adherence to the accepted models of femininity that dominated the South. This was a constraint, but if handled correctly an opportunity to manipulate the system in order to ensure their petitions were passed. After all women wanted to ensure that if a divorce petition was passed they were provided with adequate provision or alimony to ensure economic survival. There was little comfort in gaining a divorce if a woman was going to be left in a worse situation than she was in during marriage.

Property ownership and the law often overlapped. This was particularly evident at the end of the Civil War, when many previously wealthy, slaveholding families were left financially devastated by Confederate defeat and the loss of their slave property after emancipation. This was mirrored in a decline in the percentage of dowable lands, which lessened in line with the social, economic, and political changes caused by the Civil War. However, the setting up of separate estates invariably protected women from financial devastation and cushioned this loss. As women like Ruth Balderee discovered, the decision to set up a separate estate prior to marriage had been a decision that later protected her, by enabling her to leave her husband, without being left financially destitute. For widows the advantages of having a separate estate could also be of immeasurable value to them, both financially and personally. Primarily it sheltered them from the worst excesses of economic deprivation if they faced a life alone, in the event of the death of their husband.

The relationship between single women, property, and the law was constantly evolving throughout the nineteenth century. In theory single women had the power to act as a femme sole, which placed them in a more advantageous position than married women. In reality single women, particularly those who had been married and then who sought a divorce, soon learned that their quest to return to their former status as femme sole largely depended on whether or not they were perceived by the courts as having acted like "true women." Widows and divorcées often discovered that there was a lag between what they were told their rights were and how these rights were actually implemented or interpreted in different jurisdictions. In the number of divorce petitions filed and examined in this book alone, it is clear that the autonomy of the "femme sole" was subject to numerous social and cultural restrictions that operated as much to restrain women's power as for married women in the early part of the century. The easiest way that a woman could gain some modicum of agency in the southern states, prior to the Civil War at least, was to abide strictly to its codes of appropriate feminine behavior that connected back to the ideal models of womanhood. Even if a woman was seen as a femme sole in the eyes of the law, such as in the case of involuntarily single-ness or widowhood, it was still important that a woman continued to adhere to the social prescriptions of true womanhood that bound married women to it. If a woman was single, she was expected to show that she championed the ideals of domesticity and to show she believed that marriage and motherhood came first. If a woman had never married, it was important that she was prepared to show her "usefulness" as a single woman by embracing the ideals of single blessedness. For a widow this could be achieved by demonstrating "virtuous widowhood," and in divorce by highlighting the fact that a woman had been a good wife and an innocent victim of a cruel and barbarous husband.

If women wanted to gain acceptance, respect, and some modicum of personal agency prior to the Civil War in particular, the vehicle to help achieve this was to show an adherence to prevalent models of southern womanhood even in its broadest sense. An unattached planter woman was bound to the larger patriarchy of the South, even if she was not married, or had never been married. She therefore had to operate within the strict limitations and gender conventions of her time, even when it came to suing in court, petitioning for her dower share, or obtaining a divorce from her barbarous husband, if she was to have any hope of success. By working within these rigid confines, women who were single or who wanted to be single gradually chipped away at the existing frameworks of power. This led to an increase in personal autonomy, albeit slowly. This was helped by the profound social, economic, political, and demographic changes accelerated by war that culminated in important changes in the law in the postwar period. It also helped to expand and revise the boundaries of true womanhood, which elasticized in the postwar period, to include new versions of "true womanhood" into its remit. This included those women who embraced the Cult of Single Blessedness and those "tens of thousands" of new widows born of wartime.[146] As a result these slow but steady advances began to filter through and make tangible changes to single women's lives, which again mirrored the altered social and cultural scene post-Reconstruction.

CONCLUSION

The Civil War and postwar years have been described as "a crisis in gender," a period of time marked by "the reconstruction of white southern womanhood."[1] For single, slaveholding women the process of challenging traditional models of southern womanhood had begun in the Old South. This was because single women by virtue of their nonmarriage already chafed against the rigid ideologies of gender that existed for their class and race.

The evidence in this book suggests that single, planter-class women disguised their departure from traditional gender models, which required them to marry and have children, by making themselves indispensable to the family unit or within their local communities. Single women's roles in the family replicated conventional gender roles for women as caregivers, helpmeets, or maiden aunts, which coalesced with traditional notions of nineteenth-century femininity. This was partially out of choice, and in part out of necessity. By demonstrating an outward compliance with the Cult of Domesticity or Cult of True Womanhood, single women improved their self-image in southern society, gaining acceptance, respect, and paradoxically a route to greater autonomy. In the antebellum world, old attitudes of social scorn toward unmarried females remained, but these were slowly being replaced by new ideas of single blessedness that had particularly taken root in the urban centers.[2] In these areas networks of single women gradually sprung up as early as the 1830s. For elite white women who came from wealthy, slaveholding families, the advantages of their social class and race position granted them certain privileges over lower-class white people and black people.[3] As a result they benefited from the advantages of their elevated social position that afforded them the opportunity to reject marriage, but still continue to show that they were useful members of their families or communities, which enhanced other people's perception of their femininity. However, it was critical that these women clearly understood the importance of patriarchy in their lives that was perhaps most defined by their role in the family. To repeat again the words of Jane Turner Censer, the planter class "emphasized the persistence of the metaphor of family as appropriate representation for various social relations" that supported race, class, and gender hierarchies.[4] It was about more than *just* the family; it was also about the overarching patriarchy of southern society.

Within this rigid context of race, class, and gender, slaveholding women were able to form close and loving relationships with other single women. Prior to the Civil War, the model of white, southern womanhood helped to disguise the true nature of female friendship, and evidence suggests that single women found considerable freedom in their relationships with other women. This was because of the dominant ideology that perceived women to be nonsexual and pure. If this argument is followed, then the relationships shared between single women could be nothing more than innocent. In fact society often saw female friendship as a useful distraction to prevent unmarried women becoming a burden on society. As the examples in this book reveal, the form and function of female friendship was considered nonthreatening, which allowed these friendships to develop and blossom in the first half of the century. Often friendships between women were perceived as only temporary and therefore were considered to have no real chance of maturing into a more permanent form.[5] Later on in the century, when women increasingly took on paid roles at work outside of the home, female friendship suddenly became a potential threat, as it had the possibility of becoming more permanent, as women gained financial independence.

The Civil War altered the social and economic fabric of many planter-class families. As Lincoln's Emancipation Proclamation freed four million slaves in the South, planters watched on in horror as their property and wealth literally ebbed away from them.[6] As a consequence the nature of the southern family altered significantly, which led to a growing acceptance within the old elite that single women could pursue paid work in certain occupations, such as teaching.[7] This in many respects proved to be a double-edged sword as it acted as a springboard for female autonomy in the workplace but also started to threaten the male hegemony as women gained more independence. The drive for women's work thus came from a conservative ethos tied to the preservation of the southern family. However, in the postwar years the transition to paid work also threatened conventional models of femininity. By the mid-to-late 1870s, new theories of female sexuality challenged the idea that women were asexual. New interpretations of female sexuality dismissed previously held notions that women were by nature passionless.[8] This had a significant effect on female friendship between single women because their relationships were no longer viewed as nonsexual and pure. In addition to this, in the postwar years their friendships also had the capacity to become more permanent because of the possibility (and necessity) of paid work.[9]

Work was another important marker in slaveholding women's lives. Undoubtedly the war intensified social change in elite women's lives, as it forced them, on an unprecedented scale, to respond to the needs of the Confederacy. The war was a catalyst that accelerated social changes that had already begun in the antebellum era. Single women successfully managed large plantations in the absence of their husbands from the early 1800s. In so doing they clearly demonstrated an adherence to upholding conventional ideals of femininity. Kirsten Wood described this as widows' manipulation of ladyhood.[10] This seems validated, as single women used their femininity as a disguise in order to successfully manage plantations, while simultaneously adopting new characteristics and manners that were required for them to do so effectively. In other words, by being seen to operate within gender lines, widows inadvertently gained greater autonomy.

In terms of the two other main working roles discussed in this book, nursing and teaching, it is clear that the foundations for these roles were sown in the antebellum South. These vocations expanded out of fairly traditional nurturing and caregiving roles that were already present in the prewar South. They had their roots in the southern family and rapidly expanded into a more public arena during the Civil War and Reconstruction eras. The war therefore acted as a catalyst for expediting an expansion, or more accurately, a transition of women's traditional home-based roles and transposed them into a public setting. The war required women to develop a new set of feminine characteristics in support of southern independence, which rather paradoxically meant that the ideal model of southern womanhood had to be revised or expanded. The Civil War therefore helped to reshape traditional notions of what constituted femininity in a changing South, highlighting trends that had already begun in the antebellum era. As Anastasia Sims suggested, the southern lady diversified during the Civil War, and "different elements of her character" were emphasized to "suit different circumstances."[11] For women who were single this included their ability to be self-reliant, brave, and stoic, particularly in their work as nurses on the front line. For women like Phoebe Yates Pember, who worked as a Confederate nurse, it was important that women demonstrated that they could be "hard and gross" in their working lives, not as a challenge to patriarchal authority, but in order to do their job well.[12] Unmarried women had more flexibility and maneuverability than their married counterparts (as they did not have homes and families of their own), and therefore they were able to step into certain wartime roles more easily than married women were, which had both immediate and longer-term consequences.

First, it proved that unmarried women could be "useful" to their communities and devoted to the Confederate cause. It drew attention to the burgeoning trend of single blessedness that had taken root in the Old South but that came into sharper focus in wartime. As Lee Chambers-Schiller argued, the Cult of Single Blessedness reached its heyday in the South during wartime, meaning that women born in the 1840s and 1850s benefited most from the opportunities it opened up for them.[13] Some women, like the domestic novelist Augusta Jane Evans, celebrated it as an opportunity for single, southern women to cement their new place in postwar society as respectable, southern women. She even used it as a framework for her wartime novel *Macaria*.[14] In doing so she championed the view that the war and its aftermath demanded a reconsideration of women's roles and a broadening of the boundaries of true womanhood.[15] As Jennifer Lynn Gross suggested, "Evans was not a feminist visionary, she was a social visionary. Recognizing the plight the war had created for southern women, she suggested a solution—an expansion of the definition of true womanhood to allow those women who could never marry to find usefulness and social acceptance in their lives as manless women."[16] It was almost as if she was suggesting that single blessedness should also include other categories of unmarried women, including widows. Therefore it is evident that the war had a liberating effect on single women's lives, not only in the way that they were viewed, but also in regard to the opportunities and obstacles they faced as unmarried women.

Second, the longer-term impact of single women's wartime work was that it expanded women's opportunities to find self-fulfillment in work. In a postwar South that was scarred by military defeat, demographic loss, and material and cultural devastation, the reality was that women were often required to fill certain postwar roles (such as teaching and nursing). Women from the elite class found that their lives had altered beyond recognition by the end of the war. Many spoke of the changed routine of their daily lives and their contribution to the household chores in the absence of the slaves. Although this was difficult at first, women quickly fostered a new sense of satisfaction and pride in their work in a way that they had not expected to before the war. As slaveholding families suddenly became families without slaves, the altered racial and class dynamics affected the social dynamic of southern women's lives in the type of work they did but, more important, in the breakdown of the rigid boundaries of femininity. The changes brought by war meant that a new generation of women began to work to earn a living, in order to supplement their families' income and to make ends meet. The initial motivation for the expansion of single women's working roles therefore sprang from a conservative ethos of protection and provision for their families but also resulted in the gradual breakdown of patriarchy, and with it a revised version of the southern lady.

The Civil War therefore had a dual significance for slaveholding women: it challenged gender roles but also the patriarchy that was already creaking under the strain of emancipation. For slaveholding women defeat in the Civil War not only brought with it the end of race-based slavery; it also challenged the conventional definition of southern womanhood. For the typical plantation mistress, who had benefited from her position at the center of the family, the postwar years posed a combination of threat and insecurity to her elevated status in the southern hierarchy. Yet for the single, slaveholding mistress, the war should be considered in a different light, since she already proved to be an inexact fit with the existing models of southern femininity. The war and postwar years can be interpreted as an opportunity to further accelerate the pace of social change for single women. For them this opportunity was less of a "crisis of gender" but more of an opportunity for self-fulfillment and an opportunity to be recognized and praised for the good deeds done. This opportunity seized on the notion that single women of various descriptions could still be valuable and useful members of the family, community, and country, in spite of being single. As so many more women were left to manage alone in wartime, the perceptions of female singleness were forced to change in line with altered circumstances. The war shone a bright light on single women's lives and highlighted the fluidity of the boundaries between married and single women—such as in the case of widows and divorcées.

Finally, when it came to the arena of law, changes were beginning to filter through from the antebellum era that helped improve the status of single women. These changes included the right to hold property in the form of a separate estate that resulted from the Married Women's Property Acts (the most important in 1848). These led to improvements in the property rights of married women and, in turn, had important ramifications for widows and divorcées especially. It started a wave of important legislation that allowed women to hold on to any property owned, or given to them, prior to marriage, in the form of a separate estate. The initial motivation behind these reforms had little to do with granting women additional independence but was focused on the protection of male property from potential debtors in hard times. Nevertheless the long-term by-product was that it generated a measured increase in personal autonomy for women. Again, in the case of divorce, piecemeal changes had begun prior to the Civil War period, but still the number of women who sought a divorce remained low. In the early nineteenth century the grounds for divorce were narrow, and because of this women often found that they were dependent on their own jurisdiction's interpretation of events. In the antebellum period, it was imperative that married women proved that they had been a good wife and lived up to the tenets of true womanhood, in spite of their husband's cruel or unjust treatment of them. The courts therefore emulated the patriarchy of the South in that they showed empathy to elite women who demonstrated that they were dependent, pure, and submissive in their behavior. In the postwar period, the legal changes began to slowly reflect the breakdown of patriarchy that was inextricably intertwined with slavery and that had been extinguished by defeat in the Civil War. This was reflected in a slow but steady rise in the divorce rate, which correlated to the broadening of the grounds of divorce that led to married women voluntarily returning to their femme sole status more easily.

A similar pattern is clear in the plight of widows seeking protection from the courts in order to receive their dower share in their husbands' estate. In the antebellum period, widows again had to prove that they were worthy of the court's protection and that they were acting in the best interest of their deceased husband or their family, as opposed to self-interest. In other words, by operating within traditional gender conventions, widows ensured a route to enhanced personal autonomy secured by economic or material resources. Even though the percentage of dowable lands fell after the Civil War, this was counterbalanced by benefits of the married women's property acts and the separate estates for women, which afforded them both protection and enhanced personal agency.

The route to personal autonomy for single, white, slaveholding women was not always a straightforward one. Unlike any other group of southern women, the southern lady was upheld as an ideal and a myth that few women could really attain. It was a social construct that was designed to uphold the elevated social status of the planter class, a rich and privileged minority of white slave owners in the antebellum South. However, unlike the slaveholding mistress, who was revered as the central figure in the southern family, the single woman was an uneasy fit in the cultural stereotype that dominated. In the Old South, single women in some cases remained a figure of scorn, the redundant woman who had failed in her duty to become a southern wife and mother. Increasingly though this stereotype was slowly disappearing in favor of a new image of single blessedness, which promoted the idea that, while not all women could marry, they could still be useful members of their families and communities.

As traditional ideas of marriage as a means to retain wealth in the southern family were gradually challenged by more enlightened ideas of marriage for love and companionate marriage, so too did women begin to question their own choice of marriage partners. By the Civil War, these two ideas gained pace, and women began to delay or reject marriage, as they felt increasingly less concerned about remaining single. The Civil War led to a cultural reassessment of singleness that coalesced with the new economic challenges and demographic alterations. The war acted as a catalyst for accelerating important trends that were already present, and it blurred the boundaries between marriage and nonmarriage. Ultimately defeat in the Civil War led to the end of slavery and with it a reconsideration of gender roles. In the postwar period the southern lady no longer existed, and she was replaced by a new generation of women whose lives were no longer marked by slavery. For single women the end of the war marked the continuation of a process that had begun many years before and that led to new opportunities that were a pathway to female autonomy.

Notes

Introduction

1. Grace Elmore Brown Diary, 30 September 1864, in Weiner, *Heritage of Woe*, xxviii.

2. Ibid.

3. Ibid., 28 February 1863, 40.

4. The slaveholding (or planter) class are defined as planters who owned in excess of twenty slaves. Laura Edwards argues that the planter class accounted for less than 12 percent of slaveholding households in the pre–Civil War era, with fewer still holding over one hundred slaves or more. It was commonplace to hire or own one or two slaves, even in urban areas, where upper-class white people used slaves as house servants. Laura Edwards argues that this included urban slaveholders, who also benefited from the social and economic ties to slavery. Slavery supported various family members in different ways and supported their social status regardless of where they lived. The term "slaveholding" in this study is understood in its broadest possible sense. It refers to large slaveholding families and families who had owned plantations, but who gave them up, or who had turned to other ways to make a living, such as running a family hotel, or a school. Edwards, *Scarlett Doesn't Live Here Anymore*, 16.

5. The central focus will be on women who never married. A recent collection of essays analyzes singleness from a broad interdisciplinary framework as an interpretative tool to understand how society constructs various models of femininity as a means of social control over women. Singleness in this sense can be interpreted in two main ways: as a failure to achieve true womanhood in the way that it is "traditionally endorsed" or as a sign of autonomy and independence. See Bell and Yans, *Women on Their Own*, 3.

6. Clinton, *Plantation Mistress*, 36; O'Brien, *Evening When Alone*, introduction, 1. Clinton gave a much gloomier impression of unmarried women's lives within the family unit and noted that single women were expected to "repress personal wishes that would interfere with family duty," and she "must devote her time and energies to other women's families if a nurse or extra pair of hands were required." O'Brien described the single, southern lady as being tangential to the domestic world. As he observed, "above all, she was not a mother, even though she might be surrounded by children. So she stood a little aside, acquiring thereby the advantages of a double vision, of being in, but not of the domestic world."

7. See Chambers-Schiller, *Liberty a Better Husband*. Other important works have since emerged on single women: Berend, "Cultural and Social Sources of Spinsterhood"; Hill, *Women Alone*; Froide, *Never Married*; Tallentire, "'Everyday Athena's'"; C. Carter, *Southern Single Blessedness*; Bell and Yans, *Women on Their Own*.

8. Ulrich, review of *Liberty a Better Husband*.

9. Chambers-Schiller, *Liberty a Better Husband*, 22–28. More recently scholars have explored how the "Cult of Single Blessedness" affected the unmarried in wartime and in the

postwar era. Refer to Faust, "Altars of Sacrifice"; Gross, "Lonely Lives Are Not Necessarily Joyless."

10. Chambers-Schiller, *Liberty a Better Husband.*

11. Berend, "Cultural and Social Sources of Spinsterhood."

12. Ibid.

13. This viewpoint differs from C. Carter's *Southern Single Blessedness* findings that single, white, elite women from the urban centers of Charleston and Savannah from 1800 to 1865 were largely satisfied with their roles within the southern family and did not seek to expand them. Carter argued that rather than seeking autonomy, these unmarried women saw themselves as existing within the mainstream of southern womanhood, rather than outside of it.

14. Gross, "Lonely Lives Are Not Necessarily Joyless." Gross also wrote about Confederate widowhood in the postwar era. See Gross, "And for the Widow and Orphan."

15. The term "Cult of Single Blessedness" is used by Chambers-Schiller, *Liberty a Better Husband.*

16. The vast literature on southern womanhood has up until recently largely focused on the plantation mistress. See Spruill, *Women's Life and Works*; A. Scott, *Southern Lady*; Clinton, *Plantation Mistress*; Fox-Genovese, *Within the Plantation Household*; Bleser, *In Joy and in Sorrow*; Censer, *North Carolina Planters*; Friedman, *Enclosed Garden*; Bertram Wyatt-Brown, *Southern Honor*; McCurry, *Masters of Small Worlds*; McMillen, *Southern Women.*

17. Faust, "Altars of Sacrifice," 1201.

18. Jennifer Lynn Gross uses the term "manless woman" in her study of Confederate widowhood. Gross, "Good Angels," 137.

19. O'Brien, *Evening When Alone*, 3.

20. Pollit, introduction, "Writing a Woman's Life," 15. See also, Huff, *Women's Life Writing.*

21. Huff, *Women's Life Writing*, 1.

22. East, *Sarah Morgan*, 115.

23. Many southern women placed great value in keeping their personal diaries. Anne Jennings Wise Hobson, a widow from Accomac County in Virginia, confessed, "I cannot do without my journal, it proves a silent monitor and companion to me." She added, "I really need something to remind me of the many resolutions I make and break. God's grace has done wonders for me, yet if it should leave me one moment what would become of me." Anne Jennings Wise Hobson Diary, 11 October 1863, Virginia Historical Society, Richmond, Virginia (VHS hereafter).

24. Wink, "'She Left Nothing in Particular,'" 38.

25. "Race and Slavery Petitions Project," http://library.uncg.edu/slavery_petitions/index.asp (last accessed 9 June 2016).

26. Welter, "Cult of True Womanhood."

27. Cashin, "Structure of Antebellum Planter Families."

28. Jabour, *Scarlett's Sisters*, 11.

29. O'Brien, *Evening When Alone*, 2.

30. Ibid., 1 and 2.

31. Clinton, *Plantation Mistress*, 232.

32. Chambers-Schiller, *Liberty a Better Husband*, 3.

33. Gross, "Lonely Lives Are Not Necessarily Joyless."

34. Mary Susan Ker Papers, Southern Historical Collection (SHC hereafter).

35. Jabour, *Scarlett's Sisters*, and Jabour, "Female Families."

36. Smith-Rosenberg, "Female World of Love and Ritual."

37. Cott, "Passionlessness," and Smith-Rosenberg and Rosenberg, "Female Animal."

38. Sedevia, "Prospect of Happiness"; Lebsock, "Radical Reconstruction."

Chapter 1 The Construction of Femininity in the Antebellum South

1. Mary Telfair to Mary Few, 2 December 1829, in C. Johnson, *Mary Telfair*, 88.

2. Ibid.

3. B. Wood, *Mary Telfair to Mary Few*, introduction, xxvii.

4. Ibid., xi–xxxix.

5. Mary Telfair to Mary Few, 26 November 1814, in B. Wood, *Mary Telfair to Mary Few*, 18–19.

6. Roberts, "True Womanhood Revisited."

7. Chambers-Schiller, *Liberty a Better Husband*, 10–28.

8. Cooper and Terrill, *American South*, introduction, xix.

9. Ibid.

10. For more information on the southern lady see A. F. Scott, *Southern Lady*; Clinton, *Plantation Mistress*; Scott, "Myth of the Southern Lady," Fox-Genovese, *Within the Plantation Household*; Bleser, *In Joy and in Sorrow*; Censer, *North Carolina Planters*.

11. A. Scott, *Southern Lady*, 256.

12. Kleinberg, *Women in American Society*, 15.

13. Fox-Genovese, *Within the Plantation Household*, and Kerber's seminal work, "Separate Spheres, Female Worlds, Woman's Place."

14. Fox-Genovese, *Within the Plantation Household*, 203.

15. Ibid.

16. For a discussion of the place of church and religion in women's lives refer to Friedman, *Enclosed Garden*; Mathews, *Religion in the Old South*; Welter, "*Feminization of American Religion*"; Pease and Pease, *Ladies, Women and Wenches*, 115–37.

17. Friedman, *Enclosed Garden*, 19. Friedman emphasized the importance of religion, kinship, and place in the construction of self-identity. Friedman noted, "Maternity, domesticity, self-sacrifice, and religious conversion were expected of women." 39. Yet these expectations initiated "powerful internal conflicts in southern women," as they neglected "their interior being" and focused instead on the images of "belle," "mistress," and "New Woman" as opposed to the reality of southern women's lives.

18. For a discussion on the Cult of True Womanhood, see Degler, *At Odds*; Cott, *Bonds of Womanhood*.

19. The Cult of True Womanhood was a phrase coined by Barbara Welter in 1966, in reference to a wide collection of nineteenth-century women's gift annuals and ladies' prescriptive literature that repeatedly referred directly to, or else alluded to, a benchmark of acceptable female behavior. See Welter, "Cult of True Womanhood."

20. Pease and Pease, *Ladies, Women and Wenches*, 116.

21. Ibid., 132.

22. Ibid., 115.

23. Ibid., 116.

24. Laura Beecher Comer Diary, 8 January 1899, SHC.

25. Ibid., 7 November 1867.

26. Ibid.

27. Pease and Pease, *Ladies, Women and Wenches,* 116–22.

28. Ibid., 121–22.

29. Ibid.

30. Friedman, *Enclosed Garden,* 99. For a discussion on female education see Farnham, *Education of the Southern Belle;* Jabour, *Scarlett's Sisters;* Allmendinger, "Dangers of Antebellum Student Life, 75–85; Clinton, "Equally Their Due"; Schwager, "Educating Women in America"; Stowe, "Not-So Cloistered Academy"; and Ott, *Confederate Daughters,* 14–35.

31. Friedman, *Enclosed Garden,* 99.

32. Farnham, *Education of the Southern Belle,* 89.

33. Julia Tutwiler to Ida Tutwiler, (undated month) 1872, Ida Tutwiler Papers, SHC.

34. Ibid.

35. Welter, "Cult of True Womanhood," 159.

36. Ibid., 158–59.

37. The Cult of Domesticity also extended beyond the South. For a discussion of the ideological construction of gender in England see, Poovey, *Ideological Work of Gender,* and Davidoff and Hall, *Family Fortunes.*

38. Welter, "Cult of True Womanhood."

39. George Fitzhugh's *Sociology for the South* quoted in A. F. Scott, *Southern Lady,* 17.

40. Wyatt-Brown, *Southern Honor,* 254.

41. Martha Foster Crawford Diary, October 1847, in Friedman, *Enclosed Garden,* 33.

42. Grace Elmore Brown Diary, in Weiner, *Heritage of Woe,* xxviii.

43. Welter, "Cult of True Womanhood," 155.

44. Broussard, "Naked before the Law," 57.

45. Blackstone, *Commentaries on the Laws of England,* 442.

46. George Fitzhugh's *Sociology for the South* quoted in A. Scott, *Southern Lady,* 17.

47. Pease and Pease, *Ladies, Women and Wenches,* 116. For a discussion on female passionlessness, see Cott, "Passionlessness."

48. Mary Telfair to Mary Few, 26 November 1814 in B. Wood, *Mary Telfair to Mary Few,* 16.

49. Elizabeth Ruffin quoted in Michael O'Brien, *Evening When Alone,* 11; Julia M. Southall quoted in Jabour, *Scarlett's Sister's,* 275.

50. Hartog, *Man and Wife in America,* 93.

51. Friedman argued that widows and single women were in a unique position in their "sovereignty over all aspects of plantation business." Friedman, *Enclosed Garden,* 129. Likewise, Wood's *Masterful Women* demonstrates how important perceptions of femininity were to the exercise of widow's agency. If widows were seen to act in the interest of their deceased husbands, and to uphold certain standards of feminine behaviour, they benefited from a considerable degree of personal autonomy. As Wood suggested wealthy widows utilized their elevated position within the social hierarchy to reexert their ladyhood, which gilded them with an air of superiority that never-married women tried to emulate in the role of single blessedness. See K. Wood, *Masterful Women,* 158–91 and 9–10.

52. Bynum's work on poor white women in North Carolina underpins the importance of class and wealth to a woman's experience of widowhood. Bynum illustrated how slaveholding

women fared much better in comparison to their poorer counterparts, who were judged unfavorably by southerners. The various ingredients that constituted one's identity as a single white female—such as race, class, wealth, age, and personality—were all key to the experience of widowhood. See Bynum, *Unruly Women*, 16, 25, and 73–74.

53. Clinton, *Plantation Mistress*, 76–77; Fox-Genovese, *Within the Plantation Household*, 202–6, and Wyatt-Brown, *Southern Honor*, 240.

54. Lee, "Beyond Sorrowful Pride," 87.

55. Ibid.

56. Ibid.

57. K. Wood, *Masterful Women*.

58. Ibid., introduction, 1–14.

59. As Kirsten Wood noted: "Widows evicted tenants, fired overseers, and sold slaves, all in the name of obeying (dead) husbands and protecting [their] children." Likewise their "posture of dependent ladyhood . . . encouraged white men to decide that assisting a widow served their own financial interests, familial honour, or personal reputation for chivalry," which replicated existing gender patterns. If an elite, southern woman couched her demands in the language of dependence, and in the service of the family, she soon discovered that she inadvertently gained personal agency. K. Wood, *Masterful Women*, 10.

60. Fox-Genovese, quoted in Censer, *Reconstruction of White Southern Womanhood*, 2.

61. K. Wood, *Masterful Women*, 7.

62. Caroline Cocke to Martha Cocke, Cocke Family Papers, section 31, VHS.

63. Ada Bacot Diary entry, 11 February 1861, in Berlin, *Confederate Nurse*, 27.

64. K. Wood, *Masterful Women*, 1–5.

65. Ada Bacot Diary, 8 September 1862, in Berlin, *Confederate Nurse*, 145.

66. Ibid.

67. Ibid.

68. K. Wood, *Masterful Women*, 28.

69. Single Women in History: 1000–2000, at University of the West of England. Hosted by the Women's History Network, 2006.

70. K. Wood, *Masterful Women*, 27. It is not clear where the term "social widow" first originated. I first became aware of the term at a conference on Singleness in June 2006.

71. Rebecca S. C. Pilsbury Diary, SHC.

72. Ibid., 14 November 1848, microfilm vol. 1.

73. Ibid., 5 December 1848 and 2 December 1848.

74. K. Wood, *Masterful Women*, 28.

75. Ruth Hairston was widowed for a second time in 1852 when Robert Hairston died. See also the Wilson and Hairston Family Papers 1751–1928, folder 1a-8, SHC.

76. Sedevia, "Prospect of Happiness"; Censer, "Smiling through Her Tears"; Bynum, *Unruly Women*.

77. Divorce petition of Martha Smith Green to the General Assembly of Tennessee, Race and Slavery Petitions Project (RSPP hereafter), Legislative Petition Analysis Record (PAR hereafter) no. 11482911.

78. Elizabeth Kirkpatrick to the Hon. Joseph Scott Sole Judge of the Probate Court of Saline County, Arkansas, RSPP, PAR no. 20285701, http://library.uncg.edu/slavery_petitions/index.asp (accessed December 7, 2012).

79. Sarah Anne Moore to the Honorable Joshua Lewis, Judge of the District Court of the First District of the State of Louisiana, 15 April 1830, RSPP, PAR no. 20883012.

80. K. Wood, *Masterful Women*, 133.

81. Ibid., 31. Kirsten Wood explored wills and the property rights of widows from the American Revolution up to the Civil War and examined the way in which they were treated differently in regards to their dower share, in connection to their age, and according to the number and age of their dependents.

82. Ibid.

83. R. E. Coker Papers, SHC.

84. Keziah Brevard "owned four homes, at least three plantations, a grist mill and two hundred slaves." For more information see Moore, *Keziah Brevard*, introduction.

85. Ibid, epilogue.

86. Chambers-Schiller, *Liberty a Better Husband*, 13–15.

87. Welter, "Cult of True Womanhood," 169.

88. Chambers-Schiller, *Liberty a Better Husband*, 10–28.

89. "The Reverie of the Old Maid," *Southern Literary Messenger* (1862): 389–95.

90. Tickner, *Spectacle of Women*, 163.

91. Clinton calculated the age at first marriage of women in the South. This was based on a sample of "750 members of the planter elite born between 1765 and 1815." The sample reveals that 1.9 percent of women married at fifteen, 7.0 percent at sixteen, 9.9 percent at seventeen, 10.2 percent at eighteen, 9.9 percent at nineteen, and 11.8 percent at twenty, with 22 percent of southern girls married between twenty-one and twenty-five years of age. See Clinton, *Plantation Mistress*, appendixes A and B, 233.

92. Anna Elizabeth Holt Diary, 25 January 1861, VHS.

93. Pease and Pease, *Ladies, Women and Wenches*, 20.

94. Grace Elmore Brown Diary, in Weiner, *Heritage of Woe*, xxviii.

95. Clinton, *Plantation Mistress*, 180–81.

96. Lerner, *Grimke Sisters from South Carolina*, 1–12.

97. Ibid., 1–12.

98. Faust, "Altars of Sacrifice."

99. Chambers-Schiller, *Liberty a Better Husband*, 12.

100. Ibid.

101. Lebsock, *Free Women of Petersburg*, 16.

102. The rise of companionate marriage can also be linked to changes in married women's property law (and the rise of the separate estate), which allowed women to protect any property that they took into the marriage with them. This meant that wealthy slaveholding families were less concerned that their property would be put at risk if daughters married for love rather than property.

103. East, *Sarah Morgan*, xxi.

104. Susan to Hannah Wylie, undated letter, Gaston, Strait, Wylie, and Baskin Family Papers, South Caroliniana Library (SCL hereafter).

105. Chesnut, *Diary from Dixie*, 463.

106. Mary Telfair to Mary Few, 24 May 1818, William Few Collection, in C. Johnson, *Mary Telfair*, 87.

107. Mary Telfair to Mary Few, 24 July, no year (item 292), and 7 January 1828 (item 28), both in the William Few Collection, Georgia Archives, Morrow, in C. Carter, *Southern, Single Blessedness*, 1.

108. Grace Elmore Brown Diary, 13 September 1862, Weiner, *Heritage of Woe*, 40.

109. Mary Telfair to Mary Few, 26 November 1814, in B. Wood, *Mary Telfair to Mary Few,* 18–19. The phrase "single blessedness" can be traced back to William Shakespeare's *Midsummer Night's Dream*, 1:1, 20.

110. C. Johnson, *Mary Telfair*, 87.

111. Jabour, *Scarlett's Sisters*, 47–83.

112. Ibid., 10. For a discussion of single blessedness also see 83–111 and 270–77. Jabour's work builds on Joan Cashin's work that suggests that elite women had a "culture of resignation," in that they resigned themselves to the fact that they had little choice, except to silently endure the gender conventions that they knew dominated their world. This quotation is directly from Jabour, *Scarlett's Sisters*, 14.

113. Ott, *Confederate Daughters*, 116–17.

114. Jabour, *Scarlett's Sisters*, 13.

115. Gregory, *Father's Legacy to His Daughters*.

116. Throughout her long life, Susan Wylie sustained a lively correspondence with various male members of her extended family, including her nephews, who wrote to her for advice and shared conversations about politics.

117. Hoffman, "Wylie Women and Accommodating Men," 13.

118. Ibid., 17 and 14.

119. Obituary of Miss Susan Ann Wylie, 6 October 1857, Gaston, Strait, Wylie, and Baskin Family Papers, SCL.

120. Gross, "Lonely Lives Are Not Necessarily Joyless," 46–47.

121. Sexton, *Southern Woman of Letters*, xxii.

122. For further information on single women gaining respectability by promoting feminine roles in others, see Tallentire, "'Everyday Athena's.'"

123. Sarah Varick Cozens Morrison Papers, 15 September 1834, SHC.

124. Mary Susan Ker Papers, SHC.

125. B. Wood, *Mary Telfair to Mary Few*, introduction, xxv.

126. Ironically, these additional burdens often resulted in women delaying marriage—either consciously or unconsciously, as they became embroiled in caring for their siblings, at the expense of making the most of their expected coming-out season.

127. Faust, "Altars of Sacrifice," 188–90.

128. Ibid., 188.

129. Ibid.

130. A. Scott, *Southern Lady*, 81.

131. Virginia also had an older brother, John Hammett, who lived in nearby Prince William County with his wife, Lucy Carney. See Virginia Hammett Diary, VHS.

132. Ibid., 7 May 1863.

133. Ibid., 8 February 1863.

134. Ibid., 23 June 1863.

135. Ibid., 2 December 1863.

136. Grace Elmore Brown Diary, 23 November 1861, in Weiner, *Heritage of Woe*, 16.

137. Elizabeth Collier Diary, 11 April 1862, SHC; and in Faust, "Altars of Sacrifice," 176.

138. Faust, "Altars of Sacrifice," 176.

139. Ibid., 177.

140. Virginia Hammett Diary, 14 August 1864, VHS.

141. Ibid.

142. Rable, *Civil Wars*, 52–53.

143. Virginia Hammett Diary, 10 December 1863 and 3 April 1864, VHS.

144. Ibid.

145. Farmer, *American Civil War 1861–1865*, 54–55.

146. Harriett Perry to her sister Mary Temperance, 22 October 1864, in Johansson, *Widows by the Thousand*, introduction, viii.

147. Lee, "Beyond Sorrowful Pride," 84.

148. Ibid.

149. Berlin, *Confederate Nurse*, 1–15.

150. K. Wood, *Masterful Women*, 4–5.

151. Mary Telfair to Mary Few, 2 December 1829, in C. Johnson, *Mary Telfair*, 88.

152. Sims, *Power of Femininity in the New South*, 1–5.

153. For a discussion on the origins of the Civil War see Dew, *Apostles of Disunion*; Escott, *Major Problems in the Old South*; Hummel, *Emancipating Slaves, Enslaving Freemen*; Link, *Roots of Secession*.

154. For a discussion on Reconstruction see D. T. Carter, *When the War Was Over*; Ezell, *South since 1865*; White, *Reconstruction after the Civil War*, and Farmer, *Reconstruction and the Results of the American Civil War*.

155. Gross, "Lonely Lives Are Not Necessarily Joyless," 33.

Chapter 2   **Single Women and the Southern Family**

1. Inventory of DeRosset Family Papers, 1671–1940, SHC.

2. Ibid. Eliza Ann DeRosset was born in 1802 and died in 1888. Her unmarried sister, Magdalen Mary DeRosset, was slightly younger (1806–50).

3. Catherine Kennedy to Elizabeth DeRosset, 30 April 1836, DeRosset Family Papers, SHC. Catherine also added that so long as she raised her children "to be useful, holy and happy; the sacrifice of my own feelings in some respects, will not be regretted."

4. Eliza Anne to Catherine Kennedy, 13 June 1861, DeRosset Family Papers, SHC.

5. Anna Moore to Magdalen DeRosset, 13 September 1830, DeRosset Family Papers, SHC.

6. See Fox-Genovese, "Family and Female Identity"; Genovese, "'Our Family White and Black'"; Censer, *North Carolina Planters*; Burton, *In My Father's House*, 104–48 and 260–314; C. Carter, *Southern Single Blessedness*, 65–95.

7. Catherine Kennedy to Eliza Ann DeRosset, 1 November 1861, DeRosset Family Papers, SHC.

8. Ibid.

9. Ibid.

10. Ibid.

11. The term "the Cult of True Womanhood" was coined by Welter in "Cult of True Womanhood." The term "Cult of Single Blessedness" is used by Chambers-Schiller, *Liberty a Better Husband.*

12. The exclusion of enslaved black women (in addition to other groups of women, such as Native American women, frontier women, and poorer white people) is critical in understanding the racial and class dynamics of southern society. Racial and class distinctions undergirded southern relations and in doing so provided an important contrast that elevated the perceived status of elite white women. Single women benefitted from this contrast by emphasizing their womanly nature and their possession of a maternal instinct, which was denied to black women.

13. Whites, *Gender Matters,* 15.

14. Genovese, "'Our Family White and Black,'" 69.

15. Fox-Genovese, "Family and Female Identity," 18–19.

16. Burton, *In My Father's House,* 104.

17. In the war and postwar period this was to change, as the patriarchal structure disintegrated in line with military defeat and emancipation of the enslaved. As Jane Turner Censer argued the changes in the elite southern family "mirrored changes taking place elsewhere in the world" as the "patriarchal family had become weakened in much of western society —from Western Europe to the United States." As Censer argued, "women clamoured for expanded access to education, jobs, and the public sphere in the North, but it was followed albeit later in the South." See Censer, *Reconstruction of White Southern Womanhood,* 277.

18. Cashin, "Structure of Antebellum Planter Families," 56.

19. Censer, *North Carolina Planters,* introduction, xiv, and 57.

20. Cashin, "Structure of Antebellum Planter Families," 60–62.

21. Ibid.

22. Bleser, *In Joy and in Sorrow,* introduction, xxi. The northern family was not defined by race in the same way as the southern family was. A more advanced pace of industrialization and urbanization impacted family life, women's working roles, an increased age of first marriage, and a gradual reduction in family size.

23. For a discussion on the development of the North see Clark, "Household Economy, Market Exchange"; Dublin, "Rural Putting Out Work"; Henratta, "Families and Farms"; Larson, *Market Revolution in America;* Rothenburg, "Market and Massachusetts Farmers"; Sellers, *Market Revolution;* and Kulikoff, "Transition to Capitalism." For a discussion on the alleged differences between North and South refer to Pessen, "How Different from Each Other"; Shalhope, "Race, Class, Slavery"; Harris, *Society and Culture in the Slave South,* chapter 1.

24. Jane Turner Censer argued that northern and southern ideals regarding femininity "might have been closest in the 1870s and 1880s." See *Reconstruction of White Southern Womanhood,* 278.

25. Historians such as Drew Gilpin Faust have argued that the Civil War resulted in a "marriage squeeze" resulting in "a generation of southern women [facing] the prospect of becoming spinsters reliant on family support" as a consequence of the catastrophic loss of southern men during the war. This argument has been contested by J. David Hacker, who utilized the federal decennial censuses from 1850 to 1880 in order to explore the long-term demographic impact of war on marriage patterns. According to Hacker's findings, 92 percent

of southern white women who came of marriage age during the war did eventually marry. While their average age may have been somewhat higher, this coalesced with a "gradual increase in the age of marriage" tied to economics. For more information, refer to Hacker, "Effect of the Civil War on Southern Marriage Patterns," 40 and 42.

26. Catherine Sedgwick quoted in Lubovich, "Married or Single," 23.

27. Mary Kelly quoted in Lubovich, "Married or Single."

28. Ibid., 23.

29. Clinton, *Plantation Mistress*, 85.

30. Marina Oshana described autonomous persons as "beings in actual control of their own choices, actions and goals," and as a "person in possession of de facto power to govern himself." Oshana, *Personal Autonomy in Society*, 3.

31. Whites, *Gender Matters*, 91.

32. Censer, *Reconstruction of White Southern Womanhood*, 12.

33. Cousin Adelaide to Margaret Bain Cameron, 1 February 1853. Cameron Family Papers, SHC.

34. Margaret was one of eight children; Mary Anne, Thomas Amis Dudley, Paul Carrington, Margaret Bain, Rebecca Bennehan, Jean Syme, Anne Owen, and Mildred Coles.

35. Censer, *North Carolina Planters*, 81.

36. Mary Susan Ker Papers, SHC, and Holley, "'But One Dependence.'"

37. Battle, *History of the University of North Carolina*, 107.

38. Inventory of the Edward Varner Family Papers 1730–1965, Georgia Historical Society (GHS hereafter).

39. Josephine Varner Diary, 24 April 1863, Edward Varner Family Papers, GHS.

40. Ibid., 2 February 1865.

41. Ibid., 23 February 1863.

42. Family members recognized the strong relationship between the two sisters and used the metaphor of a stream to describe the relationship between them. When Amanda Varner died at age eighty, her cousin wrote to Josephine Varner that "you live running along like two sweet and useful streams—side by side down the slope into the shadows and now into the sunlight," and she referred to their "long and beautiful association together." Cousin to Joe Varner, 15 April 1915, Edward Varner Family Papers, GHS.

43. Josephine Varner Diary, 1 January 1865, Edward Varner Family Papers, GHS.

44. Ibid., 15 December 1881.

45. Ibid.

46. C. Carter, *Southern Single Blessedness*, 65–95.

47. Ibid.

48. Chambers-Schiller, "Woman Is Born to Love."

49. Smith-Rosenberg, "Female World of Love and Ritual," 9.

50. On the question of honor see: Wyatt-Brown, *Southern Honor*, and Crowther, "Holy Honor."

51. Clinton, *Other Civil War*, 43. Clinton argued that the "feminization of American religion" afforded women an opportunity to exercise control, to state a preference," and to exercise autonomy.

52. Broussard, "Female Solitaires"; Chambers-Schiller, *Liberty a Better Husband*. Since Chambers-Schiller, other important work has emerged on single women: Berend, "Cultural

and Social Sources of Spinsterhood"; Hill, *Women Alone;* Froide, *Never Married;* Tallentire, "'Everyday Athena's'"; C. Carter, *Southern Single Blessedness;* Bell and Yans, *Women on Their Own.*

53. Margaret Coxe quoted in Chambers-Schiller, "Woman Is Born to Love," 36. Note how Coxe placed mothers first and single women second.

54. Margaret Williford to Martha (Williford) Service, 23 July 1849; Carrie Holmes to Martha (Williford) Service, 3 September 1849, Emma Marie Service Papers, SHC, in C. Carter, *Southern Single Blessedness,* 84.

55. Margaret Williford to Martha (Williford) Service, 23 July 1849; Carrie Holmes to Martha (Williford) Service, 3 September 1849, Emma Marie Service Papers, SHC, in C. Carter, *Southern Single Blessedness,* 84.

56. Margaret Williford to Martha (Williford) Service, 23 July 1849; Carrie Holmes to Martha (Williford) Service, 3 September 1849, Emma Marie Service Papers, SHC, in C. Carter, *Southern Single Blessedness,* 84.

57. Frank Shaw to Mary Susan Ker, 30 October 1867, Mary Susan Ker Papers, SHC.

58. Memorandum Mary Ker to Mamie and Nellie Ker, 10 December 1871, Mary Susan Ker Papers, SHC.

59. Mary Susan Ker Diary, 11 June 1894, Mary Susan Ker Papers, SHC.

60. Ibid., 13 May 1894.

61. Ibid., 19 May 1894.

62. Mamie Ker had five children: Albert, Mary, Matilda, Catherine, and Percy.

63. In September 1894 Mary joined the staff at Mrs. Blake's school in New Orleans, where she remained for a year.

64. William Henry Ker to Mary Susan Ker, 4 February 1878, Mary Susan Ker Papers, SHC.

65. Broussard, "Female Solitaires."

66. Ibid.

67. Chambers-Schiller, "Woman Is Born to Love," 35.

68. Mary Telfair to Mary Few, 2 December 1829, in B. Wood, *Mary Telfair to Mary Few,* 93, and Chambers-Schiller, "Woman Is Born to Love," 35.

69. Mary Telfair to Mary Few, 25 [?] [? 1826], in B. Wood, *Mary Telfair to Mary Few,* 62.

70. Mary Telfair to Mary Few, 25 [?] [? 1826], in B. Wood, *Mary Telfair to Mary Few,* 62.

71. Whites, *Gender Matters,* 13–14.

72. O'Brien, *Evening When Alone,* 32.

73. Ibid., 33.

74. Ann Lewis Hardeman Diary, 8 July 1850, in O'Brien, *Evening When Alone,* 222.

75. Ann was evidently a religious woman and saw to it that the children attended church and read regularly from the Bible. She is typical of a woman affected by the Second Great Awakening and the spirit of religious revival in the early to mid-nineteenth century.

76. Diary of Ann Lewis Hardeman, 1850–67, 6 December 1860, in O'Brien, *Evening When Alone,* 314.

77. George Mordecai was born into a prominent and well-connected family in Warrenton, North Carolina, in 1801. He became the president of the Bank of the State of North Carolina in 1949. He also held a number of other titles and posts, in addition to his job as a lawyer. For further information refer to the biography in the George W. Mordecai Papers, SHC.

78. George W. Mordecai Papers, SHC. Caroline was born in 1794 and died in 1862. She married Achilles Plunkett, and the couple had three children, all of whom died in infancy. Achilles died in 1824, leaving Caroline as a young widow. During her widowhood she tried, unsuccessfully, to run the family academy in Warrenton. She taught her brother's children before opening a small school in Mobile, Alabama. Eventually she moved back to the family home in Raleigh. Following a turbulent period of poor mental health she was institutionalized in an insane asylum where she eventually died in 1862.

79. Emma Mordecai to George Mordecai, September 29, 1862, George W. Mordecai Papers. This reiterates the idea of the collective family and the reciprocal nature of single women's relationships with their siblings. For example, in a letter from Emma to George Mordecai on 18 November 1844 she expresses her deep affection for George, her "guardian brother," for whom she had the "tenderest gratitude." "Never, my dear brother, can I forget all that you have suffered for me and all your noble and touching kindness to me," she wrote with fondest affection. Microfilm series Southern Women and Their Families, GMP 522, reel 6, Wilson Library, SHC.

80. Ellen Allen to George W. Mordecai, 30 August 1860, George W. Mordecai Papers, microfilm series, subseries 1.2.4 1861–65, reels 10 and 11, SHC.

81. The Shakers were a religious sect that formed in eighteenth-century England. The group is marked by their monastic, communitarian life, which was devoted to preparing the way for God's will to be carried out on earth. For further information see Stein, *Shaker Experience in America*, 1–8.

82. Ellen Lazarus to George Mordecai, Brentwood, 23 March 1868, George W. Mordecai Papers, SHC.

83. Bingham, *Mordecai: An Early American Family*, 42.

84. Paul Cameron to Margaret Cameron, 15 March 1853, Cameron Family Papers, SHC. Paul is referring to the loss of their father and the continued ill health of their sister, Mildred Coles, who was never married and was supported by both Paul and Margaret Cameron.

85. Margaret Cameron to Paul Cameron, 15 March 1853, Cameron Family Papers.

86. Mary Scudder to John Scudder, July 20 1856, Scudder Family Papers, GHS.

87. C. Carter, *Southern Single Blessedness*, 71.

88. Censer, *Reconstruction of White Southern Womanhood*, 113.

89. Eliza Holladay to Elizabeth Travers Lewis, 22 May 1848, Holladay Family Papers, VHS.

90. Ibid.

91. Ann Lewis Hardeman Diary, 29 June 1853, in O'Brien, *Evening When Alone*, 254.

92. Ibid.

93. C. Johnson, *Mary Telfair*, 49.

94. Mary Telfair to Mary Few, 6 December 1817, quoted in C. Johnson, *Mary Telfair*, 49.

95. Mary Telfair to Mary Few, 28 March 1818, quoted in C. Johnson, *Mary Telfair*, 49–50.

96. Inventory to the George W. Mordecai Papers, SHC.

97. Ellen Mordecai to George W. Mordecai, 16 October 1868, George W. Mordecai Papers, SHC.

98. Emma Mordecai to George W. Mordecai, Columbus, 23 April 1869, George W. Mordecai Papers, SHC.

99. In a speech in March 1838, reported in the newspaper *Liberator,* Angelina spoke about her reasons for leaving the South. "I stand before you as a southerner, exiled from the land of my birth by the sound of the lash and the piteous cry of the slave. I stand before you as a repentant slaveholder. I stand before you as a moral being."

100. Edmundson Family Papers, 598a 998–1006, section 28, VHS.

101. Obituary, 16 October 1857, Gaston, Strait, Wiley, and Baskin Family Papers, SCL.

102. William Mobley to Hannah Wylie, 12 November 1859, Wylie Papers, SCL.

103. Mary Telfair to Mary Few, 2 December 1825, in B. Wood, *Mary Telfair to Mary Few,* 48–49.

104. Mary Telfair to Mary Few, 2 December 1825, in B. Wood, *Mary Telfair to Mary Few,* 49.

105. Josephine Blair Harvie to Sarah Harvie, 30 January 1852, section 3, Harvie Family Papers 1807–1913, VHS.

106. Josephine Blair Harvie to Charles Old Harvie, Dykeland, 23 December [undated year], Harvie Family Papers 1807–1913, VHS.

107. Harvie Family Papers, VHS.

108. *Macon Telegraph,* 1826, box 4, folder 54, Edward Varner Papers, GHS.

109. Broussard, "Female Solitaires," 21.

Chapter 3 **Work**

1. Virginia Hammett Diary, 1 August 1863, VHS.

2. Massey, *Women in the Civil War,* introduction, xviii.

3. Grace Elmore Brown Diary, 1 October 1865, in Weiner, *Heritage of Woe,* 48.

4. Grace Elmore Brown Diary, 13 July 1865, in Weiner, *Heritage of Woe,* 14–15.

5. Wiley, *Phoebe Yates Pember,* 105.

6. For a discussion on how fulfilling traditional gender roles led to female agency see Broussard's "Female Solitaires," 12 and 21. For the postwar era refer to Gross, "Lonely Lives Are Not Necessarily Joyless."

7. Jabour, *Scarlett's Sisters,* 279.

8. For more information on single women's roles within the family refer to C. Carter, *Southern Single Blessedness,* 65–95.

9. Young girls often aspired to be like their single female teachers, especially during their time in the female academies. Anya Jabour argued that life in the academies led to the development of female resistance to accepting conventional gender roles. Jabour, *Scarlett's Sisters,* chapter 2, and 61 and 63.

10. Mitchell, "Ann Pamela Cunningham," 11.

11. Ibid.

12. Nancy Hewitt in Mitchell, "Ann Pamela Cunningham," 5.

13. Chambers-Schiller, *Liberty a Better Husband,* 6.

14. Ibid., 5.

15. Faust, "Altars of Sacrifice," 1209.

16. Campbell and Rice, *Woman's War.*

17. Rebecca S. C. Pilsbury Diary, SHC.

18. Ibid., 20 November 1848.

19. Ibid.

20. Ibid., 2 December 1848.

21. This links to what Joyce Broussard has called the "servant ideal," which is the idea that servitude was an avenue to self-fulfillment and female agency. See Broussard, "Female Solitaires," 12.

22. Faust, Glymph, and Rable, "A Woman's War: Southern Women in the Civil War," in *A Woman's War: Southern Women, Civil War, and the Confederate Legacy* (1996) 2.

23. Laura Beecher Comer Diary, 3 December 1862, volume 1, January 1862–April 1863 and 2 January 1862, SHC.

24. K. Wood, *Masterful Women*, 4–5.

25. Ibid.

26. Laura Beecher Comer Diary, April 1863, SHC.

27. Ibid., 28 December 1867. On 6 March 1867 she also wrote about her anxiety managing the freedmen, planting, and general tasks on the plantation.

28. Ibid., 26 November 1872.

29. Clinton, *Plantation Mistress*, 109 and 179.

30. Laura Beecher Comer Diary, 16 June 1872, SHC.

31. Catherine Edwards to Charles Biddle, 4 July 1805, Catherine Edwards Papers, SCL. Likewise, Leonora Whiteside, widow of James Anderson Whiteside, inherited a vast estate in 1861. On the back of her excellent management of the estate she was reputed to be the richest woman in Tennessee. Myers, *Children of Pride*.

32. Catherine Edwards to Charles Biddle, 4 July 1805, Catherine Edwards Papers, SCL.

33. Paulina Read Le Grand to William Huntington, Edge Hill, 25 March 1838, William Huntington Papers, VHS.

34. Myers, *Children of Pride*, 1728–29.

35. Ibid.

36. Moore, *Keziah Brevard*, 1–17.

37. Keziah Brevard Diary, 30 January 1861, in Moore, *Keziah Brevard*, 83.

38. Keziah Brevard makes reference to "Jim" on a regular basis. On 7 February 1861, "Jim is an impudent Negro—and every servant knuckels to him"; 9 February 1861, "Jim is a self-willed Negro"; 13 February 1861, "I never did have such impudence offered me—I do not think I ought to let it pass without punishment." Keziah Brevard Diary, Moore, *Keziah Brevard*, 83.

39. Rable, *Civil Wars*, 117.

40. Ibid.

41. Moore, *Keziah Brevard*, 15 and 37.

42. Keziah Brevard Diary 13 October 1860, 19 October 1860, 24 October 1860, in Moore, *Keziah Brevard*, 39, 41, and 44.

43. Shalhope, "Race, Class, Slavery."

44. Moore, *Keziah Brevard*, 89.

45. K. Wood, *Masterful Women*, 92.

46. Lebsock, *Free Women of Petersburg*, introduction, xv.

47. Ibid. Lebsock's study examined black and white women in an urban center, but shades of her argument can also be seen within the planter class in the prewar South.

48. R.E. Coker Papers, 18 October 1861, SHC.

49. A Short History of Sarah Witherspoon McIver and Genealogical Record, R. E. Coker Family Papers, SHC.

50. R. E. Coker Papers, 18 October 1861, SHC.

51. Ambrose Stone to Catherine Stone, 6 March 1847, Stone Family Papers, SHC.

52. Ruth Stovall Hairston Wilson to her father, Peter Hairston, Berry Hill, 29 May 1814, Wilson and Hairston Family Papers, SHC.

53. He also grew cotton in Columbus, Mississippi.

54. Inventory of Wilson and Hairston Family Papers, SHC, 1.

55. Frances Devereux Polk to her daughter, Frances Polk Skipton, 6 June 1866, Polk Family Papers, SHC.

56. Ibid., 17 April 1868.

57. Ibid., 15 February 1869.

58. Ibid., 9 November 1869.

59. Octavia Wyche Otey Journal 1849–88, Wyche and Otey Family Papers, 1824–1936, SHC.

60. Ibid.

61. Ibid., 24 January 1871, 26 January 1871, 16 February 1871.

62. Ibid.

63. For a discussion on emancipation in the South see Daniel, "Metamorphosis of Slavery"; Foner, "From Slavery to Freedom"; Escott, *Major Problems in the Old South,* 537–57, and O'Donovan, *Becoming Free in the Cotton South.*

64. A more recent study of upper-class southern women's lives in the postwar era is Jane Turner Censer, *Reconstruction of White Southern Womanhood.*

65. Octavia Wyche Otey Journal 1849–88, Wyche and Otey Family Papers, 1824–1936, SHC. For example 25 January 1871, 20 March 1871, 16 February 1871.

66. C. Carter, *Southern Single Blessedness,* 183.

67. Ibid.

68. Anne Jennings Wise Hobson Diary, 24 October 1863, 27 December 1863, 24 January 1864, 12 November 1864, VHS.

69. Ibid.

70. Ibid., 30 April 1865.

71. Ibid.

72. Ibid.

73. McPherson in Shalhope, "Race, Class, Slavery."

74. Anne Jennings Wise Hobson Diary, 9 February 1868, VHS.

75. Ibid. Anne Hobson was a Presbyterian, a woman guided by her faith. However, she worried that her husband lacked the same belief, and in her comment on his life, she is also referring to his spiritual salvation.

76. Berlin, *Confederate Nurse,* 27–28.

77. Ada Bacot Diary, 24 February 1861, in Berlin, *Confederate Nurse,* 27–28.

78. Historian Walter Johnson warned that the meaning of "agency" has become overloaded as a term. He points to a "misleading entanglement of the categories of "humanity" and "agency." W. Johnson, "On Agency."

79. Ada Bacot Diary, 27 October 1871, in Berlin, *Confederate Nurse,* 52.

80. Ada Bacot's earlier memories at Arnmore were happy. She recalled fonder memories when she was a mistress and "a loving husband provided. Memory carries me back to the happy time, and fills my eyes with tears." Ada Bacot Diary, 1 May 1861, Berlin, *Confederate Nurse,* 32.

81. Rable, *Civil Wars,* 121.

82. Massey, *Women in the Civil War,* 44.

83. For a further discussion on the reconstruction of gender models see Censer, *Reconstruction of White Southern Womanhood,* 10–50.

84. Rable, *Civil Wars,* 121. Rable noted that while women gained self-confidence, meaning, and importance through nursing, they knew it was only a temporary role. He claims that most went back to being wives and mothers after the war, but he did not account for those women who were single.

85. Clinton, *Other Civil War,* 121. Also see 121–46.

86. Thomas, *Confederate Nation,* 225–29.

87. Wiley, *Phoebe Yates Pember,* 105.

88. Gross, "Lonely Lives Are Not Necessarily Joyless," 46–49.

89. Cumming, *Journal of Hospital Life,* 44.

90. Ibid.

91. Ibid.

92. Ibid.

93. Welter, "Cult of True Womanhood," 164.

94. In the battle of Shiloh it is reported that 23,746 Confederate and Union soldiers were killed or wounded or went missing, "Civil War Trust," http://www.civilwar.org/battlefields/shiloh.html?tab=facts (accessed July 10, 2012).

95. Cumming, *Journal of Hospital Life,* 44.

96. Ibid.

97. Ibid., 13.

98. Ibid., 44.

99. Ibid.

100. Faust, Glymph, and Rable, in E. D. C. Campbell and Kym Rice, *Woman's War,* 5.

101. Ibid., 5.

102. Wiley, *Phoebe Yates Pember,* 19.

103. Richmond was the chief medical center of the Confederacy, and many of the most important general hospitals were established in the city. Other hospitals established in Richmond included Winder, opened in 1862, and Jackson, opened in 1863. See also L. Oates, "Civil War Nurses."

104. Wiley, *Phoebe Yates Pember,* 1 and 4.

105. Ibid.

106. Ibid.

107. Ibid., 6.

108. Ibid., 31–32.

109. Rable, *Civil Wars,* 122.

110. Wiley, *Phoebe Yates Pember,* 110–11.

111. In autumn 1862 Congress set out official nursing duties and salaries. Rable, *Civil Wars,* 122.

112. Phoebe Yates Pember to her sister, Richmond, Virginia, 30 January 1863, in Wiley, *Phoebe Yates Pember,* 110–11.

113. Wiley, *Phoebe Yates Pember,* 32.

114. Ibid., 33.

115. Ibid., 38–39.

116. Ibid. 78.

117. Ibid.

118. Chambers-Schiller, *Liberty a Better Husband,* 13–14.

119. Fraise, *Florence Nightingale of the Southern Army,* 13.

120. Ibid., 39.

121. *Daily Florida Citizen,* Friday, 7 August 1894, Swann Family Papers, SHC.

122. Ibid.

123. Fraise, *Florence Nightingale of the Southern Army,* 93–95.

124. Ibid. Also refer to Faust, "Altars of Sacrifice," 1217. Evans later went on to nurse sick soldiers and based her wartime novel *Macaria* on these wartime experiences, which served as a good example of how single women could fulfill the notion of single blessedness through their wartime work.

125. Augusta Jane Evans to Ella Newsom, 28 October 1863, in Fraise, *Florence Nightingale of the Southern Army,* 93. See also 93–95.

126. Augusta Jane Evans, *Macaria,* 413, 409, in Gross, "Lonely Lives Are Not Necessarily Joyless," 46.

127. Gross, "Lonely Lives Are Not Necessarily Joyless," 46.

128. Murray, "My Sisters, Don't Be Afraid of the Words, 'Old Maid,'" introduction.

129. The Diary of Emma Mordecai, 18 May 1864, George W. Mordecai Papers, SHC.

130. Ellen Mordecai to George Mordecai, Richmond, 4 September 1862, George W. Mordecai Papers, SHC.

131. Anne Jennings Wise Hobson Diary, 24 January 1864, 12 November 1864, VHS.

132. Faust, Glymph, and Rable, in E. D. C. Campbell and Kym Rice, *Woman's War,* 9.

133. Bingham, *Mordecai: An Early American Family,* 37.

134. Ibid.

135. Ibid.

136. Ibid., 38.

137. Narcissa Clayton Papers, 19 May 1859, SHC. Likewise in September 1835 Sarah Varick Cozens (who was also unmarried) took charge of a school. She noted, "Have again taken charge of a school, how great the responsibility of my situation." 15 September 1834, Sarah Varick Cozens Papers, SHC.

138. Anne Elizabeth Holt Diary, 18 May 1859, VHS.

139. Ibid., 20 May 1859.

140. Ibid., 29 April 1860.

141. Ibid., 25 January 1861.

142. Ibid., 18 May 1859.

143. A. Scott, *Southern Lady,* 111–33.

144. Report of the Senate Committee on Education and Labor, in A. F. Scott, *Southern Lady*, 111.

145. Ralph Elliott to his mother, Mrs. A. Elliott, Charleston, 15 June 1864, Elliott and Gonzales Family Papers 1701–1898, SHC.

146. Ibid.

147. Ibid. In a letter written on 9 July 1865, Mary noted how the servants had a change in attitude and that they had "entirely turned fool and they act as if we had always been their worst enemies." Some of her old slaves had gone (Eleanor, Topsy, and Lawrence). The new attendants (Ben, Grace, and Edward) are described as "impertinent." In a letter to her mother, on 6 September 1865 she gives a detailed description of her daily chores, which include food preparation (making bread, skimming milk, cutting the meat) and being in the school room to hear the children learn (6 September 1865).

148. Ibid. Mary Johnstone to Emmaline Johnstone, undated.

149. Ott, *Confederate Daughters*, 98–99.

150. Josephine Varner Diary, 1 July 1862 Edward Varner Family Papers, GHS.

151. Laura Edwards suggested that women had to "confront the limitations and vulnerability of their legally and culturally defined dependence" as they waved their men off to war, and this resulted in feelings of despondency. See Edwards, *Scarlett Doesn't Live Here Anymore*, 74.

152. Josephine Varner Diary, 23 February 1863, Edward Varner Family Papers.

153. Welter, "Cult of True Womanhood," 169.

154. Josephine Varner Diary, 21 April 1863, Edward Varner Family Papers, GHS.

155. Julia Tutwiler to Ida Tutwiler, 1872, Ida Tutwiler Papers, 1872, SHC; Encyclopedia of Alabama, http://www.encyclopediaofalabama.org, accessed 15 January 2010.

156. Julia Tutwiler to Ida Tutwiler, 1872, Ida Tutwiler Papers, 1872, SHC.

157. Welter, "Cult of True Womanhood," 170.

158. Censer, *Reconstruction of White Southern Womanhood*, 275.

159. Mary Y. Harth to Mrs. Watson, 26 November 1865, Mary Y. Harth Family Papers, SCL.

160. Ibid.

161. She requested, "I am induced to ask a favour of you to give me the school. I have always felt the greatest interest, in their welfare and would feel it my duty as well as my pleasure to devote my time and attention to their intellectual moral and religious instruction. I am a widow with four children and a Communicant of our beloved Episcopal Church." Mary Harth, September 1865, Mary Y. Harth Family Papers, SCL.

162. A. F. Scott, *Southern Lady*, 118.

163. Mary Susan Ker was an important member of the Ker family, who worked as a governess and later a teacher in order to help contribute to her family. She also took on the guardianship of her two nieces and later two great-nieces in the role of a maiden aunt.

164. There are various letters on the topic of Mary's teaching. See also William Ker to Mary Ker, 30 August 1874; Thomas Butler to Mary Ker, 21 October 1874; William Ker to Mary Susan Ker, 20 December 1874. Mary Susan Ker Papers, SHC.

165. Ibid., 14 May 1894.

166. William Henry Ker to Mary Susan Ker, 4 February 1878, Mary Susan Ker Papers, SHC.

167. Holley, "'But One Dependence,'" 39.

168. Mary Susan Ker Diary, 8 December 1894, in Holley, "'But One Dependence,'" 39.

169. Butler, *Unhurried Years*, 106.

170. Welter, "Cult of True Womanhood," 174.

171. Chambers-Schiller, "'Woman Is Born to Love,'" and C. Carter, "Indispensable Spinsters."

172. Sarah Catherine Walthall to Fitz William Rosier, 1 May 1869, Rosier Family Papers, VHS.

173. Ibid., 28 November 1868.

174. Ibid., 25 April 1871 and 31 March 1874.

175. Ibid., 9 February 1875.

176. Ibid., 20 January 1870.

177. Ibid., 25 April 1871.

178. Ibid.

179. Cornelia Phillips Spencer in "Young Ladies' Column," *North Carolina Presbyterian*, 1870, quoted in A. F. Scott, *Southern Lady*, 105.

180. Thomas, *Confederate Nation*, 229.

181. Sims, *Power of Femininity*, 2. Sims discussed the way in which the feminine ideal had been adapted in wartime in order to be able to incorporate the new attributes that southern women had had to develop in wartime.

Chapter 4   Female Friendship

1. Josephine is regularly referred to as Joe and Josie by friends and family.

2. Elizabeth Knowlton used the term "isolated dream" to refer to Alice Baldy's daydreaming about setting up a home with Joe Varner. See Knowlton, "'Only a Woman Like Yourself,'" 40.

3. Alice Baldy to Josephine Varner, 31 January 1871, in ibid., 40.

4. Ibid., 39.

5. Josephine Varner Diary, 29 December 1866, Edward Varner Family Papers, GHS.

6. Ibid.

7. Ibid., 7 February 1867 and 31 August 1863.

8. See Vicinus, *Independent Women*, 121–62; Vicinus, "Distance and Desire," and Farnham, *Education of the Southern Belle*, 146–67.

9. Alice Baldy to Josephine Varner, 29 April 1870, Edward Varner Family Papers, GHS.

10. Ibid., 29 April 1870.

11. Ibid., 7 February 1870.

12. Martha Vicinus discussed the way in which single women embraced the idea of asexuality as a way to expand their sphere of influence, for example in religion. See Vicinus, *Independent Women*, 17–19. Conversely, in 1903 Havelock Ellis correlated the notion that "women lacked sexual passion with social repression and dysfunction." See Cott, "Passionlessness," 219.

13. There is much debate on the existence of a women's culture. Scholars who agree that it existed include: A. F. Scott, *Southern Lady*; Smith-Rosenberg, "Female World of Love and Ritual"; Welter, "Cult of True Womanhood"; Kerber, "Separate Spheres, Female Worlds, Woman's Place"; Cott, *Bonds of Womanhood*; Lebsock, *Free Women of Petersburg*, 112–45.

Scholars who have taken issue with this view include Clinton, *Plantation Mistress,* and Fox-Genovese, *Within the Plantation Household.*

14. Gross, "Lonely Lives Are Not Necessarily Joyless." For more information on how the war was a catalyst that provided single women with an opportunity to fulfill "single blessedness" see also Chambers-Schiller, *Liberty a Better Husband,* 5–7.

15. Holloway, "Searching for Southern Lesbian History," 266. For the entire chapter see 258–72.

16. Knowlton, "'Only a Woman Like Yourself,'" 36.

17. Definition of Friendship, http://friends.com/definition-of-friendship#sthash.ciy HnoUR.dpuf Friendship (accessed June 7, 2016).

18. Mary Telfair Commonplace Book 1822–29 in C. Johnson, *Mary Telfair,* 115.

19. Chambers-Schiller, "'Woman Is Born to Love.'"

20. Cott, "Passionlessness."

21. Smith-Rosenberg, "Female World of Love and Ritual."

22. Ibid., 9. Female friendship began at home, in the safe confines of the southern family, in the relationships between mother and daughter, sisters, female cousins, and aunts. The loving bonds between sisters were used as a model for female friendship. These friendships often began at school. As young girls pined and missed their home and family they often dealt with this by replicating familial ties in their relationships with nonkin. These fictive ties mirrored the form, function, and expression of sorority, blurring the boundaries between family and friendship.

23. On the question of honor see Wyatt-Brown, *Southern Honor,* and Crowther, "Holy Honor."

24. For a discussion on the alleged differences between North and South refer to Pessen, "How Different from Each Other"; Shalhope, "Race, Class, Slavery"; Harris, *Society and Culture in the Slave South,* chapter 1.

25. Farnham, *Education of the Southern Belle,* chapters 6 and 7.

26. Holloway, "Searching for Southern Lesbian History," 259.

27. Welter, "Cult of True Womanhood."

28. Smith-Rosenberg, "Female World of Love and Ritual."

29. Jeffreys, *Spinster and Her Enemies,* 112.

30. Smith-Rosenberg and Rosenberg, "Female Animal"; and Degler, "What Ought to Be."

31. Cott, "Passionlessness," and Faderman, *Surpassing the Love of Men,* 157–77. Marriage was seen in many ways as a way to "neutralize" intense forms of female friendships. Therefore women who failed to marry could be viewed, particularly in light of changing attitudes to sexuality in the late nineteenth century, as potentially subversive.

32. Mary Telfair to Mary Few, 26 January 1840 and 5 April 1840 in B. Wood, *Mary Telfair to Mary Few,* 197 and 199–202.

33. Ibsen, and Klobus, "Fictive Kin Term Use."

34. Mary Telfair to Mary Few, 16 December 1828, in B. Wood, *Mary Telfair to Mary Few,* 82.

35. Mary Telfair to Mary Few, March 1829, in ibid., 86.

36. Alice Baldy to Josephine Varner, 29 April 1870, Edward Varner Family Papers, GHS.

37. Cameron Family Papers, 19, 20, 21 November 1863, SHC.

38. Myers, *Children of Pride*, 1576. Her comment was a playful joke as the ladies shared the same name. Yet even in jest the reference to being a "blessing" and proving useful remains. Mary Taylor never married and spent most of her life on the family plantation in Worcester County, Maryland. Mary Sharpe married at the age of twenty-two and had five children.

39. Jabour, "Female Families," 90.

40. Ibid., 89–96.

41. Sarah Morgan Journal, 23 May 1861 in East, *Sarah Morgan*, 81–82, and introduction, xxiv.

42. East, *Sarah Morgan*, xxxix. Sarah Morgan married Roman Catholic Frank Dawson, editor of the *News* and *Courier*. The couple had three children, the latter of whom died at five months old. In March 1889 Frank Dawson was shot dead, leaving Sarah Morgan a widow with two children to raise. She was forty-seven years old.

43. Lasser, "'Let Us Be Sisters Forever.'" Lasser focused on the relationship between Antoinette Brown and Lucy Stone, two lifelong friends, who later became sisters through marriage. She highlights the frequency with which the two women repeatedly used sororal terms to refer to one another, long before their marital alliances gave them basis for justifying the use of such a term in reality.

44. S. L. Moore to Eliza DeRosset, 25 July 1825, DeRosset Family Papers, SHC. The DeRosset family were from Wilmington, North Carolina; they owned a rice plantation in Brunswick County, North Carolina. Eliza Ann (1802–88) and Magdalen Mary (1806–50) were the unmarried daughters of Armand John DeRosset (1767–1859) and his wife, Catherine Fullerton DeRosset (1773–1837). For more information in the family history refer to DeRosset Family Papers, 1671–1940 (in particular the inventory), SHC.

45. Jabour, "Female Families," 86. Lizzie Grove resided in Missouri and Laura Brumback in Illinois, though she was originally from Virginia. They were "faithful" lovers who remained unmarried. Their correspondence and the language they used adds a further dimension to same sex friendship that mirrored heterosexuality rather than deliberately covering it up.

46. Alice Baldy to Josephine Varner, 1870, in Knowlton, "'Only a Woman Like Yourself,'" 41.

47. Hannah Wylie to Susan and Mary Wylie, 4 May 1851, on the topic of Katherine's wedding. She added, "Aunt Kate was not much pleased with the match she said it is [some]thing she would never have anything to do with unless it was to advise if she thought they were making a bad choice." Gaston, Strait, Wylie, and Baskin Family Papers, SCL.

48. Eliza Holladay to Elizabeth Travers Lewis, 22 May 1865, Holladay Family Papers, VHS. She was responding to Elizabeth's letter in which she had declared "her exceeding liking for the delightful state of single blessedness."

49. Wink, "'She Left Nothing in Particular,'" 29. Southern society celebrated piety, purity, submissiveness, and domesticity in women. These four cardinal virtues formed the benchmark of the Cult of True Womanhood. Therefore the freedom to express oneself in writing marked an opportunity for self-expression, self-fulfillment, and personal agency in its most primal form.

50. Anna Moore to Magdalen DeRosset, 13 September 1830, DeRosset Family Papers, SHC.

51. Mary Telfair to Mary Few, 3 December 1813, in C. Johnson, *Mary Telfair*, 109.

52. Wink, "'She Left Nothing in Particular,'" 17.

53. Mary Telfair to Mary Few, 13 October [no year], in C. Johnson, *Mary Telfair*, 88. Single women always felt that they had to prove themselves in a way that married women did not.

54. Ellen Mordecai Diary, 11 November 1817, Mordecai Family Papers, 1649–1947, SHC. Ellen Mordecai (1790–1884) was an unmarried writer, teacher, and governess. The Mordecais were a Jewish family from North Carolina. See Bingham, *Mordecai: An Early American Family*, 82. Bingham noted of the family that it "seemed they would remain single yet together, always a queer, old fashioned, stiff set." Sally Hill to Virginia Holladay, [undated] ca. 1857, Holladay Family Papers, VHS. In a subsequent letter Sally again writes how she dreams of meeting with Virginia again and fantasizes about "sweet walks and sweet talks" with her. Sally Hill to Virginia Holladay, 8 February 1858, Holladay Family Papers, VHS.

55. Sally Hill to Virginia Holladay, 20 May 1857, Holladay Family Papers, VHS. "My dear Virginia, I sometimes feel as if I would give anything in my possession if I could only see you for a little while—you have no idea of how impatient I feel and when shall we meet I cannot tell." Also Broussard, "Female Solitaires," 12. Broussard argued that all women were relegated to a "servant ideal" whereby they devoted themselves to the patriarchal order of life, but by doing so they achieved agency and self-fulfillment.

56. Augusta Jane Evans to Rachel Lyons, 8 December 1859; Augusta Jane Evans to Rachel Lyons, 4 January 1860, in Sexton, *Southern Woman of Letters*, 3 and 13.

57. Ibid.

58. Augusta Jane Evans to Rachel Lyons, 29 May 1860, and Augusta Jane Evans to Rachel Lyons; 4 January 1860, in Sexton, *Southern Woman of Letters*, 13.

59. Eliza DeRosset to Magdalen Mary DeRosset, 2 July 1825, DeRosset Family Papers, SHC.

60. Diary of Mary Ker, 9 October 1895, Ker Family Papers, SHC.

61. Josephine Varner Diary, Edward Varner Family Papers, GHS.

62. Broussard, "Female Solitaires," 12.

63. Augusta Jane Evans to Rachel Lyons, 14 June 1860, in Sexton, *Southern Woman of Letters*, 13.

64. C. Johnson, *Mary Telfair*, 108.

65. Farnham in C. Johnson, *Mary Telfair*, 110.

66. W. Taylor and Lasch, "Two 'Kindred Spirits,'" 23–41.

67. Faust, *Mothers of Invention*, 142–45, esp. 144. In the nineteenth-century era women would not recognize the rigid distinctions between homosexuality and heterosexuality. "Intense—even seemingly erotic—female friendships co-existed harmoniously with male-female courtship and even marriage."

68. Farnham, *Education of the Southern Belle*, 148.

69. The reference to the word "torn" actually comes from Josephine Varner's description of losing her dearest friend, Sallie Carter, when she announced she was to marry Mr. Butler. Though she reported feeling pleased for her that she had made a good match, she also noted wistfully, "Yet how sad it makes me to give her up, although I can love her the same, I feel as used of her loving affection, yet I feel she is being torn from me." Josephine Varner Diary, 1 March 1864, Edward Varner Family Papers, GHS.

70. Holloway, "Searching for Southern Lesbian History," 262.

71. Ibid., 262–63. Estelle Freedman points out that in the 1880s "educators became suspicious of 'smashing' or same-sex crushes at women's schools." See Freedman, "Sexuality in Nineteenth-Century America," 199.

72. Farnham, *Education of the Southern Belle*, chapter 7, esp. 156.

73. Buza, "Pledges of Our Love," 16.

74. Anna Cameron Diary, 19, 20, and 21 November and 2, 3, and 8 December 1863, in Jabour, *Scarlett's Sisters*, 63–64.

75. Jabour, "Female Families," 86–103.

76. Grace Elmore Brown Diary, 30 September 1864, in Weiner, *Heritage of Woe*, xxviii. and 40.

77. Jabour, "Female Families," 86–103.

78. As Lillian Faderman argued in her book *Surpassing the Love of Men*, 240: "Love between women had been encouraged and tolerated for centuries—but now that women had the possibility of economic dependence, such love became potentially threatening to the social order. What if women would seek independence, cut men out of their lives?" Therefore as Faderman argued, "Love between women was metamorphosed into a freakishness, and it was claimed that only those who had such an abnormality would want to change their subordinate status in any way," 240–41. The rise of the sexologists therefore came about at the same time as women tried to assert their autonomy and therefore could be interpreted as a reaction to it. It could be used as a powerful weapon to stop women from gaining independence from men.

79. Chambers-Schiller, *Liberty a Better Husband*, 2.

80. Knowlton, "'Only a Woman Like Yourself,'" 40.

81. Laura Beecher Comer Diary, 20 January 1862, SHC.

82. Ibid.

83. Ibid.

84. Ibid., 8 January 1899.

85. Ibid.

86. There are a number of entries where Laura talked about the difficulties she had managing her plantation in Alabama as a widow in the years following the Civil War. On 7 November 1867 she wrote, "At my plantation in Alabama surrounded by the usual annoyances of free Negroes! Indolent, unused to their new situation, are they not intolerable?" She added, "I am striving with all my might to wind up all my worldly goods and business of every kind. I long to be relaxed and ready to depart." Laura Beecher Comer Diary, microfilm, series 1, vol. 2, SHC. Depressed, downtrodden, and weary, Comer was on the brink of despair, looking for death as an escape from her troubled life. Yet in 1872 the tone of her diary alters completely, and she appears to be a transformed woman with renewed hope and plans on the horizon, including traveling.

87. Laura Beecher Comer Diary, 6 March 1867, SHC.

88. Ibid., 28 June 1867.

89. Ibid., 26 November 1872.

90. Ibid., 8 January 1899.

91. Laura Comer also had a tendency to speak negatively about friends if she perceived that they had let her down. These negative comments often occur when her mood is depressed or when she is having a difficult time on the plantation.

92. Unknown to Mary Susan Ker, 12 June 1864, and Helen Wells to Mary Susan Ker, 9 December 1874, Mary Susan Ker Papers, SHC.

93. E. M. Reid to Mary Susan Ker, 28 March 1880, Mary Susan Ker Family Papers, SHC. Mrs. Reid's husband had recently died, and she described how she spent the days alone, while her grown-up sons were at work and her younger daughter, Annie, was at school. Mrs. Reid was reasonably well off, and her case is worth noting because it shows how single women (widows, and the permanently single) forged networks for mutual support, financial assistance, or company. Though Mary did not take Mrs. Reid up on her offer, it shows an alternative living arrangement that friends put forward and often considered. Mary's sister-in-law Josie Ker also had offered Mary a home with them ten years prior, as they were worried about the health and welfare of Mary, working long hours as a teacher in order to support herself. Also see Josie Ker to Mary Susan Ker 15 December 1873, Ker Family Papers, SHC.

94. There were many letters written to Mary from family members that demonstrate how loved, valued, and respected she was within the extended family.

95. Mary Telfair to Mary Few, 20 October [1833] in C. Johnson, *Mary Telfair,* 101; 103, 104, and 105.

96. C. Johnson, *Mary Telfair,* 99.

97. C. Carter, *Southern Single Blessedness.*

98. Eliza Holladay to Elizabeth Travers Lewis, August 1849, Holladay Family Papers, VHS.

99. Hannah Wylie to Mary Wylie, 17 November 1853, Gaston, Strait, Wylie, and Baskin Family Papers, SCL. Hannah's comment was made in reference to the slaveholding auctions (she refers to them as "Negro speculations") taking place nearby.

100. Her sister, Susan, who was eighteen years her senior, likewise discussed a frenzied prosecession rally in Lancaster in June 1851: "It was more like a corn husking than anything like I can compare it to . . . beast Rhett went forward . . . and he went illustrating the advantage of secession . . . and his gaping gang gulped it down. . . . Then came Adams amidst the loud cheering of the hoard and the greater part knew no more than the animals that brought them there." University of South Carolina Programme Guide, 16–19, SCL.

101. Susan Wylie 29 September 1847, Gaston, Strait, Wylie, and Baskin Family Papers, SCL.

102. Obituary of Susan Wylie, 6 October 1857, Gaston, Strait, Wylie, and Baskin Family Papers, SCL.

103. Harriott Middleton to Susan Middleton, 26 October [year unknown], in "Middleton Correspondence, 1861–1865." Harriott wrote about various subjects including female propriety. As a single woman she valued "propriety" and a good "self-image." In response to her letter, Susan Middleton referred to the behavior of her sister Emma, who she accused of a lack of decorum in her desire to participate in the round dancing at a local social gathering. Susan paints herself as the good southern matron, offering advice to her younger sister. Alarmed at her sister's unladylike confession of wanting to round dance, she confessed to Harriott, "That Emma should wish to set aside propriety and delicacy in this way mortifies me deeply, but I have no doubt she will do it, for she is as least as self-willed as I am." Susan Middleton to Harriott Middleton, January [date unknown] 1863. Ibid. The letters between the Middleton girls offer a window into the social scene in Charleston during the Civil War. The candor of their letters makes it easier to understand the social context during the war.

104. Caroline Kean Hill Davies Diary, 25 April 1861, VHS.

105. Augusta Jane Evans to Curry, 20 December 1862, in Sexton, *Southern Woman of Letters*, introduction, xxx.

106. Augusta Jane Evans, in Sexton, *Southern Woman of Letters*, 97.

107. For example, Augusta Jane Evans to G. Beauregard, 19 August 1863, in ibid., 97.

108. Augusta Jane Evans to G. Beauregard, 19 August 1863, in ibid., 97. See also Gross, "Lonely Lives Are Not Necessarily Joyless."

109. Vicinus, *Independent Women*, 189.

110. Ibid.

111. For a discussion of the postwar period and its effect on elite, slaveholding women see Edwards, *Gendered Strife and Confusion*, 185–86.

112. Faust, *Mothers of Invention*, 145.

113. Ibid. Faust cites the example of Nannie Haskin of Tennessee, who observed rather disapprovingly in 1863, "I have noticed girls carrying on over each other kissing each other and so on. I think it is right foolish sometimes." Other diarists noted in their journals how the standards, or behavior, of young girls was far less concerned about adhering to rigid gender conventions.

114. Holladay Family Papers, VHS; Gaston, Strait, Wylie, and Baskin Family Papers, SCL; and George W. Mordecai Papers, SHC.

115. Ibid.

116. Smith-Rosenberg noted, "Devotion to and love of other women became a plausible and socially accepted form of human interaction." See Smith-Rosenberg, "Female World of Love and Ritual," 9.

117. Duggen, "Trials of Alice Mitchell," 266.

118. Faderman, *Surpassing the Love of Men*, 240–41.

119. Ibid.

120. Chambers-Schiller, *Liberty a Better Husband*.

Chapter 5 **Law, Property, and the Single Woman**

1. Divorce petition of Mary Reid to General Assembly of North Carolina, RSPP, PAR no. 20184216.

2. Ibid.

3. Ibid.

4. Fox-Genovese, *Within the Plantation Household*, 194–210, esp. 195 and 203.

5. Jabour, *Scarlett's Sisters*, 12–13.

6. The collection includes petitions from the fifteen slaveholding states. A large number of the petitions are from Virginia (seven of twenty-three reels) and North and South Carolina (eight of twenty-three reels).

7. Originally, I had planned to use a sample of thirty-five cases, six from each state. This number was quickly revised, to include over one hundred cases.

8. Censer, "Smiling through Her Tears."

9. Bynum, *Unruly Women*. Bynum discussed how the changes in divorce law favored men in North Carolina, which again suggests that the changes in divorce laws actually found their roots in conservative soil and that they were enacted to protect women, not to liberate them.

10. Hartog, *Man and Wife in America*, 118.

11. Ibid., 115–17.

12. Bynum, *Unruly Women*, 60, and Pease and Pease, *Ladies, Women and Wenches*, 91.

13. Hartog, *Man and Wife in America*, 118.

14. Welter, "Cult of True Womanhood."

15. Hartog, *Man and Wife in America*, 93.

16. Jabour, *Scarlett's Sisters*, 13.

17. Lebsock, *Free Women of Petersburg*, 16–17.

18. Degler, *At Odds*, 168–69. Degler linked the rising divorce rate to the ideal of companionate marriage. He also views the rise in divorce rates as a sign of women's growing desire for autonomy. This contrasts to Norma Basch, who said that divorce was "the gambit of the desperate" and the pursuit of protection for women. Norma Basch, "The Emerging Legal History," 107.

19. Peter Bardaglio noted that the "profound social changes" in the South "slowly" filtered through to the legal system and became "mirrored" in the law. See Bardaglio, *Reconstructing the Southern Household*, introduction.

20. Basch, "The Emerging Legal History," 106.

21. Ibid., 107.

22. It is more difficult to ascertain what percentage of the petitions resulted in the cases being granted to women. Some of the petitions include a recorded result, but many do not. Further investigation or a more detailed study would be beneficial in the future in order to ascertain more definite patterns. For a more general figure see Degler, *At Odds*, 168–69.

23. Censer, "Smiling through Her Tears," 27. In South Carolina there were no divorce laws until Reconstruction, which in many ways reflected the conservative ethos of that particular state. See Degler, *At Odds*, 168–69.

24. Censer, "Smiling through Her Tears," 38. Censer highlighted how important it was for plaintiffs to show that they were pinnacles of "domesticity," "industriousness," and "good management" when filing for a divorce. A woman had to "prove" that she had been "wronged" but also to demonstrate that she had continued to act with "ladylike decorum."

25. Basch, "Emerging Legal History," 106.

26. Jabour, *Scarlett's Sisters*, 13.

27. Basch, "Emerging Legal History," 107.

28. Ibid.

29. Divorce petition of Julia Patterson to the judge of the circuit to Montgomery County sitting as a court of equity, RSPP, PAR no. 20986504, 3 February 1865, no recorded result.

30. Divorce petition of Rachel Miller to the Honourable Robert B. Gilliam, Davidson County, North Carolina, RSPP, PAR no. 21286608.

31. General petition information, Rachel Miller, North Carolina, RSPP, PAR no. 21286608.

32. Ibid.

33. Divorce petition of Margaret Selina Oliver to Southern Chancery Division of Alabama, Records of the Circuit Courts, Final Record Chancery Court, RSPP, PAR no. 20184216. By "her due" I am referring to a widow's dower share, which was one-third of her husband's real estate. This will be discussed in more detail later on. The role of an administrator was similar to an executor of a will. Suzanne Lebsock noted, "The administrator was obliged to

dissolve partnerships, to collect and pay debts, to pursue litigation, to distribute the estate to the proper heirs, and to manage it in the meantime." The decision of whether to take on the task of administration or coadministration was a choice a widow could either accept or decline. By accepting, widows held responsibility, but also power, over their husbands' assets. For further information refer to Lebsock, *Free Women of Petersburg*, 120–21.

34. Divorce petition of Margaret Selina Oliver, RSPP, PAR no. 20184216.

35. Ibid.

36. Divorce petition of Sarah M. Mason to the Circuit Court of the County of Franklin, 11 December 1863, RSPP, PAR no. 21686304.

37. Ibid.

38. Divorce petition of Mary Terry to General Assembly of Virginia, January 1850, Legislative Petitions, RSPP, PAR no. 11685006.

39. Ibid.

40. Ibid.

41. Censer, "Smiling through Her Tears," 37.

42. Censer quoted in Basch, "Emerging Legal History," 107.

43. Petition of Sarah H. Black to judge of the First Judicial District in Texas, RSPP, PAR no. 21585501, Brazoria County Courthouse.

44. Ibid.

45. Petition of Sarah H. Black to the judge of the First Judicial District in Texas, RSPP, PAR no. 21585501, Brazoria County Courthouse. Even in a western frontier state like Texas that was fairly liberal in its treatment of women, compared to elsewhere in the South, a definite gender bias continued to exist in divorce cases. In the Texas Divorce Law passed in 1841, men had a clear advantage if they sued for divorce. The statute of 1841 allowed a husband to divorce his wife if she "shall have voluntarily left his bed and board, for the space of three years with intention of abandonment" or if she had "been taken in adultery." While the abandonment provision was fairly standard for both sexes, the law gave far greater moral latitude to men when it came to adultery, as women had to prove not only that her husband had been adulterous, but that he had actually "lived in adultery with another woman," which was far harder to prove. No amendments were made to the Texas Divorce Law until 1873, and even then it simply added on a six-month county residency requirement. See Blum, "When Marriages Fail," 23–26.

46. Petition of Jane Brown to Court of Equity for the County of Guilford, County Court Divorce Records, RSPP, PAR no. 21286026.

47. Divorce petition of Martha Smith Green to the General Assembly of Tennessee, Legislative Petition, RSPP, PAR no. 11482911.

48. Ibid.

49. Divorce petition of Martha Smith Green to the General Assembly of Tennessee, Legislative Petition, RSPP, PAR no. 11482911.

50. Francelle Blum's study of Texas describes a rising rate of marital dissolution across the United States by the late nineteenth century. The results from the Carroll-Wright Report show that in the 1870s alone, the general divorce rate increased by almost 80 percent, but in Texas it rose by a staggering, 352 percent. Blum, "When Marriages Fail," 5–6. Texas did not follow English common law (whereas the remainder of the South, bar Louisiana, did). Yet culturally it was still very southern, even though it was a western frontier based on Spanish

law. Its frontier attitudes made it distinctive and generous in its outlook toward women's liberties. Blum, "When Marriages Fail."

51. Divorce petition of Mary Hookins to General Assembly of Tennessee, Legislative Petition. RSPP, PAR no. 114844502.

52. Ibid.

53. Bynum, *Unruly Women*, 60–61.

54. Censer, "Smiling through Her Tears," 27.

55. Ibid. Also see Hodes, *Sex, Love and Race.*

56. Divorce petition of Norfleet Perry to the Legislature of the State of Tennessee, RSPP, PAR no. 11481926.

57. Petition of John Chambers to General Assembly of North Carolina, Session Records, RSPP, PAR no. 11282504.

58. Petition of Thomas Culpepper to the House of Delegates of Virginia, Legislative Petitions, RSPP, PAR no. 11683501.

59. Censer, "Smiling through Her Tears," 35.

60. Ibid., 35.

61. Ibid., 35.

62. Lebsock, "Radical Reconstruction," 201.

63. In Georgia cruelty was not defined until 1867. Censer, "Smiling through Her Tears," 34.

64. Ibid., 27.

65. Blum, "When Marriages Fail," 25.

66. Petition of Eliza Patterson to Legislative Counsel of Florida, RSPP, PAR no. 10583901.

67. Degler, *At Odds*, 168–69.

68. Ibid.

69. Ibid., 169. According to Degler over 80 percent of men filed for divorce on these grounds alone between 1872–75. About one-third of husbands claimed adultery by their wives, 44.8 percent cited desertion, and a 4.7 percent cruelty.

70. Bynum, "Reshaping the Bonds of Womanhood."

71. Ibid. For specific examples of male plaintiffs citing cruelty as a reason for divorce, refer to Degler, *At Odds*, chapter 5. In the period 1872–76, eight hundred husbands' petitions specified cruelty on the part of their wives as a reason for divorce.

72. Historians who have emphasized the South's return to pre–Civil War values include Faust, *Mothers of Invention;* Rable, *Civil Wars,* and Whites, *Civil War as a Crisis in Gender.*

73. Virginia was one of the harshest states and stipulated a minimum length of five years in order for a divorce to be awarded on the grounds of desertion. Alabama raised its time requirement from two to three years, whereas Arkansas and Florida reduced theirs to one year. For more information see Censer, "Smiling through Her Tears," 27–28.

74. Sedevia, "Prospect of Happiness," 201.

75. Degler, *At Odds*, 168.

76. Ibid.

77. Divorce petition of Winney Jeter to Middle Chancery Division of the State of Alabama, RSPP, PAR no. 20184524; divorce petition of Sally Ballinger to the Honorable Senate and of the House of Delegates of Virginia, RSPP, PAR no. 1168304.

78. Divorce petition of Elizabeth Rea to the Honorable Judge, Mecklenburg County, North Carolina. Her petition was granted in 1866.

79. Censer, "Smiling through Her Tears," 38.

80. This argument also links to Kirsten Wood's analysis of slaveholding widows in the American Southeast and their use of ladyhood to exert authority in managing their plantations. See K. Wood, *Masterful Women.*

81. Petition of Gatsey Stevenson to General Assembly of North Carolina, Session Records, RSPP, PAR no. 11283301.

82. Ibid.

83. Petition of Hannah Crawford to District Court of Texas, Records of the District Court, RSPP, PAR no. 21586104.

84. Petition of Margaret Merritt to Northern Chancery Division, RSPP, PAR no. 20186111.

85. Petition of Lucy Norman to General Assembly of Virginia, Legislative Petitions, RSPP, PAR no. 11684814.

86. Divorce petition of Mary (Polly) Reid to General Assembly of North Carolina, Session Records, RSPP, PAR no. 11283204.

87. Petition of Mary Lawson to House of Delegates of Virginia, Legislative Petitions, RSPP, PAR no. 11684005.

88. Ibid.

89. Ibid. Before Mary married, she had a prenuptial agreement drawn up that ring fenced ten of her slaves in a lifetime estate, free from her husband's "liabilities."

90. For more information, see Bynum, *Unruly Women,* 64.

91. Ibid.

92. Petition of Ruth Balderee to Chancery Court of Alabama, Records of Circuit Court, RSPP, PAR no. 20184512.

93. Lebsock, *Free Women of Petersburg,* 200–203.

94. Petition of Ruth Balderee to Chancery Court of Alabama, Records of Circuit Court, RSPP, PAR no. 20184512.

95. Lebsock, *Free Women of Petersburg,* 77–78.

96. The Married Women's Property Act passed in Mississippi in 1839 granted married women the right to own (but not control) property in their own name. It was followed by similar acts in Texas in 1841, Florida in 1845, Alabama in 1846, and New York State in 1848.

97. Pease and Pease, *Ladies, Women and Wenches,* 3.

98. Censer, *Reconstruction of White Southern Womanhood,* 111.

99. Ibid., 112.

100. Ibid., and Cameron Family Papers 1757–1978, SHC.

101. Censer, *Reconstruction of White Southern Womanhood,* 112, and Cameron Family Papers 1757–1978, SHC.

102. Censer, *Reconstruction of White Southern Womanhood,* 113; Frances Holladay to Elizabeth Travis Lewis, August 1853. Correspondence of Frances Ann Holladay, Holladay Family Papers, VHS. Frances writes openly about the different roles that each sister took on within the family compact. "Eliza, Virgin and myself, take it a week each about to keep house, Mother always gives out dinner if she is well enough, and gives general directions. Huldah

attends to the fowls, and raises a great many. . . . We all think Virgin very much like Ann was, in appearance, and has ways like her. In sickness, she is invaluable as a nurse."

103. Pease and Pease, *Ladies, Women and Wenches*, 90–114.

104. Censer, *Reconstruction of White Southern Womanhood*, 113.

105. Holley, "'But One Dependence,'" 26.

106. Censer, *Reconstruction of White Southern Womanhood*, 120.

107. Ibid.

108. Last Will and Testament of Miss Amanda Varner, 24 March 1915, Edward Varner Family Papers, Varner Family Legal Papers, 1827–1928, GHS.

109. Lebsock, *Free Women of Petersburg*, chapter 5.

110. Memorandum to Mamie and Nellie, 20 December 1871, Mary Susan Ker Papers, SHC.

111. Hoff, *Law, Gender, and Injustice*, 106.

112. The law of dower also held an important function during marriage. As Lebsock pointed out, a wife was able to "defend" the right to her dower by blocking conveyances. Refer to Lebsock, *Free Women of Petersburg*, 24.

113. Park, *Treatise on the Law of Dower*, 3.

114. Hoff, *Law, Gender, and Injustice*, 106–7.

115. Ibid., 113–15.

116. Petition of Rebecca Cavens to Mississippi State Legislature, Petitions and Memorials, RSPP, PAR no. 11082504. The petition read, "Rebecca Caven's is entitled to dower in all the real estate of which the late Dr. Thomas K. McGrath her former husband died." She "voluntarily was relinquishing her right to dower in the lands, herein prayed to be disposed of to effect the object of this petition."

117. I am aware that this example falls slightly outside of the main period observed in this book. However, I have included it because it is an excellent example of a letter written from a slaveholding daughter to her father in the early days of her widowhood. Ruth Hairston to Peter Hairston, 29 May 1814, Wilson and Hairston Family Papers, folder 77, SHC.

118. George W. Mordecai Papers, SHC.

119. Petition of Martha Powell to General Assembly of Virginia, Legislative Petitions, RSPP, PAR no. 11683002.

120. Ibid.

121. Hoff, *Law, Gender, and* Injustice, 106–7.

122. Ibid.

123. Marena Lefevre to the Probate Court of Pulaski County, Arkansas, 15 October 1867, RSPP, PAR no. 20286701.

124. Lebsock, *Free Women of Petersburg*, 26.

125. Ibid., and Catherine Edwards to Charles Biddle, 4 July 1805, Catherine Edwards Papers, SCL.

126. This ensured that a wife was adequately provided for, but also it limited her from being able to buy and sell property, thus constraining her autonomy, which fitted in with prevalent ideas of femininity that considered women as submissive, passive, and dependent. Lebsock, *Free Women of Petersburg*, 42–44.

127. Bynum, *Unruly Women*, 62.

128. Petition of Mary Burney to Alabama Legislature, RSPP, PAR no. 10181701.

129. Petition of Miriam Porter to Tennessee Legislature, RSPP, PAR no. 21483004.

130. Petition of Elizabeth Saunders to General Assembly of Tennessee, Legislative Petitions, RSPP, PAR no. 11482203.

131. Elizabeth Latta to the Honorable Chancellor of York District, South Carolina, 26 January 1863, RSPP, PAR no. 21386330.

132. Will of Colin Clark (probated 1868) in Censer, *Reconstruction of White Southern Womanhood,* 104–5.

133. Grossberg, review of *Breaking the Bonds,* 1582.

134. Petition of Hetty Jacobs to House of Delegates, RSPP, PAR no. 11682807. Hetty Jacobs was a widow from Richmond City, Virginia, who discovered this to her peril. After her husband died, she had ongoing trouble with some of her young female slaves and children, who failed to recognize their mistress's new authority following their master's death. In a petition filed to the court of Virginia in 1829, Hetty sought permission to "dispose of the slaves belonging to the said estate" in order to pay the debts owing on the estate. She added that she had tried to pass the slaves on, but owing to their "character" nobody was willing to take them. Jacobs reported feeling constrained by the "laws of the land" that prevented her from selling them on without permission. Yet they were also of no use to her as "the conduct of the said slaves towards their mistress, the widow of said Jacobs, was so very insolent and every way objectionable as to render it impracticable for her to keep them about her household establishment."

135. Censer, *Reconstruction of White Southern Womanhood,* 103.

136. Petition of Susanna Hamm to General Assembly of Virginia, Legislative Petitions, RSPP, PAR no. 11683915.

137. Ibid.

138. Petition of Hetty Jacobs to the General Assembly of Virginia, RSPP, PAR no. 11682901.

139. Jabour, *Scarlett's Sisters,* 13.

140. Petition of Elizabeth Carter to General Assembly of Tennessee, RSPP, PAR no. 11480106. Elizabeth Carter, a slaveholding widow from Tennessee, requested that the court "pass a law to empower her to sell so much of the land belonging to the estate of the deceased as will be sufficient to pay off the debts due." Petition of Mary Larkins to General Assembly of Tennessee, RSPP PAR no. 11484601. In January 1846 Mary Larkins, the white, female widow of slaveholder Spencer Hunt, sought to "nullify a provision in his will giving a large portion of his estate of the common schools in Humphrey and Dickinson Counties." Petition of Rebecca Cavens to Mississippi State Legislature, RSPP PAR no. 11082504. She asked permission to sell land rather than slaves.

141. Petition of Caroline Johnson to Texas Legislature, RSPP, PAR no. 11584020. The result of her case is recorded as "unknown."

142. Petition of Martha Powell to General Assembly of Virginia, Legislative Petitions, RSPP, PAR no. 11683002.

143. Petition of Martha Orgain to General Assembly of Virginia, Legislative Petitions, RSPP, PAR no. 11684203.

144. Harriett Montmollin to the Honourable Chancellors of Richland District, South Carolina, 23 March 1863. RSPP, PAR no. 21386315.

145. Hoff, *Law, Gender, and Injustice,* 128.

146. Gross, "And for the Widow and Orphan," 210.

Conclusion

1. Whites, *Civil War as a Crisis in Gender,* and Censer, *Reconstruction of White Southern Womanhood.* Others have described it in similar terms, such as Edwards, *Gendered Strife and Confusion.* Historians such as Anya Jabour have manipulated the image of Scarlett O'Hara, the fictional character in *Gone with the Wind,* and fleshed out the image by use of real examples of southern women in the Civil War and postwar years. They demonstrate the changes in southern women's lives and in the altered model of southern femininity in the era of Reconstruction.

2. C. Carter, *Southern Single Blessedness,* introduction, 1–12.

3. Jabour, *Scarlett's Sisters,* 1–15.

4. Fox-Genovese, "Family and Female identity in the Antebellum South: Sarah Gayle and Her family," in Carol Bleser, ed., *In Joy and in Sorrow,* 18–19.

5. Jabour, *Female Families and Friendship,* 86–103.

6. C. Carter, *Southern Single Blessedness,* 183.

7. Ott, *Confederate Daughters,* 98–99.

8. Cott, "Passionlessness," and Smith-Rosenberg and Rosenberg, "Female Animal."

9. Jabour, *Female Families,* 86–103.

10. K. Wood, *Masterful Women,* introduction.

11. Sims, *Power of Femininity,* 2.

12. Wiley, *Phoebe Yates Pember,* 105.

13. Chambers-Schiller, *Liberty a Better Husband,* 22–28.

14. Gross, "Lonely Lives Are Not Necessarily Joyless."

15. Ibid., 46–49.

16. Ibid., 48.

Bibliography

Primary Sources

ARCHIVES AND COLLECTIONS

Southern Historical Collection, Wilson Library,
  the University of North Carolina, Chapel Hill (SHC)

Alice Lee Larkins Houston Papers

Cameron Family Papers

R. E. Coker Family Papers

DeRosset Family Papers

Elliott and Gonzales Family Papers

Elizabeth Collier Diary

Foscue Family Papers

George W. Mordecai Papers

Harrison Henry Cocke Papers

Ida Tutwiler Papers

Laura Beecher Comer Diary

Mary E. Bateman Diary

Mary Susan Ker Papers

Ker Family Papers

Mordecai Family Papers

Nancy Avaline Jarrett Papers

Pettigrew Family Papers

Polk Family Papers

Rebecca S. C. Pilsbury Diary (microfilm manuscript)

Roach and Eggleston Family Papers

Sacket and Snider Family Papers

Sarah Lois Wadley Papers

Sarah Rebecca Cameron Papers

Sarah Varick Cozens Morrison Papers / Theodore Davidson
    Morrison Jr. Papers (microfilm manuscript)

Stone Family Papers

Swann Family Papers

Emma Marie Service Papers (erroneously referred to as
    Williford Family Papers)

Webb Family Papers

Wilson and Hairston Family Papers

Wyche and Otey Family Papers

Virginia Historical Society, Richmond, Virginia (VHS)

Anna Elizabeth Holt Diary

Anne Jennings Wise Hobson Diary

Bailey Family Papers

Caroline Kean Hill Davies Diary

Claiborne Family Papers

Cocke Family Papers

Coons Family Papers

Crickenberger Family Papers

Edmundson Family Papers

Emma E. Crawford Papers

Harvie Family Papers

Holladay Family Papers

Holt Family Papers

Hughes Family Papers

Hunter Family Papers

Johns Family Papers

Judith Clairborne Hill

Mary Eliza Powell Dulany Diary

Page Family Papers,

Price Family Papers

Rosier Family Papers

Virginia Hammett Diary

William Huntington Papers

Georgia Historical Society, Savannah, Georgia (GHS)

Bolton Smith Papers

Dorsett Family Papers

Edward Varner Family Papers

Lemuel Kollock Papers

Mary Telfair Papers

Savannah Widows Society Papers

Scudder Family Papers

South Carolina Historical Society, Charleston, South Carolina

Ball Family Papers

Elizabeth W. Allston Pringle Family Papers

Harriott Pinckney Horry Diaries

Harriott Middleton Family Papers, 1848–1917

Middleton Family Papers
Pinckney Family Documents

South Caroliniana Library, University of South Carolina,
Columbia, South Carolina (SCL)
Bushart Family Papers
Catherine Edwards Papers
Cunningham and Blakely Family Papers
Gaston, Strait, and Baskin Family Papers
Johnstone Family Papers
Mary Y. Harth Family Papers
Mary Hort Papers
Mary Morse Baker Eddy Papers
Maria Alexander Sharp Papers
Narcissa Clayton Papers
William Stokes Papers

David M. Rubenstein Rare Book and Manuscript Library,
Duke University
Campbell Family Papers, 1731–1969
Craven-Pegram Family Papers, 1785–1966
David Bullock Harris Papers, 1789–1894
Hugh N. Ponton Papers, 1859–64
Isabella Anna Roberts Woodruff Papers, 1768–1865
William B. Yonce Correspondence, 1827–93

University of Reading
Schweninger, Loren, and Robert Shelton, eds. *Race, Slavery, and Free Blacks: Petitions to Southern Legislatures, 1777–1867.* Microform. Bethesda, Md.: University Publications of America, 1998. Reels 1–23 (Reels 1–2 Delaware, 3 Mississippi, 4–7 North Carolina, 8–11 South Carolina, 12–14 Tennessee, 15 Texas, 16–22 Virginia, 23 Alabama). Accompanied by Smith, Charles E, *A Guide to the Microfilm Edition of Race, Slavery, and Free Blacks.*

PUBLISHED SOURCES

Berlin, Jean V., ed. *A Confederate Nurse: The Diary of Ada W. Bacot 1860–1863.* Columbia: University of South Carolina Press, 1994.

Chesnut, Mary Boykin. *A Diary from Dixie.* Boston: Houston Mifflin, 1951.

Cumming, Kate. *A Journal of Hospital Life in the Confederate Army of Tennessee: From the Battle of Shiloh to the End of the War.* Louisville, Ky.: John P. Morgan; New Orleans: W. Evelyn, c. 1866.

Custis Lee deButts, Mary. *Growing Up in the 1850s: The Journal of Agnes Lee.* Chapel Hill: University of North Carolina Press, 1984.

East, Charles. *Sarah Morgan: The Civil War Diary of a Southern Woman.* Athens: University of Georgia Press, 1991.

Foner, Eric. "From Slavery to Freedom: The Birth of the Modern Black Community." In *Portrait of America,* edited by Stephen Oates, 416–30. Boston: Houghton Mifflin, 1994.

Fraise, Richard J. *The Florence Nightingale of the Southern Army: Experiences of Mrs. Ella K. Newsom, Confederate Nurse in the Great War of 1861–1866.* New York: Broadway, 1914.

Gregory, John. *A Father's Legacy to His Daughters.* London: T. Cadell & W. Davies, 1808.

Hobgood-Oster, Laura. *The Sabbath Journal of Judith Lomax (1774–1828).* Atlanta: Scholars Press, 1999.

King, Richard C, ed. *Victorian Lady on the Texas Frontier: The Journal of Ann Raney Thomas Coleman of Whitehaven.* London: University of Oklahoma Press, 1971.

Mathews, Donald. G. *Religion in the Old South.* Chicago: Chicago University Press, 1977.

Moore, John Hammond, ed. *Keziah Brevard: A Plantation Mistress on the Eve of the Civil War; The Diary of Keziah Brevard, 1800–1861.* Columbia: University of South Carolina Press, 1993.

Myers, Robert Manson. *The Children of Pride: A True Story of Georgia and the Civil War.* New Haven, Conn.: Yale University Press, 1972.

Norton, Mary Beth, Sharon Block, and Ruth M. Alexander. *Major Problems in American Women's History.* Fifth edition. Belmont, Calif.: Cengage, 2013.

O'Brien, Michael. *An Evening When Alone: Four Journals of Single Women in the South 1827–67.* Charlottesville: University Press of Virginia, 1993.

Rozier, John, ed. *The Granite Farm Letters: The Civil War Correspondence of Edgeworth and Sallie Bird.* Athens: University of Georgia Press, 1988.

Sexton, Rebecca Grant. *A Southern Woman of Letters: The Correspondence of Augusta Jane Evans Wilson.* Columbia: University of South Carolina Press, 2002.

Taylor, Frances Wallace, Catherine Taylor Matthews, and J. Tracy Power, eds. *The Leverett Letters: Correspondence of a South Carolina Family 1851–1868.* Columbia: University of South Carolina Press, 2000.

Weiner, Marli, ed. *A Heritage of Woe: The Civil War Diary of Grace Elmore Brown 1861–68.* Athens: University of Georgia Press, 1997.

Wiley, Bell, ed. *Phoebe Yates Pember: A Southern Woman's Story; Life in Confederate Richmond.* St. Simons Island, Ga.: McCowat-Mercer, 1959.

Wood, Betty, ed. *Mary Telfair to Mary Few: Selected Letters 1802–1844.* Athens: University of Georgia Press, 2007.

Secondary Sources

BOOKS

Ayers, Edward, and John C. Willis, eds. *The Edge of the South: Life in Nineteenth-Century Virginia.* Charlottesville: University Press of Virginia, 1991.

Bardaglio, Peter. *Reconstructing the Southern Household: Families, Sex and the Law in the Nineteenth Century South.* Chapel Hill: University of North Carolina Press, 1995.

Battle, Kemp Plummer. *History of the University of North Carolina from Its Beginning to the Death of the President Swain, 1789–1868.* Raleigh, N.C.: Edwards and Broughton, 1907.

Bell, Rudolph M., and Virginia Yans, eds. *Women on Their Own: Interdisciplinary Perspectives on Being Single.* New Brunswick, N.J.: Rutgers University Press, 2008.

Bingham, Emily. *Mordecai: An Early American Family.* New York: Hill and Wang, 2003.

Blackstone, Sir William. *Commentaries on the Laws of England in Four Books: Ninth Edition.* Book 1. Oxford: W. Strahen and Cadell and D. Prince, 1765.

Blake, Nelson Manfred. *The Road to Reno: A History of Divorce in the United States.* New York: Macmillan, 1980.

Bleser, Carol, ed. *The Hammonds of Redcliffe.* New York: Oxford University Press, 1981.

———, ed. *In Joy and in Sorrow: Women, Family, and Marriage in the Victorian South.* Oxford: Oxford University Press, 1991.

Broussard, Joyce, "'Naked before the Law': Married Women and the Servant Ideal in Antebellum Natchez." In *Mississippi Women: Their Histories, Their Lives,* edited by Martha H. Swain, Elizabeth Ann Payne, and Marjorie Julian Spruill, 57–76. Athens: University of Georgia Press, 2010.

Burton, Orville Vernon. *In My Father's House Are Many Mansions: Family and Community in Edgefield, South Carolina.* Chapel Hill: University of North Carolina Press, 1985.

Butler, Pierce. *The Unhurried Years: Memories of the Old Natchez Region.* Baton Rouge: Louisiana State University Press, 1948.

Buza, Melinda, S. "'Pledges of Our Love': Friendship, Love and Marriage among the Virginian Gentry." In Edward L. Ayers and John C. Willis, *Edge of the South: Life in Nineteenth-Century Virginia.* Charlottesville: University Press of Virginia, 1991.

Bynum, Victoria. "Reshaping the Bonds of Womanhood." In *Divided Houses: Gender and the Civil War,* edited by Catherine Clinton, 320–35. Oxford: Oxford University Press, 1992.

———. *Unruly Women: The Politics of Social and Sexual Control in the Old South.* Chapel Hill: University of North Carolina Press, 1992.

Campbell, Edward D. C., and Kym S. Rice, eds. *A Woman's War: Southern Women in the Civil War, and the Confederate Legacy.* Charlottesville: University Press of Virginia, 1996.

Carter, Christine Jacobsen. "Indispensable Spinsters: Maiden Aunts in the Elite Families of Savannah and Charleston." In *Negotiating Boundaries of Southern Womanhood,* edited by Janet L. Coryell et al., 111–33. Columbia: University of Missouri Press, 2000.

———. *Southern Single Blessedness: Unmarried Women in the Urban South 1800–1865.* Urbana: University of Illinois Press, 2006.

Carter, D. T. *When the War Was Over.* Baton Rouge: Louisiana State University Press, 1985.

Cashin, Joan. *A Family Venture: Men and Women on the Southern Frontier.* New York: Oxford University Press, 1991.

Censer, Jane Turner. *North Carolina Planters and Their Children 1800–1860.* Baton Rouge: Louisiana State University Press, 1984.

———. *The Reconstruction of White Southern Womanhood 1865–1895.* Baton Rouge: Louisiana State University Press, 2003.

Chambers-Schiller, Lee Virginia. *Liberty a Better Husband: Single Women in America; The Generations of 1780–1840.* New Haven, Conn.: Yale University Press, 1984.

Clinton, Catherine. *Fanny Kemble's Civil Wars.* Oxford: Oxford University Press, 2000.

———, ed. *Half Sisters of History: Southern Women and the American Past.* Durham, N.C.: Duke University Press, 1994.

———. *The Other Civil War: American Women in the Nineteenth Century.* New York: Hill and Wang, 1984.

———. *The Plantation Mistress: Women's World in the Old South.* New York: Pantheon Books, 1982.

Clinton, Catherine, and Nina Sibler, eds. *Divided Houses: Gender and the Civil War.* Oxford: Oxford University Press, 1992.

Cogan, Frances B. *All-American Girl: The Ideal of Real Womanhood in Mid-Nineteenth-Century America.* Athens: University of Georgia Press, 1989.

Cook, Robert. *Civil War America: Making a Nation 1848–1877.* London: Pearson Education, 2003.

Cooper, William J., Jr., and Thomas E. Terrill, eds. *The American South: A History.* 3rd ed. Vol. 1. New York: McGraw Hill, 2002.

Coryell, Janet L., Thomas H. Appleton Jr., Anastasia Sims, and Sandra Gioia Treadway, eds. *Negotiating Boundaries of Southern Womanhood: Dealing with the Powers That Be.* Columbia: University of Missouri Press, 2000.

Cott, Nancy. F. *The Bonds of Womanhood: "Woman's Sphere" in New England, 1780–1835.* New Haven, Conn.: Yale University Press, 1977.

Cott, Nancy F., and Elizabeth H. Pleck, eds. *A Heritage of Her Own: Toward A New Social History of American Women.* New York: Simon and Schuster, 1979.

Coulding, Mary P. *The Lee Girls.* Winston-Salem, N.C.: John F. Blair, 1987.

Davidoff, Leonore, and Catherine Hall. *Family Fortunes: Men and Women of the English Middle Class, 1780–1850.* London: Hutchinson, 1987.

Degler, Carl. *At Odds: Women and the Family in America from the Revolution to the Present.* New York: New York University Press, 1980.

Dennett, John Richard. *The South as It Is 1865–1866.* Baton Rouge: Louisiana State University Press, 2010.

Dew, Charles. *Apostles of Disunion: South Secession Commissioners and the Causes of the Civil War.* Charlottesville: University of Virginia Press, 2001.

Douglas, A. *Feminization of American Culture.* New York: Anchor Books/Doubleday, 1988.

Dublin, Thomas. *Women at Work: The Transformation of Work and Community in Lowell.* New York: Columbia University Press, 1979.

Edwards, Laura F. *Gendered Strife and Confusion: The Political Culture of Reconstruction.* Urbana: University of Illinois Press, 1997.

———. *Scarlett Doesn't Live Here Anymore: Southern Women in the Civil War Era.* Urbana: University of Illinois Press, 2000.

Escott, Paul D., ed. *Major Problems in the Old South,* Vol. 1. Lexington, Ky.: D. C. Heath, 1990.

Ezell, J. S. *The South since 1865.* New York: Collier-Macmillan, 1963.

Faderman, Lillian. *Surpassing the Love of Men: Romantic Friendship and Love between Women from the Renaissance to the Present.* New York: William Morrow, 1981.

Farmer, Alan. *The American Civil War 1861–1865.* London: Hodder and Stoughton, 1996.

———. *Reconstruction and the Results of the American Civil War.* London: Hodder and Stoughton, 1996.

Farnham, Christie Anne, ed. *The Education of the Southern Belle: Higher Education and Student Socialization in the Antebellum South.* New York: New York University Press, 1994.

———. *Women of the American South: A Multicultural Reader.* New York: New York University Press, 1997.

Faust, Drew Gilpin. *Mothers of Invention: Women of the Slaveholding South in the American Civil War.* Chapel Hill: University of North Carolina Press, 1996.

———. "Altars of Sacrifice: Confederate Women and the Narratives of War." In *Divided Houses: Gender and the Civil War,* edited by Catherine Clinton and Nina Sibler, 171–99. New York: Oxford University Press, 1992.

Fox-Genovese, Elizabeth. "'Family and Female Identity in the Antebellum South': Sarah Gayle and Her Family." In *In Joy and in Sorrow: Women, Family, and Marriage in the Victorian South,* edited by Carol Bleser, 15–32. Oxford: Oxford University Press, 1991.

———. *Within the Plantation Household: Black and White Women of the Old South.* Chapel Hill: University of North Carolina Press, 1988.

Fraser, Walter J., Jr., R. Frank Saunders Jr., and Jon L. Wakelyn, eds. *The Web of Southern Social Relation: Women, Family and Education.* Athens: University of Georgia Press, 1985.

Friedman, Jean E. *The Enclosed Garden: Women and Community in the Evangelical South, 1830–1900.* Chapel Hill: University of North Carolina Press, 1985.

Friend, Craig Thompson, and Anya Jabour, eds. *Family Values in the Old South.* Tampa: University of Florida Press, 2009.

Froide, Amy. *Never Married: Singlewomen in Early Modern Europe.* Oxford: Oxford University Press, 2005.

Genovese, Eugene. "'Our Family White and Black': Family and Household in the Southern Slaveholders' World View." In *In Joy and in Sorrow: Women, Family, and Marriage in the Victorian South,* edited by Carol Bleser, 69–88. Oxford: Oxford University Press, 1991.

Gordon, Lesley J., and John C. Inscoe, eds. *Inside the Confederate Nation.* Baton Rouge: Louisiana State University Press, 2005.

Grant, Susan-Mary, and Brian Holden Reid, eds. *The American Civil War: Explorations and Reconsiderations.* London: Pearson Education, 2000.

Gross, Jennifer Lynn. "'And for the Widow and Orphan': Confederate Widows, Poverty and Public Assistance." In *Inside the Confederate Nation,* edited by Lesley J. Gordon and John. C. Inscoe, 209–29. Baton Rouge: Louisiana State University Press, 2005.

———. "Good Angels: Confederate Widowhood in Virginia." In *Southern Families at War: Loyalty and Conflict in the Civil War South,* edited by Catherine Clinton, 133–54. Oxford: Oxford University Press, 2000.

Gutman, Herbert. *The Black Family in Slavery and Freedom.* New York: Random House, 1976.

Halem, Lynne Carol. *Divorce Reform: Changing Legal and Social Perspectives.* New York: Free Press, 1980.

Harris, J. William, ed. *Society and Culture in the Slave South.* London: Routledge, 1992.

Hartman, Mary, and S. Lois Banner, eds. *Clio's Consciousness Raised: New Perspectives on the History of Women.* New York: Harper and Row, 1974.

Hartog, Hendrik. *Man and Wife in America: A History.* Cambridge, Mass.: Harvard University Press, 2000.

Hawks, Joanne, ed. *Sex, Race and the Role of Women in the South.* Jackson: University of Mississippi Press, 1983.

Heilbrun, Carolyn G., ed. *Women's Life Writing.* New York: Ballantine Books, 1998.

Hill, Bridget. *Women Alone: Spinsters in England 1660–1850.* New Haven, Conn.: Yale University Press, 2001.

Hodes, Martha Elizabeth, ed. *Sex, Love and Race: Crossing Boundaries in North American History.* New York: New York University Press, 1999.

Hoff, Joan. *Law, Gender, and Injustice: A Legal History of U.S. Women.* New York: New York University Press, 1991.

Holloway, Pippa. "Searching for Southern Lesbian History." In *Women of the American South: A Multicultural Reader,* edited by Christie A. Farnham, 258–72. New York: New York University Press, 1997.

Howard, John, ed. *Carryin' On in the Lesbian and Gay South.* New York: New York University Press, 1997.

Huff, Cynthia. *Women's Life Writing and Imagined Communities.* New York: Routledge, 2005.

Hummel, Jeffrey Rogers. *Emancipating Slaves, Enslaving Freemen.* Chicago: Open Court, 1996.

Jabour, Anya. "Female Families: Same Sex Love in the Victorian South." In *Family Values in the Old South,* edited by Craig Friend and Anya Jabour, 86–108. Tampa: University of Florida Press, 2009.

———. *Scarlett's Sisters: Young Women in the Old South.* Chapel Hill: University of North Carolina Press, 2007.

Jeffreys, Sheila. *The Spinster and Her Enemies: Feminism and Sexuality 1880–1930.* London: Pandora, 1985.

Johansson, Jane, ed. *Widows by the Thousand: The Civil War Letters of Theophilius and Harriet, 1862–1864.* Fayetteville: University of Arkansas Press, 2000.

Johnson, Charles J., Jr. *Mary Telfair: The Life and Legacy of a Nineteenth Century Woman.* Savannah, Ga.: Frederic C. Beil, 2002.

Kelley, Mary. *Private Woman, and Public Stage: Literary Domesticity in Nineteenth Century America.* Chapel Hill: University of North Carolina Press, 1984.

Kertzer, David I., and Marzio Barbagli, eds. *Family Life in the Long Nineteenth Century 1789–1913.* Vol. 2. New Haven, Conn.: Yale University Press, 2002.

Kleinberg, Jay. *Women in American Society 1820–1920.* Brighton: BAAS, 1990.

Knowlton, Elizabeth W. "'Only a Woman Like Yourself'—Rebecca Alice Baldy: Dutiful Daughter, Stalwart Sister and Lesbian Lover of Nineteenth Century Georgia." In *Carryin' On in the Lesbian and Gay South,* edited by John Howard, 34–43. New York: New York University Press, 1997.

Larson, John Lauritz. *The Market Revolution in America: Liberty, Ambition and the Eclipse of the Common Good.* Cambridge: Cambridge University Press, 2010.

Lebsock, Suzanne. *The Free Women of Petersburg: Status and Culture in a Southern Town, 1784–1860.* London: W. W. Norton, 1985.

Lerner, Gerder. *The Grimke Sisters from South Carolina: Rebels against Slavery.* Boston: Houghton Mifflin, 1967.

Link, William. *Roots of Secession.* Chapel Hill: University of North Carolina Press, 2003.

Lopata, Helena Znaniecki. *Widowhood in an American City.* Cambridge, Mass.: Schenkman, 1973.

Marcus, Sharon. *Between Women: Friendship, Desire, and Marriage in Victorian England.* Princeton, N.J.: Princeton University Press, 2007.

Massey, Mary Elizabeth. *Women in the Civil War.* 1966. Lincoln: University of Nebraska Press, 1994.

Mathews, Donald G. *Religion in the Old South.* Chicago: University of Chicago Press, 1977.

May, Elaine Tyler. *Marriage and Divorce in Post-Victorian America.* Chicago: University of Chicago Press, 1980.

McCurry, Stephanie. *Masters of Small Worlds: Yeoman Households, Gender Relations, and the Political Culture of the Antebellum South Carolina Low Country.* Oxford: Oxford University Press, 1995.

McMillen, Sally G. *Southern Women: Black and White Women in the Old South.* Arlington Heights, Ill.: Harlon Davidson, 1992.

McPherson, James. *Battle Cry of Freedom: The Civil War Era.* Oxford: Oxford University Press, 1988.

Morgan, Sue, ed. *The Feminist History Reader.* New York: Routledge, 2006.

Motz, Marilyn Ferris. *True Sisterhood: Michigan Women and Their Kin, 1820–1920.* Albany: State University of New York Press, 1983.

Muhlenfeld, Elisabeth. *Mary Boykin Chesnut: A Biography.* Baton Rouge: Louisiana State University Press, 1981.

Oates, Stephen. *Portrait of America.* Boston: Houghton Mifflin, 1994.

O'Donovan, Susan Eva. *Becoming Free in the Cotton South.* Cambridge, Mass.: Harvard University Press, 2007.

O'Neill, William. *Divorce in the Progressive Era.* New Haven, Conn.: Yale University Press, 1967; New York: New Viewpoints, 1973.

Oshana, Marina. *Personal Autonomy in Society.* New York, Ashgate Publishing, 2006.

Ott, Victoria E. *Confederate Daughters: Coming of Age during the Civil War.* Carbondale: Southern Illinois University Press, 2008.

Palumbo-DeSimone, Christine. *Sharing Secrets: Nineteenth-Century Women's Relations in the Short Story.* London: Associated University Presses, 2010.

Pannell and Wyatt. *Julia S. Tutwiler and Social Progress in Alabama.* Tuscaloosa: University of Alabama Press, 2004.

Park, John James. *A Treatise on the Law of Dower: Particularly with a View to the Modern Practise of Conveyancing.* Philadelphia, 1836.

Pease, Jane H., and William H. Pease. *Ladies, Women, and Wenches: Choice and Constraint in Antebellum Charleston and Boston.* Chapel Hill: University of North Carolina Press, 1990.

Phillips, Roderick. *Putting Asunder: A History of Divorce in Western Society.* Cambridge: Cambridge University Press, 1990.

Pitt-Rivers, Julian. "Pseudo-Kinship." In *International Encyclopedia of the Social Sciences.* New York: Macmillan/Free Press, 1968.

Pollit, Katha. "Writing a Woman's Life." In *Women's Life Writing,* edited by Carolyn G. Heilbrun, 11–30. New York: Ballantine Books, 1998.

Poovey, Mary. *The Ideological Work of Gender in Mid Victorian England.* Chicago: University of Chicago Press, 1989.

Rable, George C. *Civil Wars: Women and the Crisis of Southern Nationalism.* Urbana: University of Illinois Press, 1991.

Reid, Brian Holden. *Origins of the Civil War.* London: Longman, 1996.

Riley, Glenda. *Divorce: An American Tradition.* New York: Oxford University Press, 1990; Lincoln: University of Nebraska Press, 1997.

Rubin, Anne Sarah. *A Shattered Nation: The Rise and Fall of the Confederacy 1861–1868.* Chapel Hill: University of North Carolina Press, 2005.

Scott, Anne Firor. *The Southern Lady: From Pedestal to Politics 1830–1930.* Extended edition. Charlottesville: University of Virginia Press, 1996.

Scott, Joan Wallach, ed. *Feminism and History.* Oxford: Oxford University Press.

Sellers, Charles. *The Market Revolution: Jacksonian America 1815–1846.* Oxford: Oxford University Press, 1994.

Sims, Anastasia. *The Power of Femininity in the New South: Women's Organizations and Politics in North Carolina, 1880–1930.* Columbia: University of South Carolina Press, 1997.

Smith-Rosenberg, Carroll. *Disorderly Conduct: Visions of Gender in Victorian America.* New York: Oxford University Press, 1975.

Spruill, Julia. *Women's Life and Work in the Southern Colonies.* New York & London: W. W. Norton & Company, 1998.

Stack, Carol. *All Our Kin: Strategies for Survival in a Black Community.* New York: Harper and Row, 1974.

Stein, Stephen J. *The Shaker Experience in America: A History of the United Society of Believers.* New Haven, Conn.: Yale University Press, 1992.

Stowe, Steven. *Intimacy and Power in the Old South: Ritual in Lives of the Planters.* Baltimore: Johns Hopkins University Press, 1987.

———. "'The Not-So Cloistered Academy': Elite Women's Education and Family Feeling in the Old South." In *The Web of Southern Social Relations: Women, Family and Education*, edited by Walter J. Fraser Jr. et al., 90–106. Athens: University of Georgia Press, 1985.

Swain, Martha H., Elizabeth Ann Payne, and Marjorie Julian Spruill, eds. *Mississippi Women: Their Histories, Their Lives*. Athens: University of Georgia Press, 2010.

Thomas, Emory M. *The Confederate Nation 1861–1865*. New York: Harper and Row, 1979.

Tickner, Lisa. *The Spectacle of Women: Imagery of the Suffrage Campaign 1907–1914*. Chicago: University of Chicago Press, 1988.

Tilly, Louise A., and Joan W. Scott, eds. *Women, Work and Family*. New York: Routledge, 1978.

Vicinus, Martha. "'Distance and Desire': Boarding School Friendship, 1870–1920." In *Hidden from History: Reclaiming the Gay and Lesbian Past*, edited by Martin Duberman et al., 212–29. New York: Meridian Books, 1990.

———. *Independent Women: Work and Community for Single Women 1850–1920*. University of Chicago Press, 1992.

Weiner, Marli. F. *Plantation Women in South Carolina, 1830–80*. Urbana: University of Illinois Press, 1998.

White, John. *Reconstruction after the Civil War*. London: Longman, 1977.

Whites, Lee-Ann. *The Civil War as a Crisis in Gender: Augusta Georgia 1860–1890*. Athens: University of Georgia Press, 1995.

———. *Gender Matters: Civil War, Reconstruction and the Making of the South*. New York: Palgrave Macmillan, 2005.

Wood, Kirsten E. *Masterful Women: Slaveholding Widows from the American Revolution through the Civil War*. Chapel Hill: University of North Carolina Press, 2004.

Woodward, C. Vann. *Origins of the New South 1877–1913*. Baton Rouge: Louisiana State University Press, 1987.

Wyatt-Brown, Bertram. *Southern Honor: Ethics and Behaviour in the Old South*. Oxford: Oxford University Press, 1982.

JOURNAL ARTICLES

Allmendinger, David F., Jr. "The Dangers of Ante-Bellum Student Life." *Journal of Social History* 7, no.1 (1973): 75–85.

Anzilotti, Cara. "Autonomy and the Female Planter in Colonial South Carolina." *Journal of Southern History* 62, no. 2 (1997): 239–68.

Basch, Norma. "The Emerging Legal History of Women in the United States: Property, Divorce and the Constitution." *Signs: Journal of Women in Culture and Society* 12, no. 1 (1986): 97–117.

Blom, Ida. "The History of Widowhood: A Bibliographic Overview." *Journal of Family History*, 16, no. 2 (1991): 191–210.

Cashin, Joan E. "Decidedly Opposed to the Union: Women's Culture, Marriage, and Politics in Antebellum South Carolina." *Georgia Historical Quarterly* 78, no. 4 (Winter 1994): 735–59.

———. "The Structure of Antebellum Planter Families: 'The Ties That Bound Us Was Strong.'" *Journal of Southern History* 56 (February 1990): 55–70.

Censer, Jane Turner. "'Smiling through Her Tears': Antebellum Southern Women and Divorce." *American Journal of Legal History* 25 (January 1981): 24–47.

Chambers-Schiller, Lee. "'Woman Is Born to Love': The Maiden Aunt as Maternal Figure in Ante-bellum Literature." *Journal of Women's Studies* 10, no. 1 (1988): 34–43.

Chused, Richard. "Late Nineteenth Century Married Women's Property Law: Reception of the Early Married Women's Property Acts by Courts and Legislatures." *American Journal of Legal History* 29 (January 1985): 3–35.

Clark, Christopher. "Household Economy, Market Exchange, and the Rise of Capitalism in the Rise of Connecticut Valley, 1800–1860." *Journal of Social History* 13 (1979): 169–89.

Clinton, Catherine. "Equally Their Due: The Education of the Planter Daughter in the Early Republic. *Journal of the Early Republic* 2 (April 1982): 39–60.

Conway, Jill. "Women Reformers and American Culture, 1870–1930." *Journal of Social History* 5 (Winter 1971–72): 164–77.

Cook, Blanche Wiesen. "The Historical Denial of Lesbianism." *Radical History Review* 20 (Spring/Summer 1979): 60–65.

Cott, Nancy. "Passionlessness: An Interpretation of Victorian Sexual Ideology, 1790–1850." *Signs: Journal of Woman in Culture and Society* 4, no. 2 (1978): 219–36.

Crowther, Edward. "Holy Honor: Sacred and Secular in the Old South." *Journal of Southern History* 58, no. 4 (1992): 619–36.

Cunningham, H. H. "General Hospitals: Establishment and Organization." *Journal of Southern History* 20, no. 3 (August 1954): 376–99.

Daniel, P. "The Metamorphosis of Slavery 1865–1900." *Journal of American History* 66 (1979–80): 88–99.

Degler, Carl. "What Ought to Be and What Was: Women's Sexuality in the Nineteenth Century." *American Historical Review* 79 (1974): 1467–90.

Dublin, Thomas. "Rural Putting Out Work in Early Nineteenth-Century New England: Women and the Transition to Capitalism." *New England Quarterly* 64 (1991): 531–73.

Duggen, Lisa. "The Trials of Alice Mitchell: Sensationalism, Sexology, and the Lesbian Subject in Turn-of-the-Century America.' *Signs* 18, no. 4 (Summer 1993): 791–814.

Faust, Drew Gilpin. "Altars of Sacrifice: Confederate Women and the Narratives of War." *Journal of American History* 76, no. 4 (March 1990): 1200–28.

Freedman, Estelle B. "Sexuality in Nineteenth-Century America: Behavior, Ideology and Politics." *Reviews in American History* 10, no. 4 (December 1982): 196–214.

Gross, Jennifer Lynn. "'Lonely Lives Are Not Necessarily Joyless': Augusta Jane Evan's *Macaria* and the Creation of a Place for Single Womanhood in the Postwar South." *American Nineteenth Century History* 2, no. 1 (Spring 2001): 33–52.

Grossberg, Michael. Review of *Breaking the Bonds: Marital Discord in Pennsylvania, 1730–1830*, by Merrill D. Smith. *Journal of American History* 79, no. 4 (1993): 1581–83.

———. "Who Gets the Child? Custody, Guardianship, and the Rise of a Judicial Patriarchy in Nineteenth Century America." *Feminist Studies* 9 (Summer 1983): 235–60.

Hacker, J. David. "The Effect of the Civil War on Southern Marriage Patterns." *Journal of Southern History* 76, no. 1 (February 2010): 39–70.

Hall, Jacquelyn Dowd. "'You Must Remember This': Autobiography as Social Critique." *Journal of American History* 85, no. 2 (September 1998): 439–65.

Henratta, James. "Families and Farms: *Mentalité* in Pre-industrial America." *William and Mary Quarterly* 35 (1978): 3–32.

Hewitt, Nancy. "Feminist Friends: Agrarian Quakers and the Emergence of Women's Right's in America." *Feminist Studies* 12, no. 1 (Spring 1986): 27–49.

Hudson, Jane. "From Constitution to Constitution, 1868–1895: South Carolina's Unique Stance on Divorce." *South Carolina Historical Magazine* 98 (January 1997): 75–96.

Ibsen, Charles A., and Patricia Klobus. "Fictive Kin Term Use and Social Relationships: Alternative Interpretations." *Journal of Marriage and the Family* 34, no. 4 (November 1972): 615–20.

Jabour, Anya. "'It Will Never Do to Be Married': The Life of Laura Wirt Randall, 1803–1833." *Journal of the Early Republic* 17, no. 2 (1997): 193–236.

Johnson, Walter. "On Agency." *Journal of Social History* 37, no. 1 (Fall 2003): 113–24.

Kelley, Mary. "A Woman Alone: Catharine Maria Sedgwick's Spinsterhood in Nineteenth Century America." *New England Quarterly* 51 (June 1978): 209–25.

Kerber, Linda. "Separate Spheres, Female Worlds, Woman's Place: The Rhetoric of Women's History." *Journal of American History* 75 (June 1988): 9–39.

Kulikoff, Alan. "The Transition to Capitalism in Rural America." *William and Mary Quarterly* 46 (1989): 120–44.

Lasser, Carol. "'Let Us Be Sisters Forever': The Sororal Model of Nineteenth-Century Female Friendship." *Signs* 14, no. 1 (Autumn 1988): 158–81.

Lebsock, Suzanne. "Radical Reconstruction and the Property Rights of Southern Women." *Journal of Southern History* 43, no. 2 (1977): 195–216.

Lubovich, Maglina. "Married or Single? Catharine Maria Sedgwick on Old Maids, Wives and Marriage." *Legacy* 25, no. 1 (2008): 23–40.

"Middleton Correspondence, 1861–1865." *South Carolina Historical Magazine* 63, no. 4 (October 1962): 212–19.

Moncrief, Sandra. "The Mississippi Married Women's Property Act of 1839." *Journal of Mississippi History* 47 (May 1985): 110–25.

Moore, Lisa. "'Something More Tender Than Friendship': Romantic Friendship in Early-Nineteenth-Century England." *Feminist Studies* 18, no. 3 (Fall 1992): 499–520.

Oates, Louise. "Civil War Nurses." *American Journal of Nursing* 28, no. 3 (1928): 207–12.

Pessen, Edward. "How Different from Each Other Were the Antebellum North and South?" *American Historical Review* 85 (1980): 1119–49.

Peterson, Jeanne M. "No Angels in the House: The Victorian Myth and the Paget Women." *American Historical Review* 89, no. 3 (June 1983): 677–708.

Rich, Adrienne. "Compulsory Heterosexuality and Lesbian Experience." *Journal of Women's History* 5, no. 4 (1980): 631–60.

Roberts, Mary Louise. "True Womanhood Revisited." *Journal of Women's History* 14, no. 1 (Spring 2002): 150–55.

Rothenburg, Winifred. "The Market and Massachusetts Farmers, 1750–1855." *Journal of Economic History* 41 (1981): 283–314.

Schwager, Sally. "Educating Women in America." *Signs: Journal of Women in Culture and Society* 12 (Winter 1987): 333–72.

Sedevia, Donna Elizabeth. "The Prospect of Happiness: Women, Divorce and Property in the Mississippi Territory, 1798–1817."*Journal of Mississippi History* 55, no. 3 (1995): 189–207.

Shalhope, Robert. E. "Race, Class, Slavery and the Antebellum Southern Mind." *Journal of Southern History* 37, no. 4 (1971): 557–74.

Simkins, Francis. B., and James W. Patton. "The Work of Southern Women among the Sick and Wounded of the Confederate Armies." *Journal of Southern History* 1, no. 4 (November 1935): 475–96.

Smith-Rosenberg, Carroll. "The Female World of Love and Ritual: Relations between Women in Nineteenth-Century America." *Signs: Journal of Women in Culture and Society* 1, no. 1 (1975): 1–29.

Smith-Rosenberg, Carroll, and Charles Rosenberg. "The Female Animal: Medical and Biological Views of Women and Her Role in Nineteenth Century America." *Journal of American History* 60 (1973/74): 332–56.

Stowe, Steven S. "'The Thing, nor Its Vision': A Woman's Courtship and Her Sphere in the Southern Planter Class." *Feminist Studies* 9 (Spring 1983): 67–86.

Taylor, William R., and Christopher Lasch. "Two 'Kindred Spirits': Sorority and Family in New England, 1839–1846." *New England Quarterly* 36, no. 1 (March 1963): 23–41.

Ulrich, Laura Thatcher. Review of *Liberty a Better Husband: Single Women in America: The Generations of 1780–1840*, by Lee Chambers-Schiller. *Journal of American History* 72, no. 1 (June 1985): 140.

Underwood, Betsy Swint. "War Seen through a Teen-Ager's Eyes." *Tennessee Historical Quarterly* 20 (1961): 177–87.

Waciega, Lisa Wilson. "A 'Man of Business': The Widow of Means in Southeastern Pennsylvania, 1750–1850." *William and Mary Quarterly* 44, no. 1 (1987): 40–64.

Welter, Barbara. "Cult of True Womanhood: 1820–1860." *American Quarterly* 18, no. 2 (1966): 151–74.

Wesson, Kenneth R. "Travellers' Accounts of the Southern Character: Antebellum and Early Postbellum Period." *Southern Studies* 17 (Fall 1978): 305–18.

UNPUBLISHED SECONDARY SOURCES

Berend, Zsusza. "Cultural and Social Sources of Spinsterhood in Nineteenth-Century New England." Ph.D. diss., Columbia University, 1994.

Blum, Francelle L. "When Marriages Fail: Divorce in Nineteenth-Century Texas." Ph.D. diss., Rice University, 2008.

Boswell, Angela. "'Separate and Apart': Women's Public Lives in a Rural Southern County, 1837–1873." Ph.D. diss., Rice University, 1998.

Broussard, Joyce. "Female Solitaires: Women Alone in the Lifeworld of Mid-Century Natchez, Mississippi 1850–1880." Ph.D. diss., University of Southern California, 1998.

Gross, Jennifer Lynn. "'Good Angels': Confederate Widowhood and the Reassurance of Patriarchy in the Postbellum South." Ph.D. diss., University of Georgia, 2001.

Hoffman, Jeff. "Wylie Women and Accommodating Men: Three Sisters Attempts at Asserting Autonomy in Pre–Civil War South Carolina." Unpublished paper, Constance B. Schultz Collection, University of South Carolina, Columbia.

Holley, Amy L. "'But One Dependence': Mary Susan Ker and Southern Public Education, 1876–1914." Master's thesis, University North Carolina, 1989.

Kennedy, Cynthia M. "Braided Relations, Entwined Lives: Charleston, South Carolina, Women at Work and Leisure, and the Social Relations of Urban Slave Society, 1780–1860." Ph.D. diss., University of Maryland, 1999.

Lee, Chagsin. "'Beyond Sorrowful Pride': Civil War Pensions and War Widowhood, 1862–1900." Ph.D. diss., Ohio University, 1997.

Mitchell, Judith Ann. "Ann Pamela Cunningham: A Southern Matron's Legacy." Master's thesis, Middle Tennessee State University, 1993.

Murray, Amanda M. "My Sisters, Don't Be Afraid of the Words, 'Old Maid': Demarginalizing the Spinster in Louisa May Alcott." Master's thesis, Villanova University 2009.

Tallentire, Jenea. "'Everyday Athena's': Strategies of Survival and Identity for Ever-Single Women in British Columbia, 1880–1930." Ph.D. diss., University of British Columbia, 2006.

Wink, Amy Laura. *"She Left Nothing in Particular": The Autobiographical Legacy of Nineteenth-Century Women's Diaries.* Knoxville: University of Tennessee Press, 2001.

Index

Page numbers in *italics* refer to illustrations.

CPSIA information can be obtained
at www.ICGtesting.com
Printed in the USA
LVHW081615070321
680810LV00007B/203